'Tim Butcher, one of the bravest and kindest foreign journalists who saw the Bosnian war, has written a splendid book, part memoir, part history, of that country, ingeniously using the assassin of 1914 as an anti-hero. It takes its place among classics of Balkan history.'

Norman Stone

'Lucid, passionate, urgent and above all a salient reminder that the past is not a place from which we must escape but a dynamic, living continuity to be given to our children.'

Rory MacLean

'Take a measure of well-researched history, add indelible personal recollections of the Bosnian war, season with piquant vignettes of traversing rural Bosnia on foot and mix with a light touch. The result is consistently appetizing and occasionally controversial. Tim Butcher goes from strength to strength. I enjoyed every paragraph.'

Dervla Murphy

'Rarely, if ever, can such momentous and tragic events have been sparked by such an unlikely and undistinguished a man, Gavrilo Princip. This insightful, useful and delightfully written book shines a unique spotlight on the trigger to the First World War, placing the assassin and his homeland in the wider strategic context. A great book – one to be recommended to professional and amateur historian alike.'

General Sir David Richards,
Chief of the Defence Staff

'A fabulous book that all First World War historians will now have to take account of. Tim Butcher has re-written history with his evocative and moving account of the assassin who sparked the crisis. Instead of a naive and misguided Serbian nationalist, he reveals an intelligent and determined South Slav patriot who gave his life for the cause. The research on Princip's education and motivation is outstanding, completely at odds with received historical wisdom and, importantly, it shows the Serbian state should not have been held to account. Superb.'

Saul David

'No-one has got closer into the mind of one of the key figures of the last century, Gavrilo Princip, than the journalist-turned-investigative-historian Tim Butcher. Part travelogue, part history of the Balkans, part psychological insight into the motivation of history's most famous terrorist before Osama bin Laden, this book brings an objective eye and flowing prose style to the story of what happened in Sarajevo on that June day a hundred years ago. He makes complex political and ethnic rivalries easy to comprehend, and gets to the heart of the issues, largely thanks to his personal knowledge of the region. Nor does the sheer poignancy of the tale escape his occasionally coruscating ire. This is first class history and in a year swamped with First World War centenary books it's the one you should read first.'

Andrew Roberts

TIM BUTCHER

Tim Butcher is a bestselling author who blends travel with history. His first book, *Blood River*, was a number one bestseller, a Richard and Judy Book Club selection and was shortlisted for the Samuel Johnson Prize, while his next, *Chasing the Devil*, was longlisted for the George Orwell Prize. A journalist with the *Daily Telegraph* from 1990 to 2009, he was awarded the 2013 Mungo Park Medal for exploration by the Royal Scottish Geographical Society. In 2010 he received an honorary doctorate from the University of Northampton for services to writing. Born in Great Britain, he is based in Cape Town with his family.

www.tim-butcher.com

TIM BUTCHER

The Trigger

THE HUNT FOR GAVRILO PRINCIP:
THE ASSASSIN WHO BROUGHT THE WORLD TO WAR

VINTAGE

2 4 6 8 10 9 7 5 3 1

Vintage
20 Vauxhall Bridge Road,
London SW1V 2SA

Vintage is part of the Penguin Random House group of companies whose
addresses can be found at global.penguinrandomhouse.com

Copyright © Tim Butcher 2014

Tim Butcher has asserted his right to be identified as the author of this
Work in accordance with the Copyright, Designs and Patents Act 1988

First published in Vintage in 2015
First published in hardback by Chatto & Windus in 2014

www.vintage-books.co.uk

A CIP catalogue record for this book is
available from the British Library

ISBN 9780099581338

Cover: Front top: Gavrilo Princip © Topfoto; background map: police sketch
showing the route used by Princip's assassination team to smuggle themselves
from Serbia into Bosnia, May–June 1914 © National Archive of Bosnia
and Herzegovina; bottom front: The Archduke of Austria Franz Ferdinand
(1863-1914) and his wife Sophie © Time Life Pictures/Getty Images

Printed and bound by CPI Group (UK) Ltd, Croydon CR0 4YY

For my greatest shapers
Stanley and Lisette

CONTENTS

The Western Balkans in 1914 with Bosnia
as part of Austria-Hungary

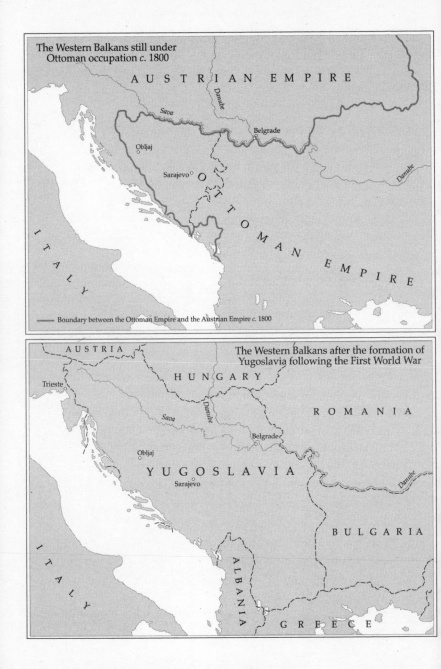

The Western Balkans still under Ottoman occupation c. 1800

AUSTRIAN EMPIRE

Sava

Danube

Belgrade

Obljaj

Sarajevo

OTTOMAN EMPIRE

Danube

ITALY

—— Boundary between the Ottoman Empire and the Austrian Empire c. 1800

AUSTRIA

HUNGARY

Trieste

Sava

Danube

The Western Balkans after the formation of Yugoslavia following the First World War

ROMANIA

Belgrade

Obljaj

YUGOSLAVIA

Sarajevo

Danube

ITALY

BULGARIA

ALBANIA

GREECE

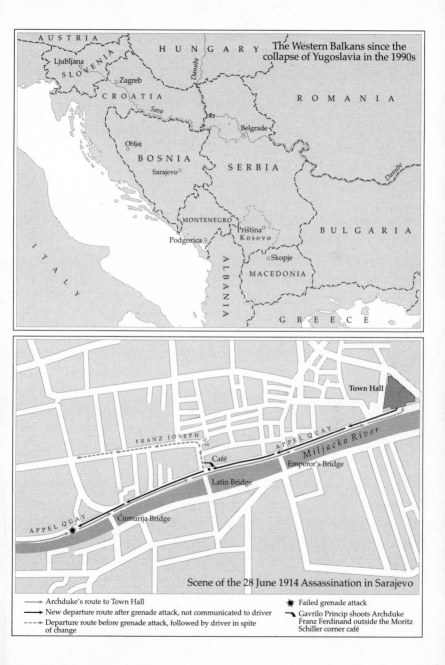

The Western Balkans since the collapse of Yugoslavia in the 1990s

Scene of the 28 June 1914 Assassination in Sarajevo

Archduke's route to Town Hall

New departure route after grenade attack, not communicated to driver

Departure route before grenade attack, followed by driver in spite of change

Failed grenade attack

Gavrilo Princip shoots Archduke Franz Ferdinand outside the Moritz Schiller corner café

NOTE ON PRONUNCIATION

The anglicised version of Bosnian, Serbian and Croatian spelling has been used in *The Trigger*. Pronunciation largely follows that of English letters although with the following exceptions:

c – is *ts* as in tsar. Hence the name Princip is pronounced *Printsip*

j – is *y* as in yam. Hence the town Jajce is pronounced *Yaitsay*

č – is *ch* as in scratch. Hence the town Glamoč is pronounced *Glamotch*

ć – is a softer *ch*. Hence the name Filipović is pronounced *Filipovich*

r – can be used as a rolled *r* vowel sound as in purr. Hence the Vrbas River is pronounced *Vurrbas*

š – is *sh* as in shin. Hence the word for tent, šator, is pronounced *shator*

dž – is a hard *j* as in gin. Hence the name Džile is pronounced *Jillay*

dj – is a soft *j* as in jack. Hence the name Hadji is pronounced *Hajee*

ž – is a yet softer *j* as in pleasure. Hence the name Draža is pronounced *Drarjer*

The Trigger

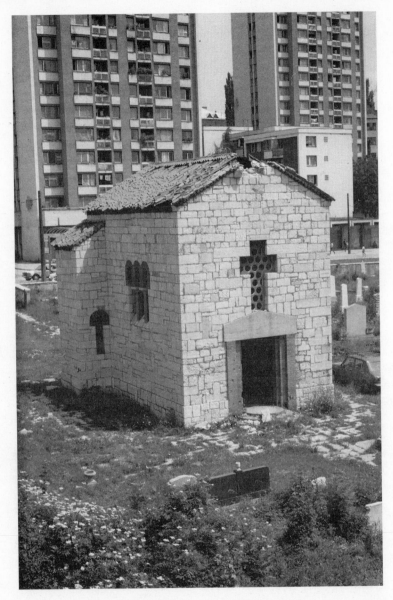

Gavrilo Princip's war-damaged tomb

PROLOGUE

This story springs from many sources, but the most powerful one for me was a discovery I made at a street market in Sarajevo, back when the city was under siege in 1994. I was a young reporter sent by the *Daily Telegraph* to cover the Bosnian War, which had begun two years earlier in this land of mountain and myth. Shelling had often made it too dangerous for civilians to venture outside in their capital city, but during a lull in the firing I joined locals as they reclaimed the streets. One afternoon I walked into an open area busy with people reduced by the war to selling possessions laid out in piles across unswept pavements. Pickings were meagre: half-worn brake pads from cars that had not run in years, a set of taps unused because of no mains water. I took a photograph of an elderly man sitting under an umbrella, shaded from the July sun, as he sold cigarettes one by one.

And then I noticed people occasionally slipping away from the market to visit a stone building on the edge of a nearby cemetery. I went to explore.

It was about the size of an electricity substation, a modest structure with a box design, easy to overlook. It wore the livery of so many wartime buildings in Sarajevo: a cavity from what appeared to be an artillery strike, terracotta roof tiles rucked out of alignment, the door ripped from its hinges, its frame pock-marked by shrapnel. I followed the market-goers and, in the summer heat, my sense of smell told me from some distance what

was going on. They were using it as a makeshift lavatory. My diary
recorded it in malodorous detail:

> The graveyard was unkempt but I was not prepared for what
> I found . . . The floor was just a sea of turds. Amongst the
> mess were dozens of used sanitary towels, a bra and lots of
> rubbish. A tombstone lay smashed in two on the floor and
> the light hung wrecked from the ceiling which had a gaping
> hole in it.

But what made me curious was that the building was clearly
some sort of chapel. A cross was visible above the doorway. Why
be so disrespectful of a religious site?

I found the answer on a piece of black marble set into an external
wall. It was a commemoration stone bearing the date 1914 and
some Cyrillic text, including a list of names. At the top of the list,
in the most prominent position, was one that jumped out at me:
ГАВРИЛО ПРИНЦИП, Gavrilo Princip.

When I went to Sarajevo for the first time as a reporter, a single
thought kept coming to me: this was where the event took place
that triggered the First World War, the assassination of Archduke
Franz Ferdinand by Gavrilo Princip. As a schoolboy I remember
struggling to pronounce the killer's name, but as I grew older my
understanding of the crisis he precipitated became clearer –
millions of lives lost in a clash so colossal it reshaped the world.
Yet the Bosnian War of the 1990s seemed far removed from the
fighting of the Great War, a localised, ethnic conflict in the Balkans,
a region synonymous in Western eyes with impenetrability, back-
wardness and violence. For much of the twentieth century Bosnia
had been one of the component parts of Yugoslavia, but when its
leaders in Sarajevo sought to create their own separate country

they clashed with the Serbian authorities who dominated the Yugoslav nation and who opposed the break-up. Tens of thousands were to die in fighting that, if you took away the helicopters, wire-guided missiles and satellite navigation systems, seemed to belong to an earlier, more brutal age: deliberate attacks on civilians, torching of homes, systematic rape, genocide.

Sarajevo was where many of the Bosnian War's defining horrors took place. In early exchanges, forces commanded by Bosnian Serb hardliners had been able to secure only a few of Sarajevo's peripheral suburbs, so they withdrew to the high ground that presses in on this cupped hand of a city and set about imposing one of the cruellest sieges in modern warfare. The lights went out, taps ran dry and supplies dwindled to a trickle, condemning 400,000 Sarajevans to survive on the collapsing skeleton of their home town. Their tormentors suffered no such supply problems and were able to dictate the nature and pace of their assault.

With their soldiers on the frontlines unable to advance, Bosnian Serb commanders sought to wear down their enemy by pounding them with artillery dug in on the nearby hilltops. When they ran out of military targets they kept on firing, wantonly destroying religious buildings, assembly halls, hospitals, newspaper offices, libraries – anything that contributed, no matter how marginally, to Bosnia's nascent sense of national identity. And when they ran out of those, they kept up their barrage, firing with deliberate cruelty – actions that were later to be successfully prosecuted as war crimes – into residential areas. With grim inevitability, many of Sarajevo's bloodiest incidents took place as civilians were cut down by shells when they emerged from cover for essential supplies: queuing for bread, waiting at a standpipe for water, crowding market stalls whenever smugglers made it into the city.

As a foreign correspondent, peacock-proud to be covering my first full conflict, I was kept busy by a city that seemed to bookend the bloodletting of the twentieth century. I was witness to a conflict that realigned the way the modern world fought. NATO would go to war in Bosnia, for the first time in its history, changing fundamentally the international community's willingness to intervene. And the Bosnian War would spill further into the future, its battlefields a training ground for jihadists who would take part in the 9/11 attacks on America.

Disturbed by what I was seeing, I read everything I could find about Bosnia's background to try and understand the source of the conflict. History seemed to loom over Sarajevo from the same heights held by the Bosnian Serb gunners, as I learned of complex colonial and religious influences that had pulled the local Slav population in different directions through the ages. Lying where Europe's south-eastern fringe comes up against influences from Asia Minor, Bosnia had a back-story dominated for hundreds of years by foreign occupation, first by the Ottoman Empire, then by Austria–Hungary (otherwise known as the Habsburg Empire). Although its people shared the same language and cultural roots, cleavages over the centuries had created three identifiable groups: Bosnian Serbs, Bosnian Croats and Bosnian Muslims. I read repeatedly how the era of foreign domination had been ended by the First World War when a new nation, Yugoslavia, emerged out of the fighting, one that allowed local Slavs to rule themselves for the first time in the modern era. In all my research the role of Gavrilo Princip appeared settled: the backwoodsman from the Bosnian hinterland who brought freedom to his people by sparking the war that finally swept away foreign control.

So why were Sarajevans now desecrating the tomb of someone who fought for their freedom? Gavrilo Princip was a Bosnian Serb – the same ethnicity as the extremists attacking the city – but spite alone could not explain what I had found. There had to be more to it.

CHAPTER 1

Fresh Flotsam

Uncle Alyn

No 62 Squadron. Uncle Alyn stands fifth from the left

In other wars more people have died, more nations been involved and the world brought closer to annihilation, but somehow the First World War retains a dread aura all of its own. The guns fell silent all those years ago, but like a refrain that stays with the audience long after the music stops, the First World War has a returning power. So monumental was the suffering, so far-reaching the influence on history that the war still generates reward not just for writers, academics and artists, but for people simply learning about themselves, their bloodlines, their place. The Great War's power lies with the suspicion that its impact has yet to be fully understood.

I was born in Britain half a century after the fighting ended, yet the First World War has always been thereabouts, a background presence shaping me and my setting, a founding sequence in my make-up. Often it was so faint it was difficult to discern: the whittling of one's own self through the loss of a distant ancestor. Occasionally it spiked: in my teens sitting with my mother as she wept through the Festival of Remembrance televised each year from the Royal Albert Hall in London. But a war from a hundred years ago remains relevant enough to intrude on our todays through a sense that closure has perhaps yet to be reached. The moral clarity that framed the Second World War's struggle against Nazi totalitarianism, or the Cold War's friction between right and left, seems to evade the earlier conflict. The question, 'Was it right to go to war in 1914?' can be answered in many ways, through bullet points or lengthy treatises, but I wonder if any answer is totally convincing.

This is what keeps the First World War so charged – the unease born of doubt as to whether the sacrifice was worthwhile. For me, this is what transforms so powerfully the words of Laurence Binyon, plain enough by themselves, but, when delivered on a raw November morning to a gathering of people wearing red paper poppies, they ache from what might have been: *We Will Remember Them*.

In the small Northamptonshire village where I grew up, the First World War was remembered in glass. Hellidon was too small to have shops, so the community revolved, as it had for centuries, around the church of St John the Baptist, a modest but stolid place of worship in keeping with the village's position at the middle of Middle England. Built of locally quarried ironstone, St John's was chilly-damp in winter, yet on summer nights the butterscotch masonry bled warmth from the day's baking in the sun. It was old enough to have known fighting; indeed, my childish imagination was fired by stories about the runnels that flute the stone arch in the portico. I was told they had been left by seventeenth-century noblemen sharpening their swords before battle in the Civil War.

As children, my friends and I would dare each other to climb the bell-tower, and for years I earned pocket money mowing the grass in the graveyard. At the village carol service one year I fought my first trembling battle with stage fright when I was called on to read the Advent message from the Archangel Gabriel. A box had to be placed in the pulpit so that I could see out as I wrestled with nerves and difficult words. The next generation of Butchers would themselves pass through St John's, with my firstborn niece being baptised there, while my own son would take snot-nosed delight in toddling up the lane to watch the bell-ringers at practice.

And each of these modest moments of a family's making were watched over by four figures immortalised in a stained-glass window that was set to catch the southern sun. Such windows are where biblical characters tend to be represented, but in the

Hellidon village church a group of decidedly unbiblical-looking male faces have stared out since their unveiling in 1920. Against a setting of rich green foliage and red petals, daylight can give the figures an authentically holy glow. They wear the pure-silver armour of chivalrous medieval knights; indeed, one is helmeted, but the other three have the pasted-down, centre-parted hairstyles of early twentieth-century England. They are portraits of the menfolk of the village who gave their lives in the First World War: two brothers, William and James Hedges, Fred Wells and John Buchanan.

It was this window that first brought me to think about the war, although my early grasp was childlike. Mostly I was interested in the sword that the helmeted figure leans on and in the stirringly heroic words of the memorial's swirling epitaph: 'The Noble Army of Martyrs Praise Thee.' These were men from my village, from my side. They died for us in a foreign place, in a cause that simply must have been noble. Now, back to the sword.

Mine was not a military family, but as I grew older it was impossible to avoid the martial osmosis that steadily gives structure to the imagery of 1914–18: troops, trenches, bayonets, barbed wire, cannon, craters, monuments, memorials. St John's held a remembrance service each year, an event that was choreographed around the symbols of the Great War and had the power to transform some of our older neighbours. I knew them as keen gardeners or dog-walkers, but for one morning each year a medal ribbon on their breasts spoke of something much more thrilling – combat that, in some way too complex for my young mind to understand, was rooted in the First World War.

The conflict would crop up more and more in my reading as the stories of Biggles landed on my bookshelves and history teachers began to fill in my understanding, one that was initially framed in terms simplistic enough for a schoolboy to grasp: Us against Them, Good versus Evil. I was taught about a clash between Britain and Germany, one fought mostly from fortified holes in the ground separated by the ominously named 'no-man's-land', a killing zone so dangerous that men would use periscopes to look out over it. Afternoons were spent playing with friends as we built earthworks of our own, dens concealed in hedgerows, underground hideouts where we too could be heroes. When my science teacher showed us how to construct a home-made periscope, it was immediately deployed on our imaginary battlefield.

At the age of twelve, I went to Rugby, a school whose alumni, they never tired of telling us, included Rupert Brooke, among the most celebrated of war poets. The school was so proud of this particular son that his great work, 'The Soldier', was read to us on every possible public occasion. It summed up perfectly any adolescent framing of the war:

> If I should die, think only this of me:
> That there's some corner of a foreign field
> That is forever England. There shall be
> In that rich earth a richer dust concealed.

The lines captured the proud early idealism stirred by the war and soon made Brooke a favourite of the Establishment. He was writing in the first months of the war, when patriotism had about it a purity yet to be corrupted by jingoism, and in his verse there was no sense of questioning the war and the way it was conducted. He died less than a year into the conflict, in April 1915, aboard a hospital ship en route to Gallipoli, and although 'The Soldier' had only just been published, Winston Churchill, in his last days as First Lord of the Admiralty, put his name to a fulsome tribute published in *The Times*:

The thoughts to which he gave expression in the very few incomparable war sonnets which he has left behind will be shared by many thousands of young men moving resolutely and blithely forward into this, the hardest, the cruellest and the least-rewarded of all the wars that men have fought.

As my schooling progressed it was the last part of this Churchillian flourish that I began to comprehend – the First World War's suicidal combination of medieval, muddy entrenchment tactics and modern, industrial-age weaponry. Entire units could be wiped out in a single engagement, dutiful infantrymen following orders not to run but to march, as they advanced against machine-gun fire; cohorts of chums churning through the slop, cringing, bleeding, drowning. Particularly haunting, for me, were the legions of soldiers who died without leaving a trace, their bodies atomised by high explosives, buried alive in artillery barrages. Could a war ever end for relatives troubled by the knowledge that the remains of a loved one had never been found? The epitaph on memorials that seeks to reassure us today, 'Known unto God', was composed by the author Rudyard Kipling, himself a father condemned to plough forlornly the post-war battlefields of the Western Front in search of his lost son, John. He never found him.

The more I read, the more I learned solemn reverence for the millions killed, disfigured and damaged, a feeling so powerful that it seeped through my young life. Hideouts that had been fun to escape to when I was younger lost their magic when I read of the vermin that infested the trenches in Flanders, the lice, the rotting corpses set into battlement walls, the gas, the shell-shocked men tormented by combat of a relentlessness never before endured. As my friends and I went through the teenage ritual of smoking cigarettes, we would lurk behind our figurative bike-shed at school and earnestly refuse a third light, a superstition we believed born of trench warfare. The myth went that on the Western Front an enemy sniper would catch sight of a match lighting the first cigarette, take aim on the second and pull the trigger on the third.

Like wreckage that floats to the surface from a colossal ocean liner that went down long ago, so links to the events of the First World War can still emerge years later. For me this happened in 1981, when my mother hung a photograph in our home. Following the death of my maternal grandmother, a sepia portrait of a young airman passed to my mother and she made sure it was put on display, prominently positioned at eye-level opposite the bottom of the stairs. From there the portrait watched over the toing and froing of my teenage years.

It showed Alyn Reginald James, my grandmother's older brother, as a young man in his early twenties wearing an infantry officer's uniform from the First World War. Uncle Alyn, as he is known to us later generations, leans casually on a cane, the very vision of dashing, the winged badge of the Royal Flying Corps visible on his breast. Before the Royal Air Force had even been founded, he was one of the first combat pilots – something that, to my young mind, marked him out with greatness, a magnificent man in his flying machine. He flew sorties against Baron Manfred von Richthofen, the Red Baron, one of the most exotic figures of the First World War. This was the stuff of childish fantasy, and for a long time that is what the portrait signified to me.

Researching this book, I found pictures of Uncle Alyn that I had not seen, fresh flotsam from the deep that still had the power to move my mother to silence. They included a pair of official photographs of his unit, No 62 Squadron, taken in the same sitting on a wintry morning in Britain, one very formal and the other smiling. In the serious one I struggled to recognise him among the glum expressions, Sam Browne belts, handlebar moustaches and medley of pre-RAF uniforms. But in the more casual picture his features stand out clearly, the same round cheeks hoisted above the wide smile I remember from the picture in Hellidon. Someone has captioned the smiling photograph with a title worthy of Biggles. It reads: 'The Cheery 62's'.

In the last image I found, he is now in France, standing alongside an informal group of airmen. The mood of the picture is different. It is cold. Several of the men have their hands in their pockets. One wears mittens. Uncle Alyn is smiling, but with not quite the same cheeky conviction as before. He stands on duckboards. The rich earth of Rupert Brooke has turned to the ruddy mud of the Western Front.

On 24 March 1918, days after this picture was taken, Uncle Alyn was lost while strafing German trenches. He was twenty-three. He has no known grave.

His parents had to endure months of uncertainty about whether he might have survived. He came down close to the Somme River during an intense German offensive and at a time when the British army was in pell-mell retreat. With thousands of casualties on both sides, the fate of a single enemy aircraft on land recently and bloodily fought over was hardly a priority for the advancing Germans. It would be months before British officialdom formally pronounced that Alyn was dead.

This is where the true power of the portrait lies: a means to earth the pain of a mother predeceased by a son, and of a sister who had lost an adored brother, an echo for those who came later of what might have been. Around the world, in picture frames, albums and scrapbooks, similar memorabilia contribute to this returning power of the Great War. As a young man I had thought of Alyn as extraordinary, someone who marked out our family in some special way. But I came to learn that, in essence, our family experience was no different from that endured by millions: a sense of loss still powerful enough to touch our contemporary world.

A few years ago my mother's brother was moved to make his own family pilgrimage to the battlefield where Alyn died. He wrote to me explaining that he wanted to see if it was possible to identify where his uncle might have been buried. 'By working out where he was probably shot down we searched a few cemeteries and did find the graves of two unidentified airmen which could easily have been Alyn and his observer. We liked to think so, anyway.'

As I matured, so did the sophistication of my understanding of the First World War. Like the trenches that started out as shell-scrapes but morphed into ever more complex military ecosystems with their own terminology – saps, berms, revetments and embra-sures – so my mental imagery of the Great War began to fill out. I started to appreciate how its impact reached far beyond the battlefield, changing the course of the twentieth century. As my history teachers drilled into me, the First World War provided the preconditions for the Second World War and thereby the tension of the Cold War. The war of 1914–18 was Ground Zero for modern history, the end of an old order that had held sway for hundreds of years, the fiery forging of a new world.

Rupert Brooke's romantic imagery no longer felt so convincing when I learned more about the senseless stalemate of trench warfare, where lives were sacrificed on frontlines that scarcely moved in years. Generals who bloodily piled unsuccessful offensive onto unsuccessful offensive could be lampooned as 'donkeys leading lions'. The starker framing of war poets like Wilfred Owen and Edward Thomas rang truer, and so I came to share in their bitterness about the way the war was run. I could get the joke when the futility of the sacrifice was satirised in films like *Oh! What a Lovely War* and television series like *Blackadder Goes Forth*.

A far-sighted teacher opened up a broader perspective when he persuaded me to read *All Quiet on the Western Front* by Erich

Maria Remarque, a veteran of the fighting, but from the 'other side'. Germans were depicted as victims of fear and suffering, living and dying in flooded trenches, ordered to make suicidal stands by commanders aloof from reality. The novel hinted at the universality of the First World War's ongoing power, as there was none of the Nazi evil or communist megalomania that made it easy to compartmentalise later conflicts. In the First World War soldiers on all sides were barely discernible from each other, fodder caught in the same murderous morass, sharing the same attrition of bullet and barrage, disease and deprivation, torment and terror. Elsewhere I learned that Adolf Hitler's psychotic German nationalism was in part forged from his own experience of trench warfare and his fury at what he perceived as the betrayal of soldiers by politicians far away from the trenches. Blood might be spilled on the battlefield, but the Great War's impact was measured in the turmoil it created far beyond the frontline through strife, civil war and revolution that ousted regimes and realigned the social order. This the First World War achieved on an unparalleled scale.

In 1982 my family went on a package holiday to Yugoslavia, a country born out of this realignment, staying at a lake resort in the north, close to the modern border with Austria. The trip was memorable because it was the first time I flew (great excitement for a fourteen-year-old) and the first time I had a holiday romance (greater excitement still), but even there the First World War also barged its way in. Before that summer I had scarcely been aware of fighting beyond the Western Front, but in our lakeside hotel in the spa town of Bled we were just a short coach trip away from the Italian Front. This was where Italy led the Allied fight against Germany's great ally, Austria–Hungary, along a frontline that climbed high into the Julian Alps, one of the most brutal theatres of the First World War. Here soldiers had to endure not just artillery barrages and infantry clashes, but winter conditions in the remote mountains. In December 1916 avalanches alone killed as many as 10,000 soldiers.

All I wanted to do on holiday was sit around the hotel pool staring at the girl I had fallen for, but my father insisted that we go on a military-history day trip. I grumbled, arguing that it would be enough for me to read Ernest Hemingway's *A Farewell to Arms*, which draws on his time serving as an ambulance driver on the nearby front. But my father would not be deterred, dragging me one afternoon onto a bus that took us deep into the mountains, up a valley with sides that got ever steeper. Summer seemed shut out from the military graveyard that we finally reached in the late afternoon. The valley floor was chill, already in deep shadow, yet there were lit candles in small glass jars flickering next to gravestones from the First World War. It was more than six decades since the fighting ended, yet the war remained alive enough for flames to be kept alight.

My education took me to Oxford, where my study of political history taught me more about the First World War's global reach. The small nation of Serbia would lose 15 per cent of its population in the First World War – compared to the roughly 2 per cent figure for Britain, where the wounds on the national psyche remain livid enough – making it apparent how the conflict had the power to redraw maps and realign history. Fighting spread to sub-Saharan Africa, as European officers led colonial conscripts into battles that ranged from the Indian Ocean coastline to others over on the Atlantic side of the continent. The Arabian Peninsula and the wider Middle East would be changed for ever as local clans rose against the decaying imperial authority of the 'Sublime Porte', the elegant soubriquet for the Ottoman Empire.

Washington would eventually be drawn in, changing fundamentally the twentieth-century balance of power and propelling America towards superpower status. Britain's pre-eminent position before the First World War was never fully restored, a slow puncture that would eventually cost Britain its empire. At Gallipoli, the theatre of war that Rupert Brooke was heading for when he died, soldiers from the other side of the world would die in such numbers that the national consciences of Australia and New Zealand would be redefined.

University studies brought home for me how the impact of 1914–18 was felt beyond the battlefield. It was a war of the masses that would change for ever how the masses viewed themselves and, crucially, how those masses were to be governed. The aloofness of assumed imperial power, the inherited *droit de seigneur* that had held sway for so long, could not survive. The Romanov, Ottoman, German and Habsburg Empires were all swept away by the First World War. For decades Europe's great dynasties had successfully fought off the rising tides of social democracy, nationalism and workers' rights that bloomed in the nineteenth century through the writings of Karl Marx, William Morris, Max Weber and so many others. From 1848, the year of Europe's failed revolutions, the *ancien régime* had prevailed because those demanding change, whether socially-minded democrats or revolutionary-minded anarchists, were outsiders. All this changed with the Great War, as insider turned on insider, empire against empire, bloc against bloc – a conflict so cataclysmic it would destroy the old order. It was out of this turbulent collapse that Bolshevism, socialism, fascism and other radical political currents took root.

I read about the origins of the First World War, a subject of such extensive academic focus over the years that Alan 'A.J.P.' Taylor, one of Britain's sharpest historians, called it 'a large-scale industry'. In the immediate aftermath of the fighting the victorious Allies laid the blame for the war solely on Germany, although later historians would develop a much wider causal kaleidoscope spreading responsibility across other combatant nations. For many researchers Luigi Albertini's magisterial opus, *The Origins of the War of 1914*, provides the mother lode with its three hefty volumes of documents, correspondence and analysis. Sifting through more than 60,000 public papers from the build-up to the war, and interviewing as many of the protagonists as possible, consumed the last decades of Albertini's life. After carefully polishing and editing his book, he would die in 1941 before completing the final chapter, on where he believed blame for the fighting ultimately lay. And ever since Albertini's opus was published, archives in Vienna, Berlin, Istanbul and elsewhere have thrown up new material for experts dissecting the mutual suspicion between the Great Powers – Germany, France, Russia, Britain, Austria–Hungary – and the sequence of events that led to the collision on the battlefields of the Eastern and Western Fronts.

From all this analysis of the Great War's origins has emerged a tragic picture of self-destruction, one that was wilful, ignorant and inexorable: wilful, in that world leaders chose to leverage up a local crisis into a world war; ignorant, in that politicians, diplomats and generals failed to grasp the consequences; inexorable, in that once the process of militarisation began, there was no dissuading the old-world regimes. Arguments of historical interpretation still rage and analysis can disagree over subplots, such as the extent to which Germany was finessed into recklessly supporting Vienna by manipulative Austrian diplomats, or by what folly Britain drew Turkey into the war. But the consensus ultimately shared by many is that the complex deterrent system of diplomatic alliances designed to balance rivalries between the Great Powers was flawed, incapable of dispersing the storm clouds massing figuratively over early-twentieth-century Europe.

My favourite, if slightly off-piste, inexorability theory was put forward by Alan Taylor, a don at my old Oxford college, Magdalen, long before I studied there. In *War by Time-Table* he argues convincingly that fixed railway schedules worsened the rush to war in 1914, especially for Germany. Railways were then the only feasible way to deploy large numbers of soldiers and materiel, but what was crucial, in Taylor's view, was that timetable rigidity made it effectively impossible to stop the escalation. For one side to avoid being overwhelmed by an enemy whose troops had already entrained, it could not hold back the full deployment of its own soldiers. Timetable rigidity contributed to mass murder in the trenches.

But the crisis still needed a spark to detonate the explosive mix of old-world superiority, diplomatic miscalculation, strategic paranoia and hubristic military overconfidence. And, like generations of young students before and since, I had been taught that the First World War began after the heir to the Austro-Hungarian Empire, Archduke Franz Ferdinand, was shot in Sarajevo by Gavrilo Princip. Academics still debate the diplomatic-political multiplier that transformed a Balkan assassination into a *casus belli* for the Great Powers, but none dispute that it was the shooting in Sarajevo that led the world to war a century ago. The assassination is so settled in the historical narrative that the exact details of Princip's actions are overlooked, even trivialised. We all smirked when Blackadder's numbskull sidekick Baldrick remembered it thus: 'I heard that it started when a bloke called Archie Duke shot an ostrich 'cause he was hungry.'

Going to Sarajevo to cover the Bosnian War brought the assassination to life for me. The street corner where Princip fired his pistol is a well-known local landmark; indeed, for years visitors used to be able to stand in two footprints sunk in the cement of the pavement, fanciful representations of where the assassin stood at his moment of destiny. But Princip's fouled tomb led me to think again. It dislodged in my mind a troubling piece of Great War flotsam: the thought that, in the eyes of some of his own people, Princip and his cause were not worth honouring. The filth I found in that memorial chapel polluted the purity of the sacrifice made by Uncle Alyn, the four men from Hellidon, the legions lost on the Western Front, the Italians buried in the snow and millions of others.

Princip was Bosnian Serb by ethnicity, but this alone could not explain what I had found. In spite of everything inflicted on them during the siege by Bosnian Serb forces, the people of Sarajevo had not given in to blanket hatred of all things Serb. During the war plenty of Bosnian Serbs had stayed in the city, bravely distancing themselves from the violent nationalism displayed by the more extreme elements of their own community, still committed to the multi-ethnic coexistence that had long been a characteristic of Sarajevo. The city's Serb Orthodox churches were largely left alone, as were Serb cultural centres and other buildings clearly linked to the Serb community. I had friends who endured the siege inside the city and who were treated no differently by their fellow Sarajevans, even though it was common knowledge they were ethnic Serbs. Through my work as a journalist I often came across a senior general defending the city from the Bosnian Serbs, a man called Jovan Divjak, who was himself Serbian.

To try to understand more about Princip, I turned to the history books. There was much to consider. There can be few turnkey moments so intensively written about as the assassination of Archduke Franz Ferdinand. In 1960 a bibliography was published that simply listed all books, articles and papers referencing the Sarajevo assassination. It was 547 pages long and had more than 1,200 entries. Like popcorn jumping from hot oil, writing about the incident has continued to emerge since that bibliography came out. But the analysis tended to focus on what happened next; on the actions of foreign powers presumed to have had influence over Princip; on who was or was not to blame for ramping up a minor political act in Sarajevo into global conflict; and on the falling-domino sequence of diplomatic blunders made by the Great Powers. None of it, to my mind, fully explained the fouled tomb.

References to Princip were common, although primary histor-ical material connected to him is incredibly scarce. He left no diary, and only a few passages of his own writing have ever been found. Austro-Hungarian legal records dating from after the 1914 assassination provide a source, with passages of Princip's own testimony recorded verbatim, although the original record of his trial was lost in the chaos of the war – a twist for conspiracy theorists who continue to pick at its origins. The paperwork, all 90 kg of it, was last recorded as being in the custody of the Habsburg imperial commandant in Vienna in around June 1915. It was kept in a chest, serial number IS 206-15, but exactly what then happened to it remains a mystery. Fortunately for historians, the two Sarajevan stenographers who covered the case had broken protocol by taking home their shorthand notes, scribbled in pencil on narrow strips of court recorders' paper, and in 1954 a transcript of the trial was published that is regarded as reliable.

In the years after the assassination a large number of friends and associates of Princip had given accounts of the young man they once knew. Some were fanciful, others frankly opportunistic, with some sources even presuming to re-create letters supposedly written by the young man. A book published in 1966 called *The Road to Sarajevo*, by a Yugoslav author, Vladimir Dedijer, does a fine job of sifting through all this hearsay to produce perhaps the most authoritative history of Princip.

Born in a village on the remote western edge of Bosnia, Princip had undergone a process of radicalisation at the schools he attended across the region, a journey that culminated in the assassination in Sarajevo. It was a deliberate revolutionary act, one that was intended to lead to the liberation of the Western Balkans. Centuries of occupation and foreign domination had drawn its Slav population in different directions, yet Princip was part of a growing cohort of locals who believed the moment was right for the locals to rule themselves. His thinking was idealistic, dreamy, woolly even – he certainly had no appreciation of how his actions might lead to a world war – and he had no clear concept of what would come after the removal of the Archduke and the Austro-Hungarian Empire he represented. Kingdom, republic, federation – whatever emerged must be better than the tyranny of the outsider. But the key question, from the perspective of the 1990s war, was whether he fired his gun only for his Bosnian Serb kin, or for the higher purpose of helping all local Slavs.

The Slav lands of the Western Balkans reach far beyond Bosnia alone, and at the time of the assassination in 1914 they were a mosaic under varying degrees of occupation or liberation: for example, Croatia towards the north had for centuries been under the control of Austria–Hungary or its antecedents, and Serbia to the east had only recently and bloodily won independence after generations of Ottoman rule, while Bosnia itself had been carved off the Ottoman Empire in the 1870s and bolted onto the Austro-Hungarian Empire. The mosaic was complex and shifting, but one constant was that its people – from the Julian Alps bordering Italy in the north all the way down to the frontier with Greece in the south – predominantly shared the same Slav bloodline. Ethnographers categorise them as 'south Slavs' to distinguish them from other Slav peoples further north (Russians, Poles, Czechs and Slovaks), although from antiquity all Slavs have some common roots.

Before the assassination, Princip had received a few days of training and some weapons through renegade intelligence officers in Serbia. For some analysts this was enough to conclude that he had purely Serbian interests at heart. However, the freedom fighting group to which he was primarily loyal, Mlada Bosna, or Young Bosnia, had members who came from all three major Bosnian ethnic groups. One of Princip's fellow conspirators on the day of the assassination, deployed with a weapon on the same mission to kill the Archduke, was a Bosnian Muslim, while another Muslim played a crucial role in acquiring the weapons used for the assassination. A Bosnian Croat family in Sarajevo was entrusted that day with disposing of the weapons after the attack.

From my reading it became clear to me that historians were remarkably casual with details concerning Princip, in particular the central question of why he took part in the assassination. So monumental were the events and aftermath of the conflict resulting from his actions that Princip's own story has been overshadowed by the onrush of what happened next – his motivations misunderstood, muddled, even misrepresented. Nothing captures better this casualness than a photograph showing a man being arrested in Sarajevo moments after the shooting on 28 June 1914. Blurry with energy, it is a dramatic image of a prisoner being frogmarched through a melee, both arms pinned as he struggles, a gendarme with a sabre trying to stop men wearing fezzes from lunging at the prisoner. It fits so well the narrative of the desperate assassin that countless historians, reporters, broadcasters and film-makers have claimed that the subject of the photograph is Princip. It is not. The subject of the picture is actually an innocent bystander, a man called Ferdinand Behr, who was caught up in the sweep of arrests following the shooting.

After the war ended in Bosnia in 1995, I was appointed Defence Correspondent for the *Telegraph* and one of my regular duties was to cover Britain's annual remembrance service, which is held each November at the Cenotaph on Whitehall in central London. I would take my place on a wooden media platform erected adjacent to the understated, yet potent stone memorial designed by Sir Edwin Lutyens and watch as the capital's principal artery of government would steadily fill on a wintry Sunday morning with members of the public, then with cadets, bandsmen, airmen, soldiers, sailors and, finally, veterans. Britain 'does' set-piece commemoration so very well, and each year I remember the immaculate timing and precision of a mass event that still managed to release an individual, private rush of solemnity.

The fallen of all wars would be commemorated, but for me the power of the service came in being drawn back to the epic sacrifice of the First World War. The poppies worn by us all were symbols born of the Western Front. Stanzas of Great War poetry would be read out by the officiating priests. Even the timing of the event kept alive the moment on Armistice Day in 1918 when the guns fell silent on the Western Front: the eleventh hour of the eleventh day of the eleventh month. The image of Princip's filthy tomb would keep coming back to me. Had all these people died for a cause so fundamentally opaque that the person who initiated the whole catastrophe could be despised by his own countrymen?

The more I read, the less clear it became. The histories all seemed to cover the same ground, worrying at the same bone of diplomatic blunders and grand strategic plans that led to mass military deployment and bloody stalemate. None seemed to address fully the catalyst of it all – Princip and his Bosnian homeland, the wellspring for conflicts of such far-reaching importance.

To understand better not just the fouled tomb, but also the ongoing power of the First World War, I decided to return to Bosnia. I would follow Princip's life path, trekking where he trekked, from the village out west where he was born; I would explore the Balkan towns and cities where he studied, worked and travelled, and would piece together as far as possible the setting and detail of the assassination, his influences and his motivations. It was a journey that I hoped would fill out my vision of the man who ghosts sketchily into the received history of the First World War. And, by grounding him in his homeland, I hoped for a clearer understanding of a place that retains, as I witnessed through the war of the 1990s, a powerful hold over some of the twentieth century's most troubling events.

CHAPTER 2

A Troublesome Teenager

The author, left, as a reporter during the Bosnian War

Light and dark loops showing minefields near Bugojno

The Balkans might today carry a reputation for remoteness, but research has revealed this to be a relatively modern attitude. In antiquity, this mountainous region on the south-eastern edge of Europe – in effect a peninsula bounded on three sides by sea – formed part of the core of the Roman Empire; indeed, one of the later Roman emperors, Diocletian, was born there. Fragments of his palace can still be seen in the Adriatic port of Split, incorporated in the tumbledown muddle of the old city on the waterfront. The region was then known as Illyria, a place name that William Shakespeare would fancy as the setting for *Twelfth Night*.

'Balkans' is a much more modern term, a Turkish word for 'a forested mountain range', which only entered common usage in the nineteenth century when the area encompassed the Ottoman Empire's territory in Europe. The Balkan Peninsula today includes Greece and Albania to the south, and Bulgaria to the east, but it was the western sector of the Balkans that came to be dominated in the Middle Ages by those who would be known as south Slavs. Before the arrival of foreign occupiers, these people ruled through a series of recognisable states with borders that fluctuated over the ages. At varying times in the Middle Ages there existed recognisable nations of Bosnia, Croatia and Serbia, states that were never powerful enough to rule the entire Western Balkan region, but which left a heritage of national identity strong enough to survive through to the present day.

Gavrilo Princip, history's ultimate teenage troublemaker, was only nineteen when he fired the pistol that killed the Archduke in 1914, and he was to die four years later in an Austro-Hungarian jail, his bones eaten away by skeletal tuberculosis. But even during so short a life, he had crossed rich contours of European geography. In the late summer of 1907, aged thirteen, he walked across roughly one third of Bosnia after his parents had decided there was no life for him in Obljaj, the impoverished village of his birth. It lies way out on the western fringe of Bosnia in the area known as Herzegovina, so it was eastwards that he and his father headed, their belongings strapped to the family's horse. A journey that would change not only Princip's life, but the course of global history, began when, as a boy, he left the famously rocky highlands of Herzegovina and climbed over the mountain passes into the tighter, greener valleys of central Bosnia.*

The overland trail eventually led Princip and his father to a railhead located in the town of Bugojno. From there they travelled by train through the fertile valleys of the Vrbas, Lašva and Bosna Rivers, the last of which rises at the foot of mountains close to Sarajevo and is the origin of the country's name. Eventually the train delivered them to the capital, then a city of roughly 50,000 people, with schools big enough to promise the young boy far greater opportunities than anything available back home. His father returned to Obljaj, leaving the young Princip in Sarajevo to embark alone on his secondary education.

---

* Over the centuries the official name of the country has referred to both Bosnia and Herzegovina, the latter being a relatively small segment of territory on the southern and western periphery, famous for its stark, stony relief and its seasonal extremes of temperature. It owes its name to a period in history when it was ruled by a *herceg* or duke, and the naming tradition continues today with the modern nation officially known as 'Bosnia and Herzegovina'. For the purposes of this book I will use the accepted abbreviation of 'Bosnia' for the whole country, unless explicitly referring to the parcel of land that makes up Herzegovina.

At this point in its history Bosnia was an outpost of Austria–Hungary, the last creaking iteration of the great Habsburg Empire that had grown to rule parts of central Europe since the thirteenth century. With its imperial capital in Vienna, the empire at the start of the twentieth century was a sprawl of peoples and languages, reaching from Bosnia in the south to Poland in the north, from the Swiss Alps in the west to the Ukrainian steppe in the east. Cherished by the novelist Joseph Roth as a 'large house with many doors and many rooms for many different kinds of people', Austria–Hungary had grown dangerously unwieldy. The 1905 edition of Baedeker's travel guide for the area noted that in some parts of the empire vehicles drove on the left, while elsewhere they drove on the right. It did not say what happened when the two driving styles collided.

As the twentieth century began, the stiff tunics worn by Habsburg imperial officials were a veneer concealing an empire in decline, home at roughly the same time and for varying periods to several figures who are key to modern history: Leon Trotsky, Adolf Hitler, Joseph Stalin and Tito. James Joyce lived there for almost ten years, teaching English to Austrian naval cadets in and around Trieste, learning to despise what he would call 'the most physically corrupt royal house in Europe'. Yet it was in schools across the empire's Balkan holdings that the green shoots of revolution were perhaps most visible. Youth politics was banned by the Austro-Hungarian authorities, so underground movements sprang up at colleges, amateurishly concealed behind a self-taught web of codenames, oaths and passwords thought up by pupils dreaming of change.

Princip may have sparked a century of turmoil, but he started out as a quiet and exemplary student from the provinces. It was while at school in Sarajevo that he first became caught up in this swirl of anti-Establishment, nationalistic idealism, reading

voraciously and learning to hero-worship Balkan assassins who
had dared to confront foreign occupiers. There were many of
those to choose from, in an era when assassination was a quite
standard driver for political change. After completing almost
three years at the Merchants' School of Sarajevo, Princip moved
on, switching to the classical grammar-school system, briefly
attending one in the northern Bosnian city of Tuzla before
enrolling at a second, back in Sarajevo. All the time his growing
radicalism made him increasingly unsettled, culminating in early
1912 when he withdrew from the Bosnian school system after
taking part in student protests against Austro-Hungarian rule.
It meant that to continue his education he would have to look
elsewhere.

Still only seventeen years of age, Princip left Sarajevo and headed
further east, crossing the Drina River frontier separating the
Austro-Hungarian territory of Bosnia from its neighbour, Serbia.
After the bunched mountainous terrain of his homeland, this
offered a very new and different environment, a flatland of eastern
European plain swept over by monumental rivers and ruled from
a capital city, Belgrade, built where high ground overlooks the
confluence of the mighty Danube and one of its largest tributaries,
the Sava. Princip arrived at a time of intense nationalistic turmoil,
with Serbia caught up in what history knows as the First and
Second Balkan Wars – short, bloody and successful confrontations
in 1912 and 1913. Through a series of clashes with Ottoman
occupiers throughout the nineteenth century, the south-Slav
people of Serbia had won freedom for themselves, re-creating part
of the medieval nation of Serbia. But they coveted parcels of territory to the south that were still under the control of Istanbul and
so, in the two brief Balkan Wars, Serbia moved to win back land
lost centuries earlier to the Ottomans.

As a result, when Princip first reached Serbia it was awash with weapons, militia, soldiers and plotters, the perfect place for a militant-minded student to complete his radicalisation. From 1912 the teenage Princip was based for long periods in Belgrade, drifting in and out of school, living on the breadline among a community of disaffected Bosnians who were dreaming of a time when their own homeland, like the new state of Serbia, might be freed from foreign control. Eventually, in the spring of 1914, Princip emerged as the leading figure in a conspiracy of young Bosnians who wanted to assassinate the heir of the Austro-Hungarian Empire that occupied their homeland.

Archduke Franz Ferdinand was due to visit Sarajevo to oversee manoeuvres by imperial troops at the end of June 1914, so in the spring of that year Princip headed home from Belgrade to Bosnia with two other would-be assassins. The route they took involved dodging border guards and wading back across the Drina under the cover of darkness. It was not just the Austro-Hungarian guards on the far side of the river of whom they were afraid. On the Serbian side, there were many elements in the Belgrade government that would have stopped them, if they could. The support that the assassins received in Serbia had come from only a small number of extremists within the military-intelligence community, and the wider Serbian establishment would have viewed any assassination plot with horror. Weakened by the bloody demands of the two recent Balkan Wars, the last thing the Serbian government wanted was to risk provoking an attack by a powerful neighbour such as Austria–Hungary.

Tension rose as Princip's gang prepared to cross back over the Drina. Now established as the group's leader, nineteen-year-old Princip ran out of patience with the bragging of one of the others, who was forced to find his own way. This left just two young men to smuggle themselves and their assassins' gear – four pistols and six grenades – all the way to Sarajevo in time for 28 June 1914

when, after the completion of army exercises, the Archduke was
due to enter the city on an official visit. The plotters judged that
the Archduke's city visit would give them their best opportunity
to strike.

I became steadily more intrigued as I worked out the route of
Princip's journey. It crossed not only rich territory, but also
contours of history that cluster tightly in this turbulent corner of
Europe. The Bosnian valleys through which he trekked were where,
three decades later, one of the subplots of the Second World War
would play out: the controversial decision by Churchill to back
partisans under Tito, a communist leader fighting against Nazi
occupation. It was a decision that had great impact on the later
Cold War, as it shifted Yugoslavia decisively into the orbit of the
communist world. For many, the stand-off between the capitalist
West and the communist East symbolically began with Churchill's
famous Iron Curtain speech at Fulton, Missouri, in 1946 when
he cited Trieste – the port city claimed by Tito's Yugoslavia – as
the divide between the two sides:

> From Stettin in the Baltic to Trieste in the Adriatic, an iron
> curtain has descended across the Continent. Behind that line
> lie all the capitals of the ancient states of Central and Eastern
> Europe . . . and all are subject in one form or another, not
> only to Soviet influence but to a very high and, in some cases,
> increasing measure of control from Moscow.

Following Princip's journey would enable me to explore this crucial
leftward lurch in Balkan history.

The route also passed places where some of the most sensitive
but unreachable moments of the Bosnian War of the 1990s had
played out. When Princip crossed back into Bosnia on his final

journey to Sarajevo, he passed through mountains north of the town of Srebrenica. This was where Europe's worst atrocity since the Holocaust took place in July 1995, when Bosnian Serbs overran a Bosnian Muslim enclave and set about systematically eradicating thousands of its men. Almost twenty years after the atrocity, the bodies of victims are still being identified from mass graves hidden in the range of hills tramped through by Princip in 1914.

By following the route from his birthplace to Sarajevo, on to Belgrade and then back again to the capital of Bosnia, I saw not only an opportunity to understand the influences that shaped Princip, but also a chance to unravel outstanding mental knots within myself, from when I first went to war.

From my home in Cape Town I began work by digging out several of the old 'set texts' from my time covering the Balkan Wars of the 1990s as a journalist, books that we outsiders dutifully lugged across the war zone. With nostalgic delight I picked up *Black Lamb and Grey Falcon*, a treasure chest of a travel book by Rebecca West, born of three brief trips through Yugoslavia on the eve of the Second World War. She famously left nothing out, taking five years to compose a tome of 350,000 words, a work that she herself described as 'an inventory of a country down to its last vest-button'. It is not just loaded with observational riches, but is on occasions irreverent, scatological, bitchy and plain batty. Much of the history within the book is unreliable, but its pluck more than makes up for this. As I reread my old paperback copy I found marginalia dating back two decades. Her complaints about the terrible quality of Bosnia's roads in the 1930s had come in for lots of underlining and ticks of approval. Some of the wartime roads I had battled along were beyond awful. One thing that stood out more clearly this time was West's hostility towards Germany, the Germans and all things Teutonic, while praising the vitality, unpredictability and

passion of local Slavs. The book is in essence an epic love-letter
to the Slavs, written at a time when one of Europe's great peoples,
the Germans, had lost their way under Nazi rule.

As I refined my plans, it was a relief not to be confronting the
risks associated with earlier trips that I had undertaken through
African war zones. At peace for more than a decade, the region I
would be travelling through was one no longer framed by war.
Ask students today what they know of Serbia and they are more
likely to mention its annual music festival, Exit, than the conflict
of the 1990s. Launched in 2000 in the Serbian city of Novi Sad,
Exit has grown raucously and exponentially each summer into one
of Europe's most popular music festivals – a sort of Glastonbury,
but without the mud.

The Internet has always seemed like the world's greatest library
opening up through my laptop and, even though I was such a long
way from the Balkans, useful leads soon began to surface. Online
search engines made it easy enough to track down old friends
whom I had known as translators, from Sarajevo to Belgrade, and
without exception they all responded positively to my emails. As
the research trail sprouted new branches, I uncovered a few words
of Serbo-Croatian lodged unused for years in a remote part of my
brain, although the language's name now had to be handled with
care. The nationalistic wars that pulled Yugoslavia apart in the
1990s have made using the old term, 'Serbo-Croatian', potentially
offensive. The different communities today speak of their own
exclusive language, whether it is Serbian, Croatian or Bosnian. It
required sensitivity when I introduced myself to local sources and
set about explaining my plan.

One of the words that came back to me clearly enough was
vukojebina, an earthy term whatever you call the language. It translates as 'where the wolves fuck', a synonym for the 'back of beyond'.
During the war of the 1990s it was a term I often heard to describe

the more remote areas of Bosnia, many of which were impossible to reach because they lay behind hostile frontlines. I was delighted to see that Princip's route cut straight across some of these, so I would be covering new territory on this trip – *terra* that had remained for me infuriatingly *incognita* when trapped inside besieged Sarajevo.

Among my favourite books had been the memoirs of a British journalist-adventurer, Arthur John Evans, who had walked extensively throughout Bosnia in the 1870s when the Ottomans were on the point of being replaced as occupiers by the Austro-Hungarians. Evans would later become world-famous as the archaeologist who discovered the Minoan civilisation on Crete, but as a young man fresh from Oxford he tramped through Bosnia and would later write on the region for the *Manchester Guardian*, the precursor of today's *Guardian*. His methods were slightly different from those of the modern-day reporter – he often carried a pistol – yet there was still much to admire. Rereading his memoirs, I found that in a letter dated February 1877 Evans described passing within a mile or so of the Princip family home at Obljaj. As I was about to embark on my own long overland journey, his description of the charms and challenges of walking through Bosnia added to my sense of anticipation:

> Those who may be inclined to 'try Bosnia' will meet with many hardships. They must be prepared to sleep out in the open air, in the forest, or on the mountain-side. They will have now and then to put up with indifferent food, or supply their own commissariat . . . those who delight in out-of-the-way revelations of antiquity, and who perceive the high historic interest which attaches to the southern Slavs; and lastly, those who take pleasure in picturesque costumes and stupendous forest scenery; will be amply rewarded by a visit to Bosnia.

Sleeping out in the open would not normally concern me, but my research showed that Princip's route touched on territory that was *vukojebina* in both the literal and figurative sense. The mountain region I would have to cross supports a significant population of wolves. I checked with local environmental groups and they assured me there had only ever been one confirmed case of a human being attacked by a wolf in Bosnia and that was because the animal was infected with rabies. I could be confident that, if I bumped into a wolf, it would most likely view me as a hunter and run away. Bears, they told me, were another story.

Bears continue to live in the mountains that I was planning to pass through, and the forests surrounding the town of Bugojno, where Princip caught his first train, have long been famous for bear-hunting. The closest I got to a bear in the 1990s was in Bugojno, when I covered fierce fighting for the town between Bosnian Croat and Bosnian Muslim forces. As the Bosnian Croats prepared to pull back they set about torching an old mountain lodge used by Tito, himself a great fan of bear-hunting. Before they left, one of the militiamen ran inside and came back out with the trophy skin of a large bear pegged out on a huge wooden board, signed by the communist dictator himself. The gunman offered it as a gift to bemused British officers attached to the United Nations peacekeeping force, and the skin remains to this day in the proud possession of the officers' mess of 1st Battalion the Yorkshire Regiment. Not to miss out, the squaddies were presented at the same time with a stuffed bear cub that is still to be found in the sergeants' mess.

Again I made contact with local environmental specialists and they assured me there had been only a handful of instances in the region when people had been attacked by bears. I was told that all would be fine, as long as I made sure I never found myself between mother bear and cubs.

But there was one other risk that I did not want to under-estimate, one that is particularly serious in Bosnia – landmines and unexploded munitions left over from the 1990s. Mines were laid by all sides then, making Bosnia one of the most mine-contaminated countries in the world. Attempts have been made to identify areas of high risk and efforts begun to clear some areas, but in spite of this around a dozen people are killed each year by wartime mines and munitions. I got in touch with the de-mining authorities in Sarajevo, who explained that it was only cost-effective to clear areas likely to be used by people. If mines were found in remoter, wilder spots, they were simply marked with warning signs and recorded on maps.

When I told the de-miners the details of my route, they sent me sheet after sheet from their map database, all as large digital files attached to an email. I clicked on the attachments and watched eagerly as the images slowly opened on the screen of my laptop, looking out for place names and features that I knew to be on Princip's route. The challenge then became to find a safe passage through the squiggly Richthofen-red loops that the experts used to mark the minefields. On the very first sheet a series of minefields was marked in the valley where Princip was born. The map for Bugojno was the most worrying, with an almost unbroken braid of black and red reaching from top to bottom of the entire page, right across the route I hoped to follow.

I spoke to the experts and to several climbers and hikers from Bosnia. They all had the same advice: away from the old frontlines it would be safe to hike in open country, but when approaching old frontline positions I should be sure to stick to tracks or paths that showed the visible signs of being used by people or animals.

As I became engrossed in my research I realised that under my feet at my desk in Cape Town was a much-loved kilim, one that

I had not really thought about in years – a large, hard-wearing piece with the repetitive fractal design common to Anatolia or the Levant. For as long as I can remember it has been on the floor of the various houses I have lived in as a foreign correspondent in Africa and the Middle East, and now as a writer in South Africa. As I went through my wartime diaries from the 1990s I was reminded of where I got it. It did not come from some shop in Istanbul's Grand Bazaar or a carpet dealer in Yemen, but was sold to me by a farmer's wife in central Bosnia.

She had spun the wool herself, dyed and woven it, using skills passed on by her mother and grandmother. I had stayed with her family for several months when the war sluiced around her tiny farming community – so close in fact that the farmhouse walls were often thwacked by stray rounds. Without electricity, we would pass winter nights sitting by candlelight around the wood-burning stove, growing strangely blasé about firefights that broke out in the nearby hills. I would read Evans or some other book that I hoped might unlock the complex local history, and she would quietly spin her wool. What was most remarkable was that she was a Bosnian Croat, a Catholic by faith orientated towards Rome and the West, and yet she maintained the proudly Eastern tradition of making Turkish-style kilims, a twist in Bosnia's rich ethnic weave.

Having worked out the route, my last concern was with the language. Happy though I was at having remembered *vukojebina*, I would need something more than a few rude words to get by on an overland trip across all of Bosnia and some of Serbia. I approached one of my most trusted Bosnian friends, Arnie Hećimović, a man who came of age during the war of the 1990s. Arnie had been just nineteen when fighting broke out in the small town in central Bosnia where he had been brought up, his family being forced to flee as neighbour turned on neighbour. He became the family's breadwinner overnight, finessing his grasp of English (largely self-taught from the lyrics of bands like The Clash) into a marketable skill; he became a translator for journalists covering the nearby deployment of British peacekeeping troops. I was one of many foreign reporters who benefited not just from Arnie's skills as a translator, but also from his role as a gatekeeper, and from his ability to help my understanding of the conflict through his local knowledge and his diplomacy at being able to persuade militiamen of different sides to let us through frontlines at awkward times.

The work allowed his family to survive those dark years, but, with the war robbing him of a university education and rerouting his life, he had joined the many thousands of Bosnians driven out of their homeland. He left in 1995 for Britain, where he has lived ever since. It had been some years since we were last in touch, but we arranged to meet to discuss my plan for working together once again. We agreed on a rendezvous in bustling South Kensington. And so it was that along a pavement crowded with museum-minded tourists I spotted the loping hulk of a man I scarcely recognised. I had known Arnie as a geeky adolescent, his eyes magnified in childlike awe by the thick lenses of the spectacles he used to wear, but here was a teenager no longer. He had filled out to fit in full the muscular Balkan stereotype.

We hugged and gossiped, teasing each other about our thinning hair and stouter frames. Then I got down to business. Would he consider coming back to Bosnia, to walk with me from Princip's village? When I first posed the question there was a pause. For Arnie, Bosnia was not a writer's project, a place to be analysed with the dispassion of an outsider. For him, it was a home that had rent itself apart and spat him out. I could tell he was not initially keen, but he was nevertheless curious, wanting to know more about my wider interest in Princip, asking questions and listening closely to the route that my research had already identified. After an hour or so I began to fret about being late to interview a research source, but it was Arnie who told me to relax, as he could get me across London in time. The years had reversed our roles completely. Arnie (the onetime Bosnian yokel) showed me (the onetime London resident) how to do something I had never done before: access a bicycle from London's rent-a-bike-on-the-street system. And so I found myself being guided deftly once more by Arnie, not along a mountain track in central Bosnia as before, but this time along a rat-run leading smartly to Victoria Station.

We parted with Arnie promising to discuss the plan with his girlfriend and see if he could find a way of taking time off from his job as a picture editor on the *Guardian*, the same paper that Evans wrote for in the 1870s. It took several weeks for him to mull over my proposal, and it soon became clear from his emails that he was most concerned about the landmine threat. In the past fifteen years Arnie had gone back home to see his family enough times to know full well the risk. Some of the woods where he used to play as a child were strictly out of bounds to modern genera-tions of children because of the mines. It was troubling him so much that he had started dreaming about them.

I did everything I could to reassure him, sharing the maps I had been given by the de-miners and explaining to what lengths I had gone to tap into the best current advice. Eventually, with the encouragement of his girlfriend, he agreed to come at least for the first weeks of my journey, emailing me his decision:

I'm sure it'll be just fine, but mustn't convince myself that it's going to be a walk in the park. The only thing we have to worry about are: landmines, poisonous snakes and quick changing weather but not the rest :-)))

We agreed a start date of mid-June 2012, and all that remained was for me to pack a rucksack, remember the lucky hat that had accompanied me on my previous adventures in Africa and say goodbye to my family. Jane – the same name, my diary informed me, as the girl I fell for all those years ago on that Yugoslavian package holiday – was as supportive as ever, but we never enjoy the impact that long periods of separation can have on our children. At the time Kit was six and Tess a year younger, so I sat them down on the eve of my departure to go through it all, emphasising that Mum alone would be around for the next couple of months. I explained that I was going to a place called Bosnia, which I used to know quite well, but now I was to explore the history of a man long dead – Princip – a man responsible for killing the Archduke of something called the Austro-Hungarian Empire. They both appeared to take it in and, as children do so wonderfully, moved on instantaneously to the next thing to grab their attention: an ice lolly from the fridge, a grubby game in the garden . . . whatever.

As Tess ran out of the room I heard her shouting to Jane: 'Dad's going away to look for a hungry ostrich.' Baldrick would have been proud.

CHAPTER 3

The Wild West

Princip's father, Petar, and mother, Marija, at their
Obljaj homestead, circa 1930

Graffiti left by Gavrilo Princip in the garden of his home in Obljaj:
his initials, in Cyrillic, and the year, 1909

The journey began with me and Arnie kneeling in roadside grit as we struggled to pack away our last supplies. We had been dropped by car in remotest Herzegovina and, with the noise of the engine dwindling, I heaved my now brick-solid rucksack onto my shoulders and looked around. To the south oozed a great lozenge of pastureland, a magnificent plain veined by watercourses and picketed tightly on all sides by foothills of high mountains. Somewhere over the peaks lay the Mediterranean, cities, motor-ways, industry and the broadband rush of the twenty-first century. But where we were standing seemed to belong to a rawer, older world order, a place of hard-scrabble rural living.

The hamlet of Obljaj, where Gavrilo Princip was born, is so small it does not register on many maps, but research had led me to the Royal Geographical Society's subterranean archive in London, where I made a breakthrough. There I found an old and very detailed military map that located Obljaj on the inland flank of the Dinaric Alps, the range that forms the spine at the top of the Balkan Peninsula. Originally printed in 1937, the map presented in rather elegant pastel colours all relevant local features: a clutch of houses built in the lee of a humpback hill offering protection from winter winds, the sweep of the plain of Pasić, the massing of Alps nearby, the meanderings of the Korana River. But this particular map sheet also hinted at something else. Originally printed with Yugoslav army markings, the map was also stamped with a Nazi swastika dated 1941, clumsily overlaid by British military hieroglyphs from the 1950s. This was a place much fought over.

It was a midsummer day, the European sun seldom more powerful, as we set off on foot, the straps of my rucksack, map case and camera bag making me feel like stringed pork-belly roasting in the oven. The village we were looking for turned out to be so small that it was no wonder many maps failed to record it. After ten minutes of walking we turned left up the only lane into Obljaj as the main road continued on its way, gently undulating along the valley floor. We ducked where trees hung low between dry-stone walls sagging with age and walked past hushed farm-houses, open doors suggesting the owners might be within, dodging the formidable heat. Bossy chickens gave the setting its only sense of movement, patrolling in complete safety a gravel track patched by weeds only occasionally disturbed by traffic.

It was the ornate fence that gave away the location of Princip's birthplace – the mere fact that it had one. No other property in this tiny community was similarly flattered, although those who had erected the commemorative railings fifty years ago might not recognise them any more. The metal was corroded, the foundation wall chipped and the entrance gate missing. The plot lay on the uphill side of the lane, so I wriggled out of my pack, dumped it on the ground to the pecking interest of some beaks, and enjoyed a relieving sense of lightness as I stepped up and into what had once been a busy family compound.

The grass had long since gone to seed, the tips crudely scythed for hay, the remainder meshed into a sprung mattress of tussock. The original farmhouse had never been much more than a hovel and now it was mostly vanished, the only structural relic a roofless, stone-built chamber set into the hillside, where livestock had originally been stabled. The Princip family had lived above, in a plain dwelling of stone walls capped by one of the steeply pitched roofs that were once characteristic of the Western Balkans. Tiled with hand-sawn shingles reaching sharply down from a high peak to a low, raggedy edge, the design always made me think of a wizard's old hat crammed onto a child's head. I had seen pictures of the original homestead, but in the wars that have washed over this region during the past century it had been targeted by those hostile to Princip's memory.

It did not take long to walk around the garden, which was little larger than a tennis court. Nettles and summer weeds grew tall inside the ruined basement, sprouting through rain-smoothed heaps of collapsed masonry and oddments of broken roof tile. At first sight there appeared to be nothing to indicate this place had any significance at all. But then I spotted the wreaths – three of them, long past their prime, with withered leaves and plastic wrappers moth-wing fragile from overexposure to the sun. Propped against the inside wall of the basement, only the tops reached out from the undergrowth, so I had to stamp away nettles and bend down to look. There were no cards, but for me they still bore a clear meaning – someone, somewhere wanted to remember.

The rear of the plot was marked by a retaining wall of rocks mostly felted with green moss. One of the larger stones was bare and on its flat, grey face my fingers were able to touch something missed by those who had sought to erase the memory of the young man born here. In three-inch-high letters I could make out the initials 'G.P.', graffiti scratched into the rock face by a young Gavrilo Princip, and the date '1909'.

The discovery was electrifying, a direct link to my quarry, so I spent several moments picturing the young boy who had earnestly left his mark here more than a hundred years ago. Arnie had been busy introducing himself to a young boy who had appeared in front of the property next door, a house that was clearly inhabited, albeit with walls unplastered and doorframes unpainted. Rural

homes in Bosnia are often works-in-progress, constantly being
developed with extensions and conversions so that members of
the wider family have a place to stay. But the war of the 1990s
had added greatly to this phenomenon, with so many communities
destroyed that, approaching twenty years since the fighting
finished, entire villages still have an air of jerry-built incompletion.

'Come over here,' Arnie called. 'You will want to meet this
family.'

People were now emerging from all corners of the house, rubbing
day-rest from their eyes. Two elderly men, one leaning heavily on
a stick, came out of the front door; a nervous-looking grandmother
in a black headscarf approached no further than the doorjamb; a
large man in his fifties bustled half-dressed down an external
staircase, pulling on a sleeveless shirt; and the young boy to whom
Arnie had first spoken had been joined by another, who seemed
to pop up from some sort of cellar. I got a strong sense that visitors were a rarity.

'May I introduce the last Princips living in Obljaj,' Arnie said,
his voice a blend of pride and surprise.

One by one, he went through the names, as chairs were arranged
for us on a shaded section of the verandah and space cleared from
a clutter of hay rakes, scythes and other equipment used for
subsistence farming. They were all members of the Princip clan.
Miljkan was the one with the walking stick, a tall man, hard of
hearing, moustachioed grey. Aged eighty-two, he sat next to his
brother, Nikola, five years his junior, much slighter and shorter,
with the habit of looking at you from the corner of his eye. The
shy woman was Miljkan's wife, Mika, also in her late seventies,
and the younger man his son, a fleshy, shaven-headed fifty-one-
year-old called Mile. It was Mile who emerged as the most talka-
tive, engaging with us enthusiastically, after Arnie's explanation
of our plan to follow the journey of his ancestor.

'I am the one who likes to keep the family tradition alive,' Mile said. 'So although I was baptised Mile, I like to use a better-known name. Have a look at this.' He showed me a book of poetry he had written in tribute to his famous forebear, the back-cover biography spelling out the author's preferred name. I have only an elementary grasp of Cyrillic, so it took a bit of lip-synching and finger-tracking to work out that he wrote under the nom de plume of Gavrilo Mile Princip. The text went on to say, rather portentously, that living in Obljaj was both 'a curse and a duty' for the writer.

My repeated mentions of their famous ancestor seemed to animate the whole group and it was Miljkan who spoke next, his voice husky from age, but his recollection convincingly sharp of the young man he referred to affectionately as Gavro.

'I was born here in 1930 and although Gavro was already dead by that time, I remember both his parents well and the house over there where they lived.' The old man was now looking in the direction of the stable-like ruin set into the hillside next door. 'His parents would sit and take coffee outside the front on sunny days and talk of Gavro. I remember listening to the stories from when I was about the same age as this chap.' He waved his cane at the youngest of the boys, his four-year-old grandson, Vuk, who was earnestly trying to follow the discussion.

I was delighted to meet them, greeting everyone formally and shaking hands. Princip had died childless and, during my months of research, I had committed a lot of time to seeking in vain any surviving relatives. From my computer terminal in South Africa I got rather excited when I found fifty-three Gavrilo Princips registered on Facebook, so I wrote to them all. All I got was a nasty note from site administrators saying that my account could be suspended for sending out unsolicited messages. The closest I had come to contacting a member of this family was tracking a distant relative, an elderly man living over the hills to the

north-east in the Bosnian city of Banja Luka. I mentioned him
and, as one, my new acquaintances dropped their gaze. Arnie
translated their collective mumblings.

'That man lost his son in the fighting of the 1990s,' Arnie said
quietly, his head tracking between the contributions emerging from
all sides. 'The young man is buried in the family plot here in the
village. Apparently the father never recovered from his grief. He
is still in mourning. He cannot move on. A sad business. A tragedy.
His anger has no end.'

I veered the conversation away from the recent war and towards
safer, older territory, explaining that Arnie and I hoped to walk all
the way to Bugojno, just as Princip had done with his father in
1907 when they trekked to the railhead before taking the train to
Sarajevo. This prompted an immediate and busy discussion. Mile
said that the closest station to Obljaj was not in Bugojno, which
lies roughly a hundred miles by road to the east, but in the opposite direction at a place called Strmica, twenty miles to the west.
People then all spoke at once, but it was old Miljkan putting his
hand on his son's knee who settled the matter. 'The railway line
to Strmica only went down to the coast of Dalmatia,' he said. 'To
go inland, to go to Sarajevo, you needed the railway that started
at Bugojno. It was the first line in the country, built by the Austro-
Hungarians.'

'In which case,' Mile said, 'you will have a tough old time. It's
a long, mountain walk to Bugojno and the most direct route takes
you right over Šator.' He pointed his arm out straight and flat in
the direction of the mountains to the south-east and then tipped
it upwards at a steep angle.

'*Šator* means "tent",' Arnie explained. 'Basically we are going
to have to climb Tent Mountain.' From the village, the edges of
the open pastureland on the valley floor appeared trimmed all
around by dark-green slopes but, over in the direction Mile was

pointing, it was possible to see a rockier peak much further away, pale and haughty above the valley sides.

The family history was kept like a rosary by the last Princips in Obljaj, polished in the retelling, a chain strung with fact, memory and myth, reassuring for later generations in its completeness and circularity. It did not presume to tell the whole history of the south Slavs, but it did give clues about key themes that shaped the development of the Western Balkans. I spent the rest of that summer day with the Princips, only moving to keep up with the shade tracking across the verandah, listening closely to the full story – the Director's Cut, if you like. It took hours as everyone, even young Novak, Nikola's eight-year-old grandson, took turns to offer up links in the chain of memories.

The Princips were not from Obljaj originally, but instead trace their roots to the rugged mountain badlands of Montenegro far to the south. Their arrival here in the middle of the eighteenth century formed part of the gradual ethnic division of the region's south-Slav population. It was a split predominantly defined not by language, culture, costume or physical appearance, all of which remained very similar across the local population, but by faith.

The modern history of the Western Balkans began roughly halfway through the first millennium, with the collapse of ancient Rome and the arrival in the area of a dominant population of Slavs, one of the many mass migrations from further east that populated much of Europe. Long before the tight modern concept of today's nation state, national identity was then defined most strongly through religion, and in the Western Balkans the south-Slav arrivals found themselves atop some of the great faith fault lines of medieval Europe. Those who were converted to Orthodox Christianity by missionaries sent from Byzantium, the eastern relic of the collapsed Roman Empire, came to identify themselves as

Serb. Those further north who converted to Catholicism, as professed by Western Christian followers of the papacy in Rome, would come to regard themselves as Croat. Other early versions of Christianity – such as Bogomilism, a medieval church that emphasised ritual over hierarchy – thrived here after the start of the second millennium, later to be denounced and persecuted as heresies by the more established streams.

Halfway through the second millennium, as the Middle Ages drew to a close, Islam would bring its influence to the Balkan Peninsula when it fell to Turkish forces from Asia Minor. These were outriders of the Ottoman Empire that replaced Byzantium, renaming as Istanbul the old Byzantine capital of Constantinople. A significant proportion of local Slavs in Bosnia would convert to Islam, progenitors of the Bosnian Muslim population of today. Jostling for pre-eminence among different streams of Christianity would come to influence the history of the Balkan Peninsula, but in Bosnia the evolution of a large Slav Muslim population added another dimension to the rivalry.

Miljkan touched on this tussle when he described how members of his family from Montenegro had ended up so much further north here in Bosnia. They were Serbs, south Slavs who had adopted Orthodox Christianity; a people who had flourished so richly in the Middle Ages that they staked some of the Western Balkans as their own nation, Serbia. It was ruled by a succession of kings, tsars and despots, with a Church so powerful that it seeded the area with some of the most venerable monasteries and reliquaries of Christendom. Independence for Serbia lasted until the occupation by invading Ottoman Turks in the fifteenth century. By the time Miljkan's ancestors moved to Bosnia in around 1750, Serbia as an independent state was almost 300 years dead, a distant source of legend and myth kept alive by stories told around the hearth.

After Ottoman forces had battled through Serbia they advanced into Bosnia, occupying the entire country in the year 1463. Their progress was swift, only easing when they reached the northern arrowhead of the Dinaric Alps. As the Ottomans consolidated their hold on Bosnia – they would stay for another 400 years – the mountain range evolved into a topographical watershed between two great rival blocs, the Muslim Turks and the Catholics from Hungary, Venice and Austria. That is not to say it was a stable or even well-marked international border. For hundreds of years it was more of a wild frontier, violated routinely by raiding parties from either side, garrisoned by troops deployed from far-off corners of empire and sluiced over by civilians fleeing a cycle of friction between the Islamic and Catholic worlds.

At different times over the centuries it suited both sides to allow a third party – Serb adherents to Orthodox Christianity – to settle in large numbers around this border zone. The Princip family then bore the name of Jovićević, a long-established Serb clan from Montenegro, and their migration northwards was part of this deliberate policy of seeding an Orthodox buffer between the Muslim Ottoman and Catholic Habsburg empires. These new arrivals on the Ottoman side were rewarded with land that they could farm as feudal serfs and, in time, with positions of responsibility in local defence forces raised on behalf of the Turkish occupiers. The new arrivals from the Jovićević family changed their name shortly after reaching the Obljaj area to Čeka, a word meaning 'to lie in wait', because they proved to be particularly adept at patiently preparing ambushes for smugglers, brigands and other raiders.

As Mile told this part of the story he struggled with a detail, gesturing with his hand as if tugging an unripe apple on a tree. 'What was the name of those really violent raiders from the coastline of Dalmatia?'

'They were known as Uskoks,' Nikola said coldly. 'Our people sorted out plenty of them.'

Through Arnie I tried to ask how they viewed today the historical reality of their forebears working as militia for the Ottomans. Could their ancestors be regarded as collaborators? But this was not one of the beads on the family rosary, so my question was passed over. Instead Miljkan wanted to explain the early nineteenth-century origins of the family's current surname.

'Our name did not become Princip until the time of Gavro's great-grandfather, a man called Todor,' Miljkan said. 'He was a big man, a strong man, and he rode a huge white horse. He was so untouchable he could cross the frontier whenever he wanted, and one day the Venetians over towards the coast of Dalmatia said his clothes were so smart and his manners so royal that they called him The Prince. We have been called Princip ever since.'

The name might sound regal, but the reality of life for the Princip clan throughout the late nineteenth century was very much at the other end of the social scale. They were serfs struggling under dire conditions of feudal exploitation.

When the Ottomans first added Bosnia to their European land holdings they valued it highly for its importance as a strategic bridgehead in their long-running battle against the Habsburgs. Turkish raids in the sixteenth and seventeenth centuries would several times reach all the way to the walls of Vienna, although the city never fell. Bosnia's value to the empire at the time earned it a glowing Ottoman epithet, 'the Lion that guards the gates of Istanbul'. And the talents of Bosnians were in great demand in the Ottoman imperial capital, at a time when it was routine for the young men of occupied lands to be forcibly removed to Istanbul for what might today be called 'reprogramming'. Far from their homes, they underwent an intense programme of education, technical training and, where necessary, conversion to Islam, creating a cadre that owed and gave everything to the empire. Although ruled by a Sultan descended from the original Turkish Osmanli dynasty, the Ottoman Empire was run by supreme administrators known as Grand Viziers and there was no dogma that these must be Turks. Through the long history of the Ottoman Empire children snatched from the Slav communities of the Balkans earned a reputation for intelligence, diplomacy and resourcefulness, so much so that they regularly succeeded in navigating the tortuous route to the very top of the Ottoman governmental machine. Several of the Grand Viziers were originally Slavs from Bosnia.

Perhaps the most famous of these was a Serb born in the village of Sokolović, close to Sarajevo, who served as Grand Vizier after converting and adopting the name of Mehmed-paša Sokolović. He held power for fourteen years during the late sixteenth century and is credited with seeking to advance his homeland through the building of bridges, mosques and other infrastructure. His most famous structure, an elegant arched bridge which spans to this day the Drina River at the town of Višegrad, has long been regarded as a symbol of Bosnia's intertwined ethnic matrix. Bosnia's greatest twentieth-century novelist, Ivo Andrić, who was just two years ahead of Princip at the same Sarajevo grammar school and would win the Nobel Prize for Literature in 1961, used the structure as a symbol for communal linkages in his historical fiction *The Bridge on the Drina*. During the war of the 1990s the old bridge was notoriously used by Bosnian Serb paramilitaries to dispose of civilians they had murdered, with bodies tipped over the edge in such large numbers that they clogged the turbines of a hydroelectric power plant downstream.

By the nineteenth century the age of Ottoman expansionism had passed, reducing considerably Bosnia's value to Istanbul. Along with other areas on the periphery of the empire, Bosnia became a remote and increasingly troublesome backwater. As part of my research I visited the imperial archive in Istanbul, seeking a flavour of the late Ottoman rule that the Princips would have known. There were no references in the entire collection to the family under any of its three names, unsurprising given their lowly peasant status. But there were several written reports that referred to the area surrounding Obljaj, painting a picture of imperial decline: the desertion of Arab troops deployed to Bosnia from the empire's Middle East holdings in Arabistan, the escape of a rebel leader, the routine execution of 'a Jew and a Christian'.

The ebbing influence of imperial authorities in Istanbul was counterbalanced in Bosnia by a rise in the power of local proxies, the south–Slav converts to Islam. To hold on to power the Ottomans had long employed 'divide and rule', the stalwart strategy of imperial regimes; and to deal with the large Christian population, local Muslim leaders had been favoured with higher social status as feudal lords known as *begs*. Furthermore, to keep the local Serb followers of Orthodox Christianity in check, Istanbul had given permission to Franciscan missionaries to work in Bosnia, maintaining monasteries and ministering to the local Catholic Croat congregation.

Down near the bottom of the pecking order were serf families such as the Princips, exploited by punitive demands for tax that rose each year, along with ever more onerous periods of military service demanded from their men. The local *begs* increasingly answered to nobody, ignoring occasional half-hearted attempts from Istanbul to legislate an improvement in the rights of Christians and setting their own arbitrary local taxes, which would routinely leave serfs destitute at the end of a working year. Peasant resentment erupted in a series of rebellions throughout the first half of the nineteenth century, led mostly by local Serbs overtaxed into penury and inspired by successful rebellions to the south-east, where the new, independent country of Serbia was being created, a modern recasting of the medieval nation.

When four centuries of Ottoman rule in Bosnia came to an end, it was through one of these uprisings – a rebellion that began in 1875 not far from where the Princip family lived. It would drag on for three years, tapping into the anger felt by those at the bottom of a regime of feudal exploitation. Several of the men from the Princip clan, including Gavrilo's father, Petar, joined the rebel groups and took to the mountains around Obljaj with their long-barrelled guns and intimate knowledge of the terrain. From there they defied not just the Ottoman troops, but also the Bosnian Muslim elite who were fighting to protect their pre-eminent social position. Violence flared across the community's fault lines that had been so artfully maintained by the Ottomans. Bosnian Muslim forces, supported from fortress towns, would launch reprisal raids deep into the countryside, burning Christian villages and slaughtering peasants suspected of giving succour to the rebels. The violence was so sweeping, Miljkan explained, that all the remaining Princip non-combatants were forced to flee from Obljaj, along with tens of thousands of other Serbs, mostly women, children and the elderly, heading west across the frontier, seeking sanctuary in Habsburg-occupied territory.

'The *begs* were so ruthless it was not safe for our family here,' Nikola said in support of his older brother. 'And when our people came back, once the Turks had finally left, they found all the houses here had been burned. So for the first time, but not the last, they had to rebuild everything.'

The mountainous region around Obljaj, including the forests cloaking the lower reaches of the tent-like Mount Šator, were rebel hot zones, close enough to the frontier to attract the attention of outsiders. They included Adeline Irby, a redoubtable Englishwoman from Norfolk whose Victorian sense of Christian charity drove her to come to the assistance of Serb refugees in this remote corner of south-eastern Europe during the rebellion of 1875. Miss Irby, as she is still referred to affectionately in Bosnia, was a pioneer aid worker, a nineteenth-century prototype for the legions spread across the world's combat zones today. Her doggedness in battling through winter snowstorms, sleeping in vermin-infested hovels and defying Ottoman attempts to hinder aid deliveries won her a huge following among Bosnian Serbs. It also generated wide publicity in Britain, especially when her cause was publicly endorsed by her good friend, Florence Nightingale. Miss Irby would dedicate the rest of her life to the advancement of Bosnian Serbs, running a school for Orthodox Christian girls in Sarajevo, where she would make her home for more than thirty years. She died there in 1911 at the age of seventy-nine and is buried today just a few yards from Princip's tomb. Her gravestone bears a carving in profile of her doughty – some might say battleaxe – face, with an inscription describing her as 'a great benefactress of the Serbian people in Bosnia-Herzegovina'.

The uprising that began in 1875 brought an end to Ottoman rule in Bosnia but, as became clear from the Princip family's reminiscences, this did not herald freedom for its south-Slav population. The Great Powers, gathering in 1878 for the Congress of Berlin, which was convened to decide the fate of territory lost by the weakening Ottoman Empire, still viewed Europe as a chequerboard of land parcels to be occupied, exploited and occasionally bartered. The interests of local populations were not nearly as important as higher, strategic concerns balancing the interests of the established powers: the Russians, the Austro-Hungarians, the Germans, the British, the Ottomans, the Italians and the French.

The imperial Habsburg rulers were deeply hostile to the establishment of a new, stand-alone country in Bosnia where south Slavs might enjoy self-rule. The Habsburg Empire already had a significant south-Slav population in territory it had long ruled across the Northern Balkans. Independence for Bosnia, Vienna believed, threatened to destabilise the empire by fomenting similar calls for self-rule from Slavs within the empire. Instability was a threat that all the Great Powers shared an aversion for, so Vienna's representatives were able to convince the other statesmen gathered at the Berlin conference that she should be allowed to occupy Bosnia. Within weeks Austro-Hungarian troops had crossed the old frontier and marched on Sarajevo.

The Foreign Minister of Austria–Hungary, Gyula Andrassy, boasted at the time that Bosnia would be taken 'with a company of men and a brass band at their head', but events proved him guilty of hubris. It would ultimately require the deployment of 300,000 troops by Austria–Hungary to fulfil the occupation and, later, the full annexation of Bosnia. They took the towns quickly enough, but out in the rural areas they came across entrenched hostility, mostly from the Bosnian Muslim community. Official figures showed that in the first few months alone 5,198 men from the invading Austro-Hungarian force were killed or wounded. In keeping with its history of resistance, Herzegovina was one of the last regions to fall to the new occupiers.

The Austro-Hungarians claimed their occupation of Bosnia was a philanthropic act of civilisation, a 'cultural mission', as they put it rather prosaically. Like so much colonialism of the era – the Scramble for Africa was taking place at the same time – outsiders routinely presented themselves as being committed to upliftment, promising to modernise, reform and advance the local population. But, just as in Africa, the philanthropy turned out to be largely a sham. Furthermore, the Ottoman legacy in Bosnia brought out many Western prejudices against Islam, the implicit message being that a Christian nation would necessarily make good the cruel, corrupt, conservative incompetence of Muslim rule.

The supposed altruism of the Habsburgs did not reach far in

Bosnia. A few hundred miles of road were built by the new occupiers, but mostly out of the simple military necessity for swift
mobilisation and the deployment of troops. Railway lines were laid
but, again, the primary motivator was hardly to help the local
community. The railway was needed in order for Austro-Hungarian
investors to profit from commercial exploitation. Timber from
Bosnia's rich forests was a target of this new trade, so within a
few years narrow-gauge railway tracks snaked across the country
and up into the forests, where felled trunks could be loaded for
export. The character of town centres and cityscapes changed
dramatically as European architects were encouraged to express
themselves through new buildings of modern Western design.
Within a few years the ancient *hans*, *caravanserais*, *souks* and *turbes*
left by the Ottomans had been overshadowed, symbolically and
literally, by an architectural avalanche of governors' palaces, military barracks, university buildings, cathedrals, museums and the
occasional brewery.

Aside from these cosmetic changes, the fundamentals of life did
not alter for the vast majority of Bosnians spread across the rural
hinterland. Academics have carried out detailed studies of the
Austro-Hungarian occupation of Bosnia after 1878, revealing how
the new occupiers failed to modernise the country for which they
were now responsible. They barely touched the old feudal system,
meaning that serfdom continued here well into the twentieth
century. They did not fundamentally tackle the social structure in
the rural areas, where *begs* were still able to demand taxes set at
arbitrary levels. And they set up yet further tiers of state fees that
kept the peasants in penury. Their schools, built with great show
in the larger urban areas like Sarajevo, made so meagre an impression on the population that by 1910, after more than three decades
of Austro-Hungarian rule, 88 per cent of the Bosnian population
could not read or write.

In Obljaj the arrival of the Austro-Hungarians was a long drawn-out disappointment for the Princips. Sitting in the village listening to their history brought home to me the disconnect that so often separates policy from reality. The statesmen leaving the Berlin Congress smugly convinced themselves that the people of Bosnia would benefit from the diplomatic finesse of having the Western Austro-Hungarians replace the Eastern Ottomans. What they had actually done, however, was quite the opposite, sowing seeds of resentment that would eventually destroy the status quo of the entire Western world.

'Our people came back home to the village after the uprising and they thought things would get much better,' Nikola said, shaking his head. 'They built their homes again here in Obljaj and thought that, as Christians now ruled by Christians, they would be better off. But nothing changed. It was still a tough life of survival, struggling to live off this land and paying tax, tax and more tax.'

Just as under the Ottomans, various family members survived by working for the occupiers, retained as border guards or policemen for the foreign empire. I asked the family about the claim made by one historian that Princip's uncle, Ilija, eldest brother of his father, had served for a time as an Austro-Hungarian gendarme – a question I felt was potentially important, as an influence on the young boy's motivation for the assassination. Once more, the family memory was blank. Instead they emphasised the dire conditions of life for their forebears at the dawn of the twentieth century, and to do this convincingly all they had to do was relate what happened to six of Princip's siblings.

'First there was Bosiljka, who died as a child,' Nikola said. 'Then there was Koviljka who was next to die, and Djuradj after her, and Branko after him and two others who were never christened and died without a name.' It was well over a hundred years

since six out of nine children from one family had died, but for
the Princip clan that would be too soon to forget.

After two hours of intensive listening, note-taking and tallying
what I had read about Princip against what his family remembered,
we all needed a break. I could not help noticing that the Princips
had not offered Arnie and me coffee – a cultural ritual for visitors
that I knew to be almost sacred. They were not being unfriendly.
They were simply too poor.

I arched my back extravagantly, and Mile picked up on the cue.
'Let's go,' he said. 'I need to walk a while and I want to show you
something that might teach you a little about Gavro's parents.'
Mile led Arnie and me back through the village and out onto the
approach road where we had been dropped earlier that day. The
sun was low in the sky and two teenage boys were walking across
the fields carrying fishing rods. 'Trout,' he said, catching my
interest keenly. Trout-fishing is a love of mine. 'They are going
after trout in the Korana. It's a beautiful fishing river.'

There was an enthusiasm about Mile that I was beginning to
enjoy, a curiosity about my interest in his ancestor. 'So many people
have said so many things about Gavro over the years,' he said.
'But they forget he was a country boy from this village. His world
was a small world, basically the fields and forests and mountains
you can see from where we are standing. He would have gone
fishing, I am sure, just like those boys over there. He would have
walked the hills I walked, shepherding the family's flock of sheep
like I did when I was a boy. But in those days, people from a place
like this never left. They were born here, married here, worked
here, died here.

'Look at Gavro's parents. His father, Petar – but everyone called
him Pepo – was from this village. His mother was Marija – everyone
called her Nana – and where did she come from? Well, if you look

over there you will see where.' He was now pointing along the valley to a collection of farm buildings less than a mile away. 'Don't laugh, but that is known as Little Obljaj because it is smaller than where we are now, Greater Obljaj. Nana came from there. You basically lived your whole life within walking distance of where you were brought up. And when you ended your life you still didn't leave.'

He had led us into the local graveyard, weaving his bulky frame through grass and weeds that grew waist-high in places and past clutches of gravestones, many of which were penned behind railings inside family plots. 'This is where Gavro's parents lie today,' Mile said, pointing over a black iron fence.

Some history books tell you that Princip's father married late and was a lot older than his mother. Their shared headstone suggested otherwise. It recorded them being born in the same year, 1860, which would have made them teenagers when the rebellion of 1875 disrupted their rural lives. While Petar went up into the hills to fight, Marija headed west as a refugee to the area around Knin, a town just across the frontier inside Austro-Hungarian territory, where Miss Irby focused most of her aid effort. The headstone recorded both their baptised and familiar names, so I was able to read that Marija (Nana) died in 1945, five years after Petar (Pepo). That meant that Princip's mother would have experienced at first hand one of the long-term after-effects of the assassination committed by her son: the Second World War. It brought another round of disruption to life in Obljaj.

'The Germans and Italians occupied this area, and in the fighting Gavro's house was totally destroyed,' Mile said. 'Poor Nana had to flee along with the others for a while. By the time she died she had suffered so much because of the actions of her son and was drinking a lot. They say it was the drink that killed her in the end.'

We were now out in a recently mown hayfield, with clear sight
of the red tiled roofs of Obljaj that run along the hinge between
the valley floor and the rocky hillock behind. Take away the power
lines and replace the stone tiles with shingles, and the view had
not changed since Princip's time. Mile stood still for a moment
and started to speak. 'The thing that still amazes me about Gavro
is how a child from this small place and from that closed time
could change the world.' Down on the river bank I could see a
boy sitting patiently and watching his fishing line drift in the
slow-moving current.

As we walked back into Obljaj I thought about how static life
had been over the centuries for a family such as the Princips.
They had been chained to this upland valley, not in the sense of
being anchored and given stability, but more in the sense of being
trapped, hocked, unable to escape its demands. We, in the twenty-
first century, so often romanticise the idyll of pre-urban, agricultural simplicity, but the existence led by the Princips, as for
peasants across Europe down the centuries, was far from idyllic.
Theirs was a living defined by a crushing yearly battle, trying to
husband enough crops and livestock to survive the deprivations
of winter and the demands of feudal obligation. As Serbs, theirs
was an identity most strongly preserved by the annual cycle of
devotions enshrined by their Orthodox Church and by stories told
around the fire about the medieval heroes of a long-gone Serbian
state. Little wonder those tales were worked up into legends of
mythological dimension – the chivalrous deeds of Serbian nobles
fighting for good against the evil of occupation.

Gavrilo Princip was born in the summer of 1894, a busy time for
a peasant family living off the land in Herzegovina. Marija had
spent the day in the fields bundling hay by hand and milking the
family cow, when her labour pains came. She had only just made

it back into the house when the baby arrived. Family lore has her mother-in-law biting through the umbilical cord. It was 13 July, a day sacred in the Orthodox calendar for the Archangel Gabriel, and although Marija wanted to name the newborn Špiro, in honour of her late brother, the parish priest insisted the child be named for the saint. Gavrilo is the name Gabriel in Serbian. The baptism was carried out swiftly. Nobody could be confident that the new baby would not suffer the same fate as many of his siblings.

'He was born just up there,' Nikola told me after we had returned to the house. Miljkan was too immobile to comfortably leave the verandah, but at seventy-seven years of age his younger brother was still sprightly enough to lead me to the next-door plot and was now standing in front of the roofless void where the old stable had been set into the slope of the hill. 'Up there, just behind, was the main room where the family lived and the food was prepared.' Nikola was now pointing to a flat section of grassy ground at the same level as the top of the stable. 'They used to have a hearth in there for cooking, and the smoke went out of a hole in the roof. The floor was made of earth and used to be swept clean every day. The other room, where they slept, was towards us, above where the animals lived, with a wooden floor.'

Nikola's description prompted me to rethink my understanding of what had once been a two-roomed home lived in by a family of five. This had been a European dwelling inhabited by an entire family at the start of the twentieth century, but it brought to my mind hovels that I routinely come across in rural Africa. The principle was exactly the same: a beaten-earth floor in a dwelling constructed out of stone walls, under a roof made of wood, thatch or branches gathered locally. A rate of child mortality that could kill six out of nine children from Princip's family sounded more like Africa than Europe. The developed world might despair at modern Africa's systemic problems, but standing in that garden in Obljaj taught me how recently much of Europe was in a similar position.

With the plot of land as his stage, Nikola began almost to act out this part of the family story. 'Most of the time the family had a horse, a cow, a few chickens and sometimes some sheep. They were all kept down here.' He was now peering inside the door of the underground chamber with the collapsed roof. 'Gavro's father used to earn money as a postman, delivering packages and letters around the area. His horse was important, so he would be well looked after in there, especially in the winter.' Bosnian winters have a well-justified reputation for extreme conditions, so much so that in the novel *Brideshead Revisited* Evelyn Waugh has Charles Ryder's mother dying 'of exhaustion in the snow in Bosnia' while serving there as a nurse in wartime. From personal experience I knew how hazardous winters can be in Herzegovina. In 1994 I had made a good attempt to kill myself by sliding off an icy road in that wintry country, rolling my armoured Land Rover and knocking myself out.

Nikola then led me up the slope to where the living quarters had been. 'Nana used to have a beautiful voice,' he reminisced. 'She sang in a choir, and all the time as she worked around the house. And she always wore traditional Serbian folk dress, with a little bag of sugar tucked away down here.' He was now gesturing to his waistband. 'She used to give it to her favourites. Sometimes she gave me some when I was a little child. She always said that she used to give sugar to Gavro because he was such a special boy.'

Special indeed was a boy who made it through childhood in these living conditions. The tuberculosis that would eventually kill Princip in 1918 was most likely contracted while being brought up in these stark conditions, although as a youngster he had been strong enough to suppress the disease. His only surviving older brother, Jovo, was seven years old when Gavrilo was born and there would be one more surviving child, a younger brother, Nikola, born three years after Gavrilo.

Gavrilo is remembered as having inherited his mother's sharp chin, blue eyes and casual attitude towards religion, while from his more pious father, Petar, came his physique: short and wiry, as befits a farmer scratching out a hard-scrabble living in the highlands of Herzegovina. The most religious member of the family, Petar was known for never drinking, a noteworthy rarity in a community where the making and consuming of plum brandy, or *šljivovica*, was – and remains – a ritual enthusiastically embraced to ease the hardships of rural life. Petar clearly had something that marked him out within the community. He served for several years as the elected head of the *zadruga*, the association of local households. For generations across the Western Balkans the *zadruga* system was the foundation of rural life, a way of sharing earnings, dividing tax obligations and dealing with problems so as to help the maximum number of people. In his journalism Arthur Evans praised it lavishly for being fair and democratic, even communistic. The fact that Petar Princip had the vision to earn extra income as the village postman also suggested that he was more than just another peasant farmer. On official forms such as his school reports Gavrilo Princip would take care to describe his father not simply as an agricultural labourer, but as 'an entrepreneur'.

Looking at Nikola as he wandered around the plot declaiming the family history, I convinced myself that I recognised his chin. It seemed to have the same sharpness as the one I had seen in the handful of surviving photographs of Princip. I felt I was looking at how the assassin would have appeared, had he reached old age.

Princip grew to take on the household tasks expected of a young boy in the village, tending the chickens, helping his mother around the homestead, working with his father in the fields and watching over the sheep. The rich local pastures of the Pasić plain, still named after an overlord from the feudal period, remained privately owned, but some of the barer hillsides higher up were common land and Princip would spend whole days up there minding the flock as it scrabbled among the rocks for nourishment. Mile said that wolves were an occasional hazard and a shepherd boy would be expected to use a stick or stones to protect his animals.

'Nana used to say that Gavro might have been a quiet boy and a small boy, but he was tough,' Nikola told me as we walked around the garden. 'He learned up on the hills how to throw a stone like a bullet and, if anyone picked on him, all he had to do was throw one stone. It always hit the target. After that they would leave him alone.' Nikola was chuckling now. 'He kept himself to himself, but he always fought to defend those who could not defend themselves. There was a story that when a teacher at the primary school in the nearby town of Grahovo was punishing a boy in class by caning, Gavro hit the teacher over the head with a pencil case. He might have been small, but the village boys all knew he was ferocious if you tried to wrestle him.' Nikola was now beaming with pride.

'As he grew older he became more and more resentful of the foreign rulers here, the Austrians,' he continued. 'We were always told that he came back to the village for the winter before the assassination because he had got into a fight with an Austrian policeman. The gendarme had forced himself onto a girl, and Gavro beat him up. The cops were looking for him, so he came here. But that was his way. He took on the bullies.'

Primary school was as far as most children's education reached in rural Bosnia under Austro-Hungarian rule at the start of the twentieth century. For Serbs it backstopped a significant, yet un-official cultural education from within their own community, one that proudly passed on ethnic identity through the sharing of folk stories and epic poetry about the heroes of ancient, pre-Ottoman Serbia. Mile sought to rekindle that same spirit when he offered to read some of his own verse written in honour of his famous ancestor. His relatives nodded approvingly, and both Arnie and I were keen to listen to him and so, in a deep baritone, Mile recited a work he had entitled 'The Hand of Gavrilo'. Laden with references to blood, bones and death, his performance briefly transported me from the verandah of the Princip family home in the summer of 2012 to the *zadruga* age a hundred years earlier, when members of all Serb households would formally gather to polish myths from an era long gone.

As he grew up, Princip would attend such gatherings in his own home, where on occasion he was encouraged to use the skills acquired at primary school by reading to the assembled group from Serbian history books. With illiteracy commonplace among the feudal peasantry, a recital by a young reader must have been quite an event. I could picture his parents standing tall with pride. In winter time, when temperatures in these high villages plummet so dramatically, the meetings would have been crowded, smoky and, no doubt, malodorous affairs. According to a passage attributed to the young Princip by a contemporary, Dobroslav Jevdjević, he found the gatherings disturbing, as if they served to encapsulate the inward-looking, forlorn reality of a people browbeaten by poverty:

The wet logs on the open fire gave the only light to the closely packed serfs and their wives, wrapped in thick smoke. If I tried to penetrate the curtain of smoke, the most I could see were the eyes of human beings, numerous, sad and glaring with some kind of fluid light coming from nowhere. Some kind of reproach, even threat, radiated from them, and many times since then they have awakened me from my dreams.

To escape peasant life under Austro-Hungarian rule would not
have been easy. But the same spirit that drove Petar Princip to be
an entrepreneurial postman had passed to all his sons.

Gavrilo's older brother, Jovo, was the one who made the break
first. Being not as bookish as Gavrilo, it was money that drove
Jovo to leave Obljaj in search of a living. After drifting through
various menial jobs he ended up near Sarajevo working in the
timber industry, which was booming at the time, with demand for
wood coming from all over the Austro-Hungarian Empire. He
settled in Hadžići, a village outside the city at the foot of the
thickly forested slopes of Mount Igman, where he earned enough
to set himself up with a pair of horses to drag felled trunks down
to his own modest sawmill. Jovo had been working there some
years when he saw a notice in a local newspaper offering places at
secondary schools in Sarajevo for suitable candidates. He sent
word back to Obljaj.

'Gavro loved his books,' said Mile after we had joined the others
once more on the verandah. 'From the time he went to primary
school just up the road in Grahovo he read and read and read.
He always had his head in a book. Nana used to get cross with
him sometimes because he could forget about the sheep and the
other chores. But then it was Nana who wanted the best for her
special son, and she was the one who said he must leave and go
to school in Sarajevo. His father was not so keen, but Nana was
able to persuade him.'

Up to this point the orbit of Princip's life had been tight. He
had never left the immediate area of the valley, rarely strayed further
than Grahovo, which is just two miles away, and scarcely had any
contact with Bosnians who were not ethnic Serbs. The stories he
heard would have centred on Serbian legends, and after the divide-
and-rule of imperial control the other local communities of Bosnian

Croats and Bosnian Muslims were a relative unknown. Under occupation first by the Ottomans and more recently the Austro-Hungarians, the different rural communities kept themselves mostly to themselves, and while there were Bosnian Croats living in and around Grahovo, before Princip left to further his education he had never met a single Bosnian Muslim.

Listening to Mile, I too found it extraordinary that a boy with a childhood of such limited horizons could go on to precipitate events that would change the world. Where did his revolutionary zeal come from, his hatred of the Austro-Hungarians, his anger at the indignity heaped on his people throughout history? And were his interests purely Serb, as some observers have claimed, or was he acting on behalf of all south Slavs? If so, where did this wider interest come from, for a boy brought up within only one of the Slav ethnic groups? With Arnie's help, I asked the family what they thought had happened to Princip once he left Obljaj, but from this point on the story dried up. Miljkan shook his head and looked at the ground. Nikola fell silent, glancing at me repeatedly from the corner of his eye. They told me they did not know. Instead they preferred to keep alive the image of the tough little farm boy who had a thing about reading and helping the weak, not the person described by some for his later actions as a ruthless assassin.

'He left as a little boy in 1907 and something happened that changed him,' Mile said. 'During the long holidays from school he would sometimes come back here. It was on one of these visits in 1909 that he left his initials on the rock at the back of the garden. We were always told that while he was leaving his mark on the stone, a friend of his called Špiro Marić asked him why he was doing it. He said it was because "one day people will know my name".'

For the first time since we arrived, Miljkan's elderly wife, Mika, now ventured out onto the verandah, mumbling to her husband and handing him a piece of paper, before slipping back to the safety of the doorjamb. Her steps made no sound in her thick, knitted woollen socks, traditionally worn all year round in rural Bosnian homes as house-slippers. Nikola glanced at the sheet, a black-and-white photocopy of a page from a book. It showed a picture of Princip's coffin as it was prepared for burial in Sarajevo. Nikola's eyes flared and he flicked the paper with his hand.

'There you are.' There was clear anger in his voice. 'They say he was a terrorist, they say all these bad things about him. But look at this. He was buried a boy. He was only nineteen when they sent him to die in jail. All I know is that he always stood up to fight for those not strong enough to fight for themselves, he stood up to fight against injustice.'

It was a noble thought for the descendants of Princip to cling to. The assassination of the Archduke had ill-served the family, bringing them no fortune and making their home a target over the years. Austro-Hungarian police rounded up Princip's parents days after the shooting on 28 June 1914 and jailed them without charge. Even though the First World War ended in defeat for the Austro-Hungarians and the founding of Yugoslavia – a country where south Slavs could run their own affairs – the new government was slow to recognise Princip's family. Petar and Marija lived out the rest of their lives in the same poverty they had always known under foreign occupation. After being destroyed in the Second World War, the family house was rebuilt as a national monument under the communist rule of Tito and opened to the public in 1964. It lasted until 1995, when Croat troops destroyed it for being too closely associated with their Serb enemies. I began to understand why Mile described living in Obljaj as both 'his curse and his duty'.

To understand better the change Princip underwent when he

left Obljaj, I would cross the mountains as he did and head towards Sarajevo. It was through this overland journey that the young boy's horizons shifted as he was fully exposed for the first time to the other component parts of Bosnia's ethnic mix. With my de-mining map showing the presence of many minefields on the slopes of our first major obstacle, Tent Mountain, I asked Mile what he thought about the scale of the threat. He told us there were definitely some mines on the mountain, but he would be willing to guide us up the foothills in the morning and start us off safely on our way. I was delighted. To persuade Arnie to come on the trip I had promised that we would only proceed with local guides, and I could think of no better guide in Obljaj than someone whose full name was Gavrilo Mile Princip.

Then Mile made me even happier by saying we could camp for the night in front of the ruins of Princip's old house. Team morale soared as Arnie and I unpacked our gear and erected our tents side-by-side on the wiry grass. It was a clear summer night, the stars blurry through the gauze of my mosquito net, the village of Obljaj noiseless, dark and at ease. For some time I lay on my sleeping bag, thrilled at this unexpected start to my journey: discovering graffiti left by Princip himself, finding the last surviving Princip family members, exploring his birthplace with people of his bloodline. With dew forcing me under the covers, I fell asleep with the family history churning through my mind – the story of generations of Princips who had lived out centuries in this remote, rough rural place and of the teenage outlier who had left to change the world.

CHAPTER 4

Over Tent Mountain

Arnie beginning the ascent of Mount Šator

Arnie passing a minefield warning sign, west of Kupres

The crowing of Obljaj's cockerels woke me at dawn and the next sound I heard was that of Mile snuffling in the half-light outside his house, heaving on stout walking boots and calf-length socks beneath long hiking shorts. His bustling roused Arnie and me out of our sleeping bags, but just to make sure we really were taking down our tents, Mile walked across to offer us Bosnian coffee served in handleless containers as small and fragile as eggcups. I suspected that a family member had been sent out overnight to beg beans from a neighbour.

'It's a long way to Mount Šator, so we want to get started as soon as possible,' Mile urged. 'It does not look like there is going to be much cloud in the sky, but if we are lucky we will get to the cover of the trees before the sun becomes too strong.' I smiled in recognition. The Forest of Šator was significant enough to earn several mentions in the journalism of Evans from the 1870s when he toured rebel positions during the Bosnian uprising. With Mile's permission, I stepped into the house to use the bathroom. The other family members had not yet stirred, but the downstairs had the same yeasty, warm aroma I recalled from farmhouses I stayed in almost twenty years ago. It spoke of cheap soap and honest elbow-grease.

'We need to get going.' Mile was beginning to sound a little cross. 'Your journey only starts now.' I thought of a line from Rebecca West's travelogue from Yugoslavia. She spent time on the Adriatic coast, exploring various offshore islands, but she wrote that it was only when she reached this area, Herzegovina, that 'the really adventurous part of our journey began'.

Cramming biscuits into our mouths as breakfast, Arnie and I loaded our rucksacks onto our backs and made to walk back down to the road that followed the valley floor. But Mile had chosen a more direct route, striding up the sloped garden and barging through the hedge on top of the dry-stone wall that bears Gavrilo Princip's graffiti. 'Come on, my friends. We've got work to do,' he said, disappearing from view.

After wrestling through the bushes at the top of the garden I found myself looking up at a steep heath, a vast rug of coarse upland grass reaching far and away to the horizon, seemingly held down by grey rocks scattered everywhere. We were heading towards a rising sun still low enough in the sky to make glowing lanterns out of seed-heavy heads among the long grass stems. As we contoured steadily up and across the slope, the rouge from the tiled rooftops of Obljaj eased itself into our wake, soon followed by that from the hamlet where Princip's mother had been courted by his father in the 1880s. As I got used to the weight on my back and settled on a comfortable rhythm for my stride, the only sound I could hear over my breathing was the distant bleating from a flock of sheep minded by a shepherd on the lower flanks down by the flat valley floor. Mile and Arnie were discussing the livestock when I caught up with them at the first break.

'All of us Princip boys spent time up here minding the family flock,' Mile explained as he leaned heavily on his shoulder-high walking stick, planted on the downward slope. His eyes followed the distant flock with interest and approval. 'Gavro would have come up here to do the same thing, and this is where he would have learned to throw stones as straight as any bullet. He would have started at an early age. When I was just seven years old I remember being trusted with the village's herd of a hundred sheep. And all I had for protection was a stick like this and a catapult for stones. Once a wolf came down and grabbed a lamb, but I held the lamb by its leg and we had a tug of war. I won! The wolf ran away and the lamb survived.'

Those hours we spent with Mile were a masterclass not just in route-finding, but in Herzegovina highland husbandry. He showed us how to choose safely from mushrooms the size of dinner plates that sprouted on the open hillside. After picking a few he would always break each specimen, scrutinising carefully the flesh inside before deciding whether to pop a piece into his mouth.

'You only eat the ones that have trails from weevils inside.' He spat out the words along with flecks of mushroom mush. 'If they are good enough for the weevils, they are good enough for us and do not have any toxin.' I had picked up a large, plump example, all white on the outside and pure pink within. Too pure, in Mile's opinion, so he batted it out of my hand and instead gave me one that was darker and flatter. It squeaked faintly when he twisted off a fragment and tasted of smoke.

Arnie and he chatted as we continued steadily on our way, my dark socks yellow with pollen dusted from alpine flowers growing ankle-deep among the grasses. I gave up keeping notes and fell back on simply enjoying the view out over the plain of Pasić, trying to guess the route Princip might have taken in 1907 when he left home for the first time. After a short while I realised I would have done better keeping an eye on the ground in front of me, as I tripped spectacularly over a rock. Mile immediately sprang into action, leading us straight to a sheltered cleft on the hillside where a stand of stocky trees grew as thick as a hedge. Taking off his rucksack and unsheathing a knife from his belt, he plunged into the thicket to the sound of snapping, grunting and sawing. After a few moments he emerged holding triumphantly two pieces of hazel about the length of snooker cues. The straight one he handed to me, the one with a crook at one end to Arnie.

Chuffed to receive my own Bosnian walking stick, I immediately took out a pocket knife and began whittling away bark that was bronze and brailled with the tiniest of blisters. To give the stick a handle I ringed it about six inches from the top, taking care that my whittling strokes did not cross this top line. Within a few minutes I had what I regarded as an elegant cream-coloured hazel walking stick with a handle of original bark. Perfect, so I thought.

Mile watched my efforts and then, without fanfare, set about a more authentic, functional barking of Arnie's new walking stick. He ringed the branch, much as I had, to preserve the bark on the handle, but instead of scraping the rest off like a carrot being prepared for the pot, he carefully dug the tip of his knife into the bark on the line where it had been ringed and then turned the branch so as to etch a single, deep cut that spiralled down its entire length. He then used the knife point to lever up the bark's top lip and proceeded to strip it in one continuous pig's-tail coil. I was impressed, but even more impressed by what he did next.

Rolling the strip of bark tightly into a cornet, he used a small twig to peg the wide end in place and then bent down to select a particularly succulent blade of grass. This he threaded as a reed into the narrow end, which he then put to his lips and blew. The shrill trumpet sound that emerged from his hazel-bark horn would not have shamed a huntsman summoning a pack of foxhounds in the English shires.

'We used them sometimes in an emergency to bring help,' Mile said, swinging his pack up onto his back. 'You would be amazed how far the sound can travel. I learned to make these as a child, and I bet you Gavro would have learned exactly the same.'

With all three of us now using walking sticks, our pace picked up as we went over a final rise and began a slow descent in the direction of a distant farmhouse at the foot of hills massing beneath

Mount Šator's distant peak. The last hint of early-morning cloud had now been burned off by the June sun and the heat was ganging up. Mile told us the farmhouse had the last spring at which we could replenish our water bottles.

'At this time of year the streams on the mountain are dry until you reach a large lake just below the peak,' he explained. 'Water has always been a problem in this part of the valley in the summer, although as children we were always told about the magic spring of Strbci – a tiny village about an hour's walk north of here. There are sinkholes there, and we were told that once in a lifetime you would see them flood with water, creating a deep stream of pure, cool water that flowed across the valley here. I don't think I can remember it ever actually happening in my entire childhood, and people used to talk about it like a sort of miracle.

'Well, do you know what happened during the war in the 1990s?' Arnie and I were now listening carefully. 'The Strbci sinkholes began to flood every year, year after year. And the way to tell it was going to happen was when snakes – thousands and thousands of them, by the truckful – would emerge sliding out of the holes as if they knew the water was coming.'

Mention of snakes had me gripping my new walking stick tighter as Mile began to speak for the first time about his involvement in the fighting.

For a significant chunk of the 1990s this entire region had been a no-go area for outsiders, a vipers' nest of extreme Bosnian Serb nationalism. Between the spring of 1992 and the summer of 1995 this land had been held by Bosnian Serbs, although it would be wrong to say it was captured through regular combat. A more accurate explanation is that the local Bosnian Serb community, with the support of militant Serb nationalists within the Yugoslav government based in Belgrade, had unilaterally staked the territory as exclusively Serb. Non-Serbs were no longer welcome, and were moved on with menaces.

The process did not involve fighting in terms of one army against another; it was more a process of one-sided bullying, underwritten by a very real sense of terror. Legend, myth and prejudice combined to create a matrix of cherry-picked historical truths used by the Bosnian Serb extremists to camouflage what amounted to that most base of human failings: racism. Non-Serb businesses were blown up, houses burned, women raped, men corralled in camps, innocents murdered. Bosnian Muslim and Bosnian Croat families, whose roots are dug just as deeply in this land as those of Bosnian Serbs, were declared aliens and kicked out, a strategy that became a defining hallmark of the war in Bosnia, one that would earn itself a neologism in the lexicon of war crimes: ethnic cleansing. Although the Bosnian Serbs were the first to use this tactic, by the time the war finished the Bosnian Croats and Bosnian Muslims would also come to employ it.

In the summer of 1993 I had approached this area as closely as was possible, coming no nearer than a field about thirty miles to the south, at the bottom of the plain that we were skirting today. Under the auspices of local Red Cross officials, an event was being organised that was grandly called a 'prisoner exchange'. I was still new to Bosnia, able to move freely enough on the Bosnian Croat side of the frontline, and I remember arriving that hot July day with an expectation of what I was about to see. Perhaps these POWs would be combatants who had been lost to the other side in fighting, or walking wounded with blood-smudged bandages and threadbare uniforms. It turned out to be somewhat different.

For several hours I waited in a field under the burning sun as buses crammed with women, children and the elderly, pale-faced in terror and uncertainty, lined up on the main road running along the valley floor. The Bosnian Serbs might have started the process of ethnic cleansing, but the Bosnian Croats had picked it up and run with it. After a final round of negotiations the buses carrying Bosnian Serb victims of ethnic cleansing by Bosnian Croat forces disappeared from view northwards and came back an hour later carrying near identical-looking passengers, this time Bosnian Croat victims of Bosnian Serb ethnic cleansing. They had been driven out of towns and villages in the area that I was now standing in – the only difference separating one group of terrified civilians from the other being their ethnicity. When I called my editors that day to offer a story, they said it was too routine to justify coverage.

'Yes, I served with the Bosnian Serb army,' Mile said. 'Those years were difficult and, for a Serb man in his thirties like me, there was no choice. I had to join up. But all I really wanted was to be a farmer back home. Twice I quit the army, and twice they caught me and took me back. It was a period of madness, and look how it ended.'

In the late summer of 1995, after three years under Bosnian Serb control, this area was overrun by soldiers from Croatia, a nation reborn out of the collapse of Yugoslavia on the other side of the old Habsburg–Ottoman frontier, the Catholic side. The assault that came to be known as Operation Storm was the largest military coup of the entire war. This time it was Bosnian Serb civilians who were bullied, forced to flee en masse, their homes torched, the country lanes choked with terrified women and children. After three years in which the Bosnian Serbs had acted with such cruelty, there was little international compassion for them as victims.

Operation Storm began the endgame of the Bosnian War, finally breaking the resolve of local Serb nationalism and forcing to the negotiating table the sorcerer's apprentice politician who had unleashed it, Slobodan Milošević. An avowed communist during Yugoslavia's red period under the dictator Tito, Milošević had switched sides as global communism waned in the late 1980s, wrapping himself instead in the flag of historic Serbia and picking at the seams of ethnic rivalry within the Yugoslav nation. It was a strategy that delivered Milošević short-term gains, but in the long term he released forces too strong for one man to control.

With Serb forces battered by Operation Storm, Milošević was forced in November 1995 to sign the Dayton Peace Accords that ended the war. Street protests in Belgrade would eventually drive Milošević from office, and he died from a heart attack in 2006 facing trial for war crimes – in many eyes, the single politician most responsible for releasing the nationalist extremism that pulled Yugoslavia apart. The tragedy was that tens of thousands of lives were to be lost in his opportunistic and, ultimately, failed attempt to retain power.

'It has been seventeen years now since the Croat army came here, and the Bosnian Croats still have power as the local authorities. To be honest, under these circumstances only a few Bosnian Serb families like ours have dared to come back,' Mile said. 'The ones who return are mostly the old, and for years now it has only felt safe enough for me to visit here from time to time, coming to see my old dad, Miljkan. I live over in an area that is still controlled by the Bosnian Serb government as recognised by the Dayton treaty, but all I want to do is come back here permanently and farm. A flock of sheep is all I need, and we could try to go back to life as it was.'

As we walked, my mind turned back to when I had reported on Operation Storm. It had been an intensely turbulent time, when frontlines set for so many years had shifted dramatically; when Bosnian Serb military dominance was blown away, the international community being willing to use NATO firepower for the first time on a large scale. The moment when frontlines change is the most dangerous time for a war reporter, and I recall hearing the news when a colleague from the BBC was killed by Croat soldiers a short distance to the north. Now I was walking across one of the mountain valleys stormed by Croat forces, with a reluctant Bosnian Serb soldier from those times who liked to be called Gavrilo Mile Princip, and who put greater value on sheep-farming than on nationalism.

The farmhouse with the freshwater spring was still some way in the distance when we passed a ruined building down in the valley. The second floor was missing and the plastered walls at ground level still bore graffiti left by Croatian soldiers back in the summer of 1995. Mile saw that I had spotted it and gave the slightest of shoulder shrugs, as if to say, 'See what I mean.' His next words were about a more immediate threat.

'Don't move,' he said, raising his walking stick as if he were preparing a bayonet charge, his eyes fixed on something moving fast in the middle distance. Mile had spotted an animal running towards us and he looked worried. 'Do not run, do not run.' He was now shouting, his anxiety cross-pollinating instantly to both Arnie and me. We all stood our ground, raising our walking sticks like pikemen, as the largest, most aggressive-looking dog I have ever seen rushed at us. I was secretly glad Arnie and Mile were both slightly in front of me. In the distance I could see the farmer's squat-looking wife running as fast as her short legs could carry her in our direction, screaming at us not to move.

I did what I was told – just.

'Get away, get away,' shouted Mile. I tried to sound fierce by making a growling sound and thrusting out my hazel stick, struggling with that most ancient of human inner conflicts: flight or fight. Just at the point when the dog was upon us, it stopped running and changed direction, circling us instead at walking pace, its mask menacing, eyes furious.

'Mile, Mile. What do you think you are doing?' panted the woman as she finally reached us. 'You know how aggressive Alba is. She is the best guard dog, but you know you should tell us when you come and visit.' Mile smiled unconvincingly and did not take his eyes off the animal, a magnificent female specimen of the *tornjak* breed, a local type of mountain sheepdog, which now shepherded our little group with throaty growls that I swear should have registered on the Richter scale. Alba followed us noisily all the way to the farmhouse before taking up a vigilant position under a nearby plum tree.

Arnie and I shook hands with Sonja Aćamović, who turned out to be related by marriage to the Princip clan, as she welcomed us to her home, dragging some plastic chairs onto the shaded front lawn. She then disappeared inside the house, coming out moments later with a tray of cups brimming with coffee and a bottle of cordial made from a local berry called *drenjak*. After serving us she sat herself down on a thick, heavy disc of tree trunk, carried nonchalantly in her meaty arms from a pile of firewood nearby, and caught up with Mile's news. Her children watched silently from overhead, peering at us through the metal grille of a first-floor balcony. It was not just in Obljaj that visitors were a rarity.

Arnie and I drank our coffee eagerly. Coffee in Bosnia is served piping hot, prepared in the old Turkish style, with the coffee grinds swirling thickly inside the mixture as it is brought to the boil in a pan, before being poured unfiltered into cups. The trick is to let the grinds settle before taking your first silent whistle of a sip, or else risk a gritty mouthful. Some drinkers use a single drop of cold water from a spoon to draw the grinds to the bottom, but I prefer simply to wait. Never stir.

And never, in post-war Bosnia, make the mistake of calling it Turkish coffee. Just as the name of the local language has become loaded, so it is with coffee. When sitting with Bosnian Serbs, you drink Serbian coffee; with Bosnian Croats, Croatian coffee; and with Bosnian Muslims, Bosnian coffee. Such linguistic gymnastics feel unnecessary, obscuring as they do the historical roots of coffee. It was Ottoman traders who spread its magic from where it was first enjoyed in distant Yemen, at the south-east extreme of the empire. Camel trains slowly cast the beans across the Arab world, through Anatolia and eventually into Ottoman holdings in Europe. Much of the spread was driven by pure commerce, but occasional accidents added happily to its dispersal. When one of the Ottoman sieges of Vienna was broken, the story goes that sacks of coffee beans were discovered in abandoned Turkish positions. They were taken as war booty into the city by an enterprising Austrian – the origin of Vienna's famous coffee-house culture.

Already thirsty from the morning's efforts, while our 'Serbian' coffee cooled I helped myself to extra servings of *drenjak*, a drink I had never tried before. It was sweet without being sickly, perfect to rehydrate with. 'Home-made,' Sonja said proudly, swinging her arm in the direction of Tent Mountain. 'We gather the berries up there in the hills. We have our own orchard for plum brandy, our own hives for honey and a big vegetable garden. We have to look after ourselves because the winters are hard. Last winter we had three metres of snow and could not get out of the valley for weeks.'

The self-sufficiency of local families was intriguing, although I found it double-edged. It might chime with modern theories of back-to-basics rural living, but I could not help thinking how it contributes to the turbulent history of this land. An atomistic society of individuals or small family groups provides a seedbed for ethnic rivalry – communities that see no virtue in coming together in the spirit of the modern nation state, defining them-selves not by their similarity to the next community along the valley, but by their distinctiveness, their ability to survive alone.

Mile explained to Sonja that we were planning to walk to the top of Mount Šator, a venture she found a little strange, pointing out that there was a serviceable jeep track up to the lake that Mile had already mentioned. Mile said something about us wanting to travel on foot, as Princip had done, and Sonja beamed. Mention of the valley's most famous son was something she clearly approved of. Their conversation drifted on, and after a polite interval I raised the question that weighed on my mind: could Sonja say if there were any landmines left over from the war on our route?

'Oh yes, there are mines up there,' she said. 'But the trail through the forest is safe enough, if you see it has recently been walked on. Lower down in the meadows make sure you walk where the grass has been scythed. After the war we did not know for sure where the mines were, but every year we cut more and more ground for hay. Wherever you see the hay has been cut you will be safe.' It is from the farming community of Bosnia that a dozen or so victims are killed each year.

The long walk ahead left us no time to dawdle, so after filling our water bottles in the kitchen – another room yeasty from energetic home-making – we said our goodbyes to Sonja and her family, her children nodding mutely at us from the balcony. We headed through the garden, past old car tyres that had been elegantly cut and tulipped inside-out to make flower pots. The footpath we were aiming for could be seen snaking up a hillside above an orchard of fruit trees. I was glad to see Sonja had a firm hold of Alba's collar, but just to make sure, I kept half an eye looking back over my shoulder until we were safely through the orchard and off Aćamović land.

The gradient stiffened and we adopted the slow and steady method for hills: little steps, lots of them, without resting. In places the grassy hillside had been worn through to the gravel below, and the path grew so steep it scrunched into a concertina of hairpins.

Soon we were too breathless to speak, climbing, climbing, climbing. After an hour Mile's mobile phone rang and I was glad for the break as he took the call, turning round for what would be my last look at the plain of Pasić. It was the rural European idyll in snapshot, a fertile valley dogtooth-checked by fields, threaded by a single track used by farmers and fringed by mountains. It felt a peculiarly peaceful backwater for the epicentre of the First World War. With Mile's mumbling in the background, I remembered a monumental map of the Austro-Hungarian Empire that I had seen on display at Artstetten Castle in Austria, the private estate of the assassinated Archduke, Franz Ferdinand. The map was enormous, a swaggering imperial inventory of the Habsburg project at its height, charting every feature then valued by the empire: cities, towns, churches, factories, bridges, rivers, mountains reaching right across land that we now know as Poland, Austria, Hungary, the Czech Republic, Slovakia and beyond. But what it missed was the birthplace of the person who would bring it all crashing down. Obljaj was much too small to be marked.

As Mile continued speaking on the phone, I wondered if Princip had also turned and taken a last glance at the valley as he and his father had trudged through these hills – the bibliophile teenager with a highlander's pedigree and a feeling for the underdog. Could he have had any idea of the changes that his horizons would undergo?

The man who today proudly keeps alive his name, Gavrilo Mile Princip, finished his call and announced a change of plan. 'I am sorry, but I really have to leave you now,' he said. 'My son, Vuk, is only four, and Nikola tells me he won't stop crying for me back in Obljaj. Good luck with the rest of the walk and, if you get to the top of Šator, say hello to Milan. He is a friend of mine and is looking after the old bear-hunting lodge up there. Tell him you know me and he might give you some help.'

It was a disappointment to be losing Mile, but at least he had started us safely on our way. We shook hands warmly and I urged him to thank his family for their hospitality, before he turned and skittered down the hill at a speed that belied his age. The last I saw of our Princip guide was Mile waving his walking stick and shouting, 'Remember the mines – stick to the path.' Arnie and I turned back up the slope.

After six more exhausting hours of climbing along a track that wormed through thick forest, we reached the lodge Mile had told us about. An A-framed structure from the late communist era, it commanded the view across the lake below the peak of Mount Šator. We had not seen a soul on the path and, as we dumped our gear on benches in front of the building, there was no sign of Mile's friend, Milan. I left Arnie recovering from the day's exertions and walked by myself down to the water's edge, delighted to be free at last of my rucksack. There was no wind to disturb the surface of the lake, set in a dell beneath the rocky summit of the mountain. Scree slopes protecting the peak reflected in its green water as I approached and, with nobody around, I took off my filthy hiking gear and waded in. The lake was bath-warm, the dark motionless water heated by the long summer day's sun. I kicked out, happily plunging my face into the murk, unable to see the bottom.

The aches of the day's hike were flushed away by the time the first tickles from underwater weeds indicated that I had reached the far side. I turned over and floated slowly back towards my clothes, all sound muffled by the water in my ears, my skyward view framed by rock fields frozen overhead in mid-cascade. By the time I had dried and returned to the lodge, the hike's exertions had been forgotten.

'Milan has turned up,' Arnie said when I got back. A compact, capable-looking man in his early forties stepped forward to shake my hand. He wore military camouflage trousers and a khaki vest. 'Milan's an ex-soldier from the war. He looks after this place in the summer and there is nobody else here but his son, Stefan.' A teenager emerged from within, as Arnie went on. 'When I told him we had met Mile, he said we are welcome to stay. We can camp outside or sleep indoors on the floor.'

I went inside and found the lodge to be little more than the shell of a building. Outside stood Milan's van, a rusty wreck from the 1980s parked facing down the slope of the gravel track. The ignition did not work properly and gravity was needed to roll it to a bump-start. Inside the building was a long wooden counter that would once have served as a fancy bar, but all the cupboards and surfaces had no stock now, apart from a few waxy jam jars carrying stubs of candles and a generous sprinkling of mice droppings. A loaded shotgun was leaning up against the fireplace, proof that we were definitely in bear country. On the wall there were patches where pictures had once hung. 'There's no power here, but Milan uses one room out the back to sleep in and keeps a fire lit in a stove in another room. He says we can cook there if we want to.'

Arnie had followed me inside, sharing what he had found out. 'It used to be a smart lodge for hunting parties coming after bears. But now it is used only from time to time. The last big group to come here was a bunch of bikers from the Czech Republic. They rode huge motorbikes laden with crates and crates of booze and had a wild time. But Milan says nobody has come this season, so he just keeps it ticking over.'

With the sun now low in the sky, the altitude was such that the temperature began to dip quickly. From my pack I retrieved warm clothes, food and cooking gear, leaving Arnie to debrief Milan further. My nose led me to the 'kitchen' where a cast-iron, enamel wood-burning stove belted out heat inside a cell of a room with a dingy window and no running water. A roasting tray of chicken pieces was already sizzling temptingly for Milan, so I set about mixing up our own meal, a broth of soup and pasta. Arnie had forgotten to bring a bowl, but I retrieved an old yoghurt tub from a dusty cupboard, rinsed it clean and served my companion. There were some grumbles about it being too salty, but I could tell from his smirks that he was teasing. After such a tough opening day it was a relief simply to recharge our energy levels.

'Milan was telling me that the path over the mountain goes across that big patch of rocks.' The last sunlight of the day rouged the rocky flanks of the upper mountain, its lower reaches already in darkness, and I could just make out the scree field that Arnie was pointing to on the far side of the lake. 'He says the path is easy enough to follow, but that most people have a car to pick them up on the other side. If we are going to make it all the way to the next town, it will take all day.'

Milan's advice tallied with what my map suggested. After crossing the mountain we would be dropping down onto the plain of Glamoč, the next of Herzegovina's wide valley floors, and to reach the small town of Glamoč itself the map indicated a hike of close to twenty-five miles. The lodge was now in total darkness, disturbed only by traces from our head-torches as I made a round of tea for everyone and we chatted. I asked Stefan if he had ever heard of Princip.

'Sure,' the young boy said. 'He was the man who killed the Archduke. We learned that at school. The teachers called him a terrorist.'

Milan piped up. 'When I was at school, things were different,' he said. 'That was back in the time of communism, and we were taught Princip was a national hero.' I found the malleability of history intriguing, as I scribbled away in my notebook.

I was tired, struggling to keep up with the conversation, and fell back on watching Arnie chatting by candlelight with our hosts – something that a few years ago would have been impossible. Arnie is a Bosnian Muslim, transformed by Milošević's 1990s nationalism into the mortal enemy of a Bosnian Serb soldier like Milan. But instead of power politics they talked of trophy bears that were once hunted in the forest through which we had walked, of how Milan as a boy had climbed up to an eagle's nest on Mount Dinara to kidnap a chick that he then reared as a pet, and a whole stream of other tall mountain tales. As the stories grew, I went inside and unrolled my sleeping bag. The sound of scurrying mice could not keep me from sleep.

It proved impossible to kick-start Arnie the following morning, so I decided to begin without him. I fancied climbing to the top of Tent Mountain, a challenge that Arnie was happy to miss. His new boots had blistered him cruelly during the climb to the lake, so I left him with a packet of anti-rub plasters and the agreement that he would follow me after exactly two hours. From Milan's description, the path sounded clear enough and we settled on a rendezvous at its highest point, just where it crossed the shoulder below the peak before beginning its long descent towards Glamoč. Working with Arnie years before had taught me he was not a morning person, so this seemed a better plan than fretting about him emerging from his sleeping bag. After breakfasting on dried fruit, peanuts and tea, I left him to rest some more.

A cuckoo sounded from within the forest as I loaded up on the porch of the lodge, the mountain peak barely visible through the chill, early mist. Cloud had built up overnight, dark enough to threaten rain but thin enough to deliver, so far, only the flimsiest of showers. I put on my rain jacket, jiggled my stiff shoulders to settle my pack and swung my hazel stick for the first of that day's many iterations.

The path cut up and across the scree field. Scree is never the easiest surface to hike on, small gravelly stones giving the impression that each step loosely slides back down as far as it has just reached up. Fortunately rain had washed most of the looser stones away and my progress was quicker than I expected. Catching my breath for the first time, I turned round to take what I had hoped would be a fine photograph of the lodge reflecting in the lake, but the mist had closed in. I hiked on, wondering if splitting up from Arnie on a cloudy day was such a good idea, only for the visibility to improve all of a sudden at the shoulder. Breaking right from the main path, I followed a fainter trail up the ridge, which my map promised would lead me to the summit. With historical irony, painted markings left on rocks to guide hikers were red squares with a white strip across the middle, a rather good impression of the flag of Austria. The foreign country that had ruled Bosnia in the run-up to Princip's assassination of Franz Ferdinand is today memorialised countless times along the country's hiking trails.

Fun though it is to walk with companions, I still find there are times when it is satisfying to go by oneself, following one's own pace, and nobody else's. My legs felt strong as I climbed for that hour or so, the clouds playing games with me, coming and going on the wind, promising wonderful views one second, then shutting them away the next. Sadly, by the time I reached the trig point marking the summit at 6,100 feet, all around me was a mucky grey. I might as well have been stumbling around at sea-level in a foggy quarry.

A wind shelter had been built out of rocks around the trig point and, tucked amongst them, I found a notebook where climbers logged their achievement in reaching the top of Mount Šator. I took the book out and saw its earliest entry was dated 2004, and was curious that it might have taken so long for the first recreational climber to reach here after the war ended in 1995. I thumbed through to the most recent entry, already almost two years old, adding my own message: 'British author in search of Princip's ghost – safe travels.'

Comfortably out of the wind, I snacked and took a long drink from my water bottle, hoping the cloud would lift. No luck, so after a rest I picked up my gear and headed down again to begin my search for Arnie. Within twenty minutes the cloud rose once and for all, revealing a scene that reminded me of cherished holidays in Scotland as a teenager. The southern summit flank of Mount Šator was one huge great moor, a rolling, treeless expanse of tundra-like tussock, yellowed in places by flowering patches of small plants that could double perfectly for Scottish gorse. In contrast to the previous day's low alpine terrain, this was a starker, treeless zone reaching in a south-easterly direction for many open miles, before coming up against another slab of thick Bosnian forest stretching to the horizon.

It proved easy enough to reconnect with Arnie on the main track, although he was full of apology for turning up a little later than planned. 'Sorry, sorry, sorry,' he grovelled when he came into view. 'Milan got talking. And then he made coffee. Serbian coffee, of course. And then he offered me his own-brew plum brandy, in which he soaks fresh mint leaves. It would have been rude to say no. I don't normally like plum brandy, but his was really special.'

No apology was needed. We had plenty of time, the sun was now shining and we were back together on Princip's trail, hiking over terrain that felt more and more familiar. Larks exploded noisily upwards in alarm from either side of the winding track, and all around was the same barrenness I remembered from hiking in Argyll. It looked so much like the Highlands I would not have been surprised to come across a gaggle of British ramblers or a shooting party in tweed banging away at grouse. But as the track finally reached the trees once more, we found evidence of a very different type of shooting activity.

Soil had been piled up to make breastworks to protect artillery positions. Prefabricated concrete doorways were set into a series of defensive underground bunkers. All around lay wooden pallets, the sort of thing you see in factories and round the back of super-markets where the delivery trucks go. They seemed so banal, so civilian, so out of context in a war zone. But then again, what better way was there to deliver heavy items, whether they are sacks of flour or high-explosive 120mm artillery shells?

'Don't go in there,' Arnie said with a firmness I had not previ-ously heard in him. I had approached one of the bunker entrances, but his words stopped me. 'These are positions dating from Operation Storm. Milan warned me to look out for them next to the path. They were built by the Croat army and there is no telling if there is unexploded ordnance still in there.'

I took his advice, viewing the scene instead from the security of the beaten track. Over the intervening years long grass had grown over the earthworks, and the timber of the pallets was bleached pale with age. In August 1995 Croat forces would have valued the high ground around Mount Šator, commanding as it does the valley of Glamoč over to the east. This would have made a fine position in which to dig in artillery, supporting Croat forces working their way deeper into Bosnia. Those would have been summer days and the gunners would have enjoyed the same scene as us: the edge of a high mountain moor, under a blue sky, with a nearby beech forest offering restful shade.

For the next few hours Arnie and I prattled away happily as we made good progress under the cover of trees along a jeep trail that had clearly not been used for a long while. Branches overhung the track so thickly it was reduced in places to a footpath for a single person, and the gravel where tyres once ran was covered with a filigree of moss. My de-mining map showed a minefield on the right-hand side of the track, perhaps a defensive position to protect the approach to the gunnery position back up on the moor. This might once have been a recreational area for hikers, but it was clear that today it was rarely used. Perhaps the meagre record in the logbook at the top of Mount Šator indeed comprised the full picture of who had climbed in this area these past years. We were yet to meet anyone on the trail, even though the terrain was as beautiful as any I have ever enjoyed for hiking.

The thought of food and drink is a stalwart motivator for long hikes, so Arnie went off on a riff about what he would most like to have, if we made it to Glamoč that evening. The map suggested we still had about fifteen miles to go, and although it was now well after midday I was relaxed as the various landmarks we were passing suggested that we were making steady progress. At a break in the forest we passed a mountain meadow of such size it warranted a reference on the map: Medjugorje, a name that translates as 'between the mountains'. With my children I had recently and repeatedly sat through one of their favourite stories, *Heidi*. Medjugorje could have doubled nicely for one of the high alpine pastures where the goatherd had lived with her grandfather.

The track continued on and on through the forest, all the time making an almost indiscernible descent. As the hours passed Arnie's blisters started to trouble him and I heard him grumbling about his footwear. 'Bloody boots! What was I thinking, buying shit like this? They are good for strutting around Shoreditch, nothing more. I've only used them for a day or two and the soles are already shredded to nothing.'

There comes a time on a trek when it's best just to let it all out, so I eased off the commiseration and let Arnie get on with it. We rested every hour or so, and after a while the forested terrain began to feel very same-ish, the trees crowded so thickly that it was difficult to spot any landmarks as reference points. We were deep in the forest, on an old jeep track, and the compass alone was telling us that we were heading in the right direction for Glamoč. There were no indicators of progress except for the passing of the hours, no sign of any local people we could ask to check we really were on the right path. Arnie's morale was beginning to dip, his footfall now painful to watch as he shifted his weight all the time to try and protect those worsening blisters. He started complaining about the tepid water in our bottles.

'I could really do with a fresh, cold drink,' he said at one point. 'Anything but this shit!'

And then, from around the corner, without any forewarning, came a silver jeep. The forest had muffled the sound of its approach, and the driver was as surprised to see us as we him. The vehicle slewed to a halt in a modest cascade of gravel and he gave us a cheery greeting, nonchalantly handing over two large bottles of water, so newly taken from a fridge that they still had condensation on the outside.

'You see, out in the remote areas of Bosnia there is magic at work,' said Arnie. 'The first guy we see on the trail in two days, and what does he have for us? Ice-cold water. Magic, I tell you.' He was smiling now, his cheerfulness restored, and so carefree in his drinking that spilled water gushed down his chin. But then he looked at me out of the corner of his eye, with a flash of seriousness about the power of the supernatural in Bosnia.

As evening approached we finally reached the edge of the forest, with the Glamoč valley opening up beneath us as wide and green as the plain around Obljaj back over on the other side of the Šator massif. I was grateful for the gentle breeze that now reached us and we paused to breathe deep, enjoying what appeared on the surface to be another paradisical agricultural tableau. In peaceful times Glamoč, now visible just a few miles to the south, was known as 'potato town' for the large-scale cultivation and processing of that vegetable. But from our viewpoint, looking out over the plain, something jarred. Many of the houses dotting the landscape were in ruins – roofless, their walls blackened from fire, their gardens overgrown through abandonment.

The track descended sharply and, as we came around a hairpin bend, we found ourselves at a modest roadblock. It was manned by an elderly figure sitting outside one of those shipping containers that are used to move goods all round the world. On this Bosnian hillside it served as a hut. His name was Zaim and he too was enjoying the late-afternoon cool, his seat facing down the slope towards the approach road climbing up from the valley floor. The sound of our sticks striking the ground caught his attention and he looked round over his shoulder, surprised.

'I don't often get people walking from out of the forest like you,' he said cheerfully. He raised his eyebrows when he heard we had walked all the way from Mount Šator and then offered to give us a ride into town at the end of his shift. There were still about four miles to go and, while Arnie was willing to accept his offer, I preferred to keep going.

'Why do you have the checkpoint anyway?' I asked.

'It's to do with the logging. You need a licence to cut timber up in the mountains, but some people try to do it without paying for the licence. I am employed by the local council to check that the loggers have the proper paperwork.'

I smiled. During the war checkpoints were a monumental pain, manned by militia who took routine pleasure in blocking foreign reporters – an irksome feature of life, as you could easily fritter away whole days negotiating your way through. It felt like progress to come across a checkpoint set up for sound environmental reasons. As I prepared to set off I caught sight of a Union Jack stencilled on the side of the container, an unexpected sight in rural Bosnia.

'The container belonged to British forces when they were based down in the valley after the war ended in 1995,' Zaim said. 'They left it when they eventually pulled out a few years back, and it was donated to Glamoč town council. Nice guys, mostly, the British soldiers. I had a job for years cooking for them in the officers' mess. Nobody eats finer than the British soldier!'

His words stayed with me as I set off for those last few miles into Glamoč, a town big enough to promise a restaurant where we could enjoy a good meal. After a day of ferocious heat, louring clouds promised a summer storm and accelerated the onset of dusk. I left Arnie to wait for his lift and had only my thoughts for company as the sky darkened and the gravel track morphed first into a tarmac lane, then into a main road with painted lines and a hard shoulder. It was Saturday evening, but traffic was scarce. The storm was yet to hit, the air growing steadily more charged. In a hillside pasture three men lay next to scythes on turf freshly shorn, smoking cigarettes and talking next to ricks newly constructed. I raised my hand in greeting, but they looked through me without response. Half a mile later four large *tornjak* dogs erupted from slumber, charging towards me, a barking blur of fangs and saliva. By reflex I tensed, but thankfully the farm compound had a fence.

Another mile later and I began to hear the intermittent thwack of wood being hewn. A pile of tree-trunk sections had been dumped in the front garden of a modest-looking home and four people were busy splitting them into pieces of firewood, which were then being carefully stacked under cover in readiness for the winter. Again I waved, again no answer. The person wielding the axe was a woman, in her sixties perhaps, her scrawny, tanned arms showing puffs of white skin as her dress rode up near the shoulder with each firm downward cleave. It brought to my mind a traumatic moment in 1993, when the driver of an aid convoy in central Bosnia had been attacked by local Croat farmers armed with agricultural tools, incensed at what they perceived to be help going to their enemies. The man was eventually finished off by a farmer's wife wielding a pitchfork.

The reaction to me, a stranger arriving in town, was at the hostile end of indifference. I felt sure Princip and his father would have met the same response as they passed through towns like this on their trek. Outsiders were to be treated with suspicion, potential threats to the status quo – a characteristic captured memorably by the writer Ivo Andrić. In his novel *The Days of the Consuls* Andrić's fictional description of Westerners passing through the central Bosnian town of Travnik has, for me, more than a whiff of authenticity to it:

> Then as soon as they reached the first Turkish houses they began to hear curious sounds: people calling to one another, slamming their courtyard gates and the shutters of their windows. At the very first doorway, a small girl opened one of the double gates a crack and, muttering some incomprehensible words, began spitting rapidly into the street, as though she were laying a curse on them . . . No one ceased working or smoking or raised his eyes to honour the unusual figure and his splendid retinue with so much as a glance. Here and there a shopkeeper turned his head away, as though searching for goods on the shelves.

On the edge of Glamoč I walked into a garage to buy a cold drink and the man at the till asked me where I had walked from that day. When I told him, he broke into the florid vernacular of the British soldier. 'No fucking way!' he said in perfect squaddie English as he handed me my change. The British army's impact on local Glamoč society clearly went beyond the donation of a few old shipping containers.

The sound of a car driving along the hard shoulder had me glancing anxiously behind me. Did local unfriendliness extend to running over strangers? But it was only Zaim slowing down, with Arnie grinning from the passenger seat and saying he would go into the town centre and find us a place to eat. By now I was done in, past caring for a meal that was more appealing in anticipation than in reality. After wolfing down veal accompanied by a sample portion of Glamoč's famous potatoes – starchy, wholesome and tasty – all I wanted was a bed.

My expectations were not particularly high, remembering the Baedeker guide's description of the inadequacies of Bosnian accommodation in the early twentieth century. 'Travellers who do not expect too much will, on the whole, find the inns very tolerable,' it said. I was too tired to be fussy, grateful to hear from the waiter that, although normally closed, the old guesthouse in the town centre could be opened up just for us.

I hoisted my bag onto my back one final time and set off, Arnie now hobbling at my side, just as the first drum roll of raindrops announced the storm's arrival. The lights at the guesthouse were off, but a man emerged from the dark, sharp-eyed and shrewish, to open up just in time, fumbling his keys under a strobe of lightning flashes. As he opened the door we jostled in out of the deluge, gratefully taking keys for rooms up on the first floor. At the top of the stairs was a picture that made me feel nicely at home, a kitsch oil painting of a local landmark: Mount Šator.

CHAPTER 5

Fishing in a Minefield

Piscatorial Imams, Muzafer Latić, left, and Kemal Tokmić

FOREIGN SECRETARY

Mr. Fitzroy Maclean, M.P., is a man of daring
character with Parliamentary status and Foreign Office
training. He is to go to Yugoslavia and work with
Tito largely for S.O.E.   The idea is that a Brigadier
should be sent out to take command later on.   In my
view, we should plump for Maclean and make him the
head of any Mission now contemplated, and give him a
good military Staff officer under his authority.
What we want is a daring Ambassador-leader with these
hardy and hunted guerillas.

If you agree, please act in this sense with the
War Office and S.O.E., and use my influence, for
what it is worth.

W.S.C.

28.7.43.

Memo from Winston Churchill,
authorising Fitzroy Maclean's Mission to Tito

The walk from Glamoč to Bugojno, where Gavrilo Princip caught the train to Sarajevo, took five more days through a landscape that was sometimes wild, often beautiful and always charged. Crossing a high pass in the mountains one morning, we glimpsed the tufted, pale-eyed mask of a wolf watching us intently from the edge of a clearing. Long enough for us both to see it, not long enough for me to take a photograph before it ghosted away to the cover of wooded darkness. On another day we hiked through country the like of which I have never experienced, a boundless, exposed dragon's back of a plateau without a single tree, its pelt of long grass combed backwards and forwards by the shifting wind. 'Middle Earth,' declared Arnie, surveying a scene that could easily pass for Tolkien's fantasy world. I looked at my mobile phone and registered a modern-day indicator of remoteness: no signal.

Formidable mountain ranges kept coming, occasional rainstorms washed through and we both had periods of footsore exhaustion. But the magic of the journey for me came from the rich overlay of history we touched on, the metronome click on the ground of our hazel sticks marking progress not just along Princip's trail but through terrain where other key episodes had played out.

I relished the sense of sharing the same physical setting that framed Princip's journey in 1907: skylines, forests, pastures, medieval ruins that he would have been familiar with. Baedeker's 1905 travel guide recorded a daily stagecoach, or 'diligence', all the way to Bugojno from the valley where Princip was born, a one-way ticket costing ten crowns in the currency of the Habsburg Empire. The price appears to have been too much for him and his father, as they trudged all the way, as we did, on foot. Princip would have recognised the high-sided valleys concertinaing the land that we traversed, the summer heat and the rural simplicity that lay all around us. We skirted north of a town called Livno, where a poster advertised a highlight of the 2012 summer season: a scything competition for local farmers.

Under Austro-Hungarian rule, Livno was the administrative centre for the area where Princip was born, and it was here that a police report was compiled by local officials after the assassination in 1914. The form comprises a list of boxes where standard details are recorded: name, occupation, parents' particulars. Under the 'reputation' category, a colonial officer had written simply: 'a weak boy'. Another of the boxes indicated the extent to which the colonisers from Vienna had failed to improve conditions for Bosnia's peasantry at the start of the twentieth century. The typed rubric demanded to know 'to whom does this serf belong?'. This time the official recorded that Princip was the feudal subject of two local lords, one named Jović, the other Sierćić.

It was during Princip's overland trip that his rage against the foreign ruler took root. He saw how the poverty he had known in Obljaj was replicated right across the country, regardless of the ethnicity of the rural community. The Austro-Hungarian authorities used to boast of how, under their rule, Bosnia benefited from new schools, industry and infrastructure, and they even goaded Princip at the trial that followed the assassination into describing the quality of life for Bosnian peasants. His answer leaves no doubt about how he regarded their plight:

'Of what do the sufferings of the people consist?' he was asked by a lawyer.

'That they are completely impoverished; that they are treated like cattle. The peasant is impoverished. They destroy him completely. I am a villager's son and I know how it is in the villages,' he answered.

The natural beauty I found impressive but what really moved me was that latent sense of charge in the landscape, the knowledge that we were crossing through an area powerful enough to have impacted modern history not just at the start of the twentieth century but at other, later turning points. Tension rose when for the first time we passed through a minefield. On the opening day, we were deep in a forest when we spotted red plastic warning signs nailed to tree trunks on both sides of the track, each bearing a skull and crossbones in white along with text printed in both Latin and Cyrillic script: 'Warning – Mines'. A less tangible sense of unease would manifest itself whenever we passed through towns. The skylines indicated Bosnia's three-way mix, with Catholic bell-towers, Islamic minarets and Orthodox spires often clustered in the same view, but the nationalist war of the 1990s had had the polarising effect of leaving only one group dominant in any particular place. Just as like electrical charges repel each other, so these south-Slav communities, which shared so much history, are now driven away from each other.

Before we even set off, the atmosphere in Glamoč gave us a strong sense of how fierce ethnic loyalties remain in the twenty-first century. Even though the town lies some way inside Bosnia, the flags of the neighbouring country of Croatia hung from shop fronts around the town square, and the peal of bells from a huge and newly-rebuilt Catholic church swamped completely the call to prayer from a local mosque. The guesthouse where we spent the night was right in the town centre where three roads merge around a small, paved triangle shaded by plane trees and surrounded on all sides by houses, bars and corner shops clad in the pale, weathered masonry that is common in nearby Dalmatia. Rinsed by the previous night's rain, the whole scene sparkled in the early light of a hushed summer Sunday. Insects flew holding patterns in air too still to even waft the flaccid flags with the vivid red-and-white chequerboard shield of the Croatian coat of arms. With the bells and muezzin falling silent, the peace was broken only now and then by the sound of a badly-tuned motorbike engine being gunned nearby by some teenage off-road riders. I watched as a nun parked her boxy Yugo car next to the triangle before bustling off purposefully in the direction of the town's large Catholic church.

There is a mild schizophrenia about the Balkans, a sense of identity that swings between Oriental and Occidental, old world and new. On a gentle summer morning in a town such as Glamoč one could be forgiven for believing you are deep in western Europe. The town square, with its corner shops and pavement cafés, would not look out of place deep in the south of France or high on the Spanish sierra. The owner of the guesthouse, Zdravko Lučić, sat with me that morning on the terrace while I ate a breakfast of eggs sunnyside up or, to use the local wording, 'on your eyes'. A Bosnian Croat, originally from the town of Bugojno, Zdravko had served as a soldier in bitter fighting there.

When the Bosnian War began in 1992, the conflict had initially been a two-way struggle between Bosnian Serbs and all other Bosnians – that is to say, Bosnian Muslims and Bosnian Croats. Surprised by the speed of the Bosnian Serb land-grab, the two other communities were forced into a working alliance, one that went as far as the two sides fighting alongside each other. But tensions worsened steadily between the Bosnian Croat and Muslim allies, and eventually became all-out war. Just as Serbs reminisce about the glories of medieval Serbia, so Croats venerate their own long history, one that records with pride the existence of an independent kingdom of Croatia. No matter that the nation effectively lost its freedom 900 years ago, becoming first a vassal state of Hungary and later a component of the Habsburg Empire, legends of self-rule were kept alive over the centuries by Catholic Croats just as keenly as stories of early Serbian nationhood were preserved by Orthodox Christian believers.

Epic tales of past glories would be told in Croat hovels, as they were in simple Serb dwellings like the ones in Obljaj. Peasants from both communities then relied on the same *zadruga* system, gathering families into parish groups where issues could be worked through and burdens shared. They were also the platform where resentments against feudal overlords could be vented and self-pity could fester, occasionally erupting into rebellion. Just as the Ottoman occupiers of Bosnia faced occasional uprisings from disaffected locals throughout the eighteenth and nineteenth centuries, so the various elites imposed on Croatia by Hungary and Austria often faced revolts. In both cases the response was very similar: peasants executed, villages burned, communities destroyed, anger fuelled.

In its fundamental details Zdravko's family story was identical to that of the Princip clan, two days' walk away on the other side of Mount Šator. The only difference was that one was a narrative of Croat victimhood, the other of Serb. Much as the local communities here in recent times have sought to emphasise their differences, this shared experience shows how the south-Slav peoples of the Balkans have a common historical narrative of suffering, one that is transitive between the different communities.

It was largely a sense of righting past historical wrongs that led to the founding of an independent Croatia when Yugoslavia fell apart in the 1990s. In 1991, a year before the Bosnian War began, the Croatian War had started, as the Croatian republic that used

to be part of Yugoslavia broke away in a struggle that would eventually lead to the creation of today's independent country. In the
flush of this success, a small but influential contingent of extreme
Croat nationalists saw the subsequent war in neighbouring Bosnia
as an opportunity to grab land that might restore what they held
to be their birthright, a Croatian state reaching far into Bosnia,
as history shows was the case at its territorial zenith roughly 1,000
years ago. When these ultra-nationalists made their move in late
1992, following months of plotting and preparing, there was only
one possible outcome: the Bosnian Croats and Bosnian Muslims
turned their guns against each other.

Throughout 1993 the Bosnian Serbs largely sat back and watched
their two once-united opponents rip each other apart. Some of the
most hateful atrocities and episodes of ethnic cleansing took place
that year between these two former allies – incidents that I covered
as a reporter. On one occasion I had to drive away wild dogs from
eating a corpse in the village of Stupni Do, where Bosnian Croat
extremists had slaughtered Bosnian Muslim farmers on an autumn
day. An already complex war had become a lot more complicated,
something that made reporting it a challenge. For example, in the
central Bosnian town of Vitez a small pocket of Bosnian Muslims
in the old town centre found itself surrounded by a hostile enemy
made up of Bosnian Croats, who were then themselves surrounded
by more Bosnian Muslims, who were in turn confronting a wider
Bosnian Serb enemy. Newspaper stories became more and more
convoluted and, inevitably, mistakes were made.

In October 1993 I was one of the last foreign correspondents
to see up close the famously graceful bridge in Mostar. This
southern city was then torn apart by some of the worst fighting
between Bosnian Croats and Bosnian Muslims. One morning I
cowered inside a Spanish armoured personnel carrier from the
UN peacekeeping force being driven into the Bosnian Muslim

half of town, where I was to spend one of the most terrifying nights of my life. My diary recorded that the city's airfield was a no-man's-land separating the two sides, so we roared across the tarmac at high speed from the Bosnian Croat frontline positions to find:

> . . . the first Bosnian Muslim trenches, First World War-style with tin helmets bobbing up and down every 15 ft and mounds of earth, barbed wire and timber. One nice touch was several feet of trench that were crowned with grapevines sending their tresses down and round the men.

Mortar shells were raining down so heavily that the personnel carrier did not move for the entire duration of its twenty-four-hour-long deployment, parked for safety under the protection provided by an overhanging building. Pumped with adrenalin, I ventured out on foot to an improvised hospital set up in the basement. An old Mercedes taxi roared to a halt outside just as I arrived, its passenger door already flung open as a Bosnian Muslim civilian desperately dragged out a woman who had been hit by mortar shrapnel. As she was bundled out of the car I can remember my reflex of embarrassment at seeing her left breast exposed in the bloody confusion. She made no move to cover herself. She would not move again.

The beautiful single-span bridge was then barely recognisable, crudely covered with a roped web of old tyres, a forlorn attempt to protect the 400-year-old masonry. To cross it was to risk your life, so you had to sprint, doubled-over, all the time knowing that you might be in the cross-hairs of Bosnian Croat snipers hidden in houses just a few yards away on the west bank.

A few days later the bridge came tumbling down, a catastrophically symbolic moment when a dream died – the dream of all southern Slavs living as one. The tyres could offer no protection against a salvo of shells deliberately aimed by a Bosnian Croat tank. So deep ran the hatred between the two former allies that Bosnian Croat commanders ordered to be destroyed anything that hinted at a Bosnian Muslim cultural connection to this land. The bridge had been built by Ottoman occupiers in the late sixteenth century and, in the poisonous atmosphere of the 1990s, that was enough to condemn it through historical linkage – no matter how disingenuous – to the Bosnian Muslim side. Bosnia's Muslims are just as much southern Slavs as Bosnian Croats and Bosnian Serbs, the key difference being their faith. They were not foreigners and certainly not descendants of Turkish Ottoman occupiers.

The bridge's destruction was big news, but *Newsweek*, the reputable American magazine, would famously blunder in a prominent picture-led account of the incident. The magazine wrongly blamed Serbian forces for shelling the bridge. This muddle seemed to capture, for me, the sense of the war becoming too complex for outsiders to decode. Some Western policymakers at that time gave the impression of giving up on Bosnia, as if the violence were too historically rooted ever to be resolved.

As Zdravko, owner of the guesthouse in Glamoč, told me his own story it became clear that during this period our paths had passed perilously close to each other. His home town, Bugojno, was then being fought over fiercely by his own side, the Bosnian Croats, and that year's enemy, the Bosnian Muslims. In July of 1993 things were going badly for the Bosnian Croats, with their forces preparing for a retreat. 'They were coming at us from all sides and I was deployed to man a checkpoint to block the road that leads into Bugojno from the south,' Zdravko said. 'It was in a place called the Pajić field.'

'But I remember your checkpoint on that road well,' I explained. 'There was a British UN position nearby, and I joined a column of their Warrior armoured troop carriers heading up to Bugojno from the south during the fighting. The first day we tried, it was too dangerous to pass your checkpoint. There were no people on the road, but it was covered in rubble and blocked with a jack-knifed truck loaded with wood. The next day, really early in the morning, I drove my armoured Land Rover straight past you, sandwiched between two Warriors that managed to push past the lorry and the rubble.'

With the faintest of smiles Zdravko then said: 'Well, if I had seen you that day I would have shot you.' I am still not sure if he was joking. 'Those UN bastards,' he continued, his voice sharpening with anger. 'All they did was help our bloody enemies. They did not give a damn about us Croats.' His rage against the foreign forces from Britain, France, Canada, Holland, Spain and elsewhere – peacekeepers who found themselves in Bosnia without any peace to keep – was replicated across all combatants in the war. If there was one common feature between the otherwise bitterly divided forces with whom I had contact, it was their hostility towards the outsider, the phenomenon that Ivo Andrić, writing in the 1940s, observed so acutely in his historical novels. In the 1990s the different communities each blamed the UN for working against them: helping their enemies unfairly. I had seen how untrue this was, but self-pity is a powerful force, blinding in its reinforcement of victimhood.

I was intrigued that Zdravko and I could remember the same situation so differently. He was convinced the UN forces had given up on the Bosnian Croat civilians forced out of Bugojno by the fighting. But I remember clearly the risks taken by these foreigners as they did whatever they could to help those same civilians. A British officer would be killed patrolling nearby when his vehicle hit a mine. At the height of the fighting for Bugojno, I watched the local British commander negotiating at length with Bosnian

Muslim forces so that he could provide whatever help he could to civilian Bosnian Croats huddling for safety in a small village just outside the town.

Fighting between Bosnian Muslims and Bosnian Croats lasted for more than a year before the leaders of the two groups, under diplomatic pressure from the international community, agreed a peace deal. So from spring 1994 the two sides reunited once more in a common front against the Bosnian Serbs, one that would culminate in joint operations during Operation Storm, which was so decisive the following summer. The Croat–Muslim fighting had achieved nothing except claiming thousands of lives and picking scabs off old rivalries. For Zdravko, it meant that he no longer felt at home in his birthplace, preferring to live in Glamoč, a town set firmly under the control of the Bosnian Croats following the Dayton peace deal that ended the war.

After hearing the Bosnian Serb perspective from Mile's family back in Obljaj, and that of the Bosnian Croats from Zdravko, our first major encounter with Bosnian Muslims came unexpectedly on the third day of walking from Glamoč. We had just climbed the mountain pass known locally as the Gates of Kupres, which takes its name from a nearby highland town, famous for its ski resort. The pass is well-known for marking the frontier between the rocky open wastes of Herzegovina and the tighter, greener valleys of central Bosnia, and no sooner had we crested the rise than we heard something we had not encountered so far on the journey: running water. Herzegovina is famously dry in the summer months but having crossed through the Gates of Kupres we already had proof of change – a perennial mountain stream within the watershed of the Vrbas River. An hour or so later we came across an old climbers' refuge deep in the forest where we met two Bosnian Muslim imams dressed in clothing I do not normally associate with mullahs: rubber waders, battered green hats and waistcoats covered in small pockets from which bundles of fishing line nosed. They were mad-keen fishermen about to go trout-fishing.

In 1957 Lawrence Durrell published a thriller about the Balkans, *White Eagles Over Serbia*, following his service as a diplomat in post-Second World War Belgrade. The book's swashbuckling hero, Methuen, manages to outwit the state security services hunting him by surviving on trout caught in mountain streams. I love fly-fishing, but when I read this book twenty years ago the idea of going fishing up a Bosnian mountain stream was simply unfeasible. Today it was a different story.

'Can I join you?' I asked, after introducing myself to Kemal Tokmić and Muzafer Latić. Of course, they said; and so, leaving Arnie to rest outside the climbers' hut, I then embarked on an extraordinary fishing safari. Clambering down the bank, we came to a stream no wider than a table-tennis table, a chain of tiny pools, cascades and eddies that gurgled down through a muddle of forest obstacles: fallen tree trunks, overhanging ferns, exposed roots and patches of boggy silt. Right there, next to where the mullahs planned to set up, was a red mine-warning sign nailed to a tree. Now I am no expert, but twenty or so years after mines were planted in this area, gravity, rain, landslides and the attention of passing wild animals could only have had one effect, if those devices were dislodged: they would surely have worked their way down the gully towards the stream where we were now standing. I pointed at the mine sign and asked Kemal if he thought it was safe to fish.

With a shrug of his shoulders that marked him out as a truly committed fisherman, he turned away from me and began to concentrate on the next little pool, reading the current for where a fish might lie. 'God will provide,' he whispered.

We spent a few hours stalking mountain trout. They were tiny little things, no longer than the span of your hand, spectral-white on the underside and camouflaged dark-brown on top, the boundary between the two colour schemes marked by a plimsoll line of bright-red polka dots. These were not stocked fish bred in tanks, but wild, canny little blighters that it took skill to land. I have fished lakes in New Zealand and rivers in the Falkland Islands, but this piscatorial mission was as challenging as any: approaching each tiny pool in silent stealth, threading the rod through an overhead web of leafy branches, keeping one's footing on the uneven river bank and trying to land the bait where the water was moving just enough for its touchdown plop to be hidden, but not so much for the line to be swamped.

Kemal was the first to have a strike, but as he jerked the line upwards his weight shifted and the old log on which he was balancing collapsed. The fish escaped in a tangle of leafy, gritty cursing that would have brought blushes to his congregation.

My own attempts were even clumsier, so I was mostly happy to watch and learn from the local experts. Their concentration was intense, their skill level high, their passion tangible. As we crept up the stream bed I thought about the fishermen I had seen on the first evening we arrived in Princip's village – Bosnian Serb teenagers. I thought of Bosnian Croat boys I had seen fishing near Glamoč. In Bosnia the love of fishing knows no boundaries.

When we got back to the hut I found that Arnie had made a plan. 'It's another four hours' walk from here to Bugojno and, as it is already late, I have arranged for us to sleep here,' he said. The refuge had been built in the early 1960s when Yugoslavia was ruled by the communist dictator, Tito. Inside was a large common room with a horseshoe of benches constructed around a wood-burning stove, the walls decorated mostly with maps showing local trails. Among the maps were a few photographs of the lodge's construction team from 1962, lean, bare-chested men, and women in flowery dresses, proudly sharing in the communal project.

I invited my two new angling friends to join us for a meal and we spent the evening chatting around the barbecue built out the front near where the mountain stream tumbles down a waterfall. The woodsmoke blended with the smell of spicy mince nuggets, *ćevapčići*, hissing fat onto the coals. As a final flourish, flat bread rolls known as *lepinja* were placed on the grill to toast. Leathery to the touch and dusty with flour, they soaked up the fragrant oil when stuffed with the meatballs and dressed with freshly chopped onion.

The two mullahs showed great interest in my project to follow Princip and were intrigued by the Bugojno connection. They both came from the area. Kemal's mother had been killed by Bosnian Croat shelling during the fighting of July 1993, but they had no idea that Princip had taken the train from here as a youngster to begin his schooling in Sarajevo. As with others on this trip, the mention of Princip could unlock people's views about not only the 1914 assassination, but much that had followed in this country.

'We live in an age where in the rest of the world Muslims are regarded as terrorists,' Kemal said, after gnawing his way through one of the rolls. 'But look at the assassination of 1914 in Sarajevo – there were no Muslims involved. The assassin was this young man Princip and he was a Bosnian Serb. He shot dead the Archduke and he shot dead his wife. That makes him a terrorist. But the world does not say all Bosnian Serbs are terrorists, does it? Of course not. It is just the Muslims that all become terrorists when one Muslim does something stupid.'

While I could agree that the Western world can today be clumsy in its portrayal of Islam, I had to point out that one of Princip's fellow conspirators in Sarajevo on the day of the assassination *was* a Bosnian Muslim, a man called Mehmed Mehmedbašić. He was armed and committed to the same goal as Princip: to kill the Archduke as he passed through the streets of the city on his official visit. Kemal and Muzafer both said they had never heard of Mehmed Mehmedbašić or his role in the assassination. They were both highly educated men, but on this basic historical point they were ignorant, believing instead a narrative that suggested the assassination was exclusively a Bosnian Serb exercise designed only to serve the interests of that one ethnic group.

Our conversation brought home the polarising effect of Bosnia's ethnic rivalries, a phenomenon re-energised so corrosively by the events of the 1990s. Kemal had lived through that conflict, and indeed had buried his own mother under cover of darkness in Bugojno because the intensity of the shelling had made it too dangerous to hold a funeral in daylight. If you have endured such an experience perhaps it is understandable that you might blindly emphasise the differences, and not the similarities, with rival ethnic groups within your community. As we sat drinking coffee, our discussion moved on to the period of Tito, the age when community projects such as the mountain lodge outside which we were sitting were built. Again, the sense of victimhood felt by Muzafer and Kemal outshone everything else.

'Tito was not interested in the Bosnian Muslim population,' Kemal said. 'He kept power to himself at the centre and did not care at all about our people here in Bosnia.'

Arnie could not let this pass. 'Come on,' he said politely. 'What about the constitution of 1974, which guaranteed full republic status to Bosnia for the first time within Yugoslavia? The country had always been the poor cousin inside Yugoslavia, next to the federal republics of Serbia and Croatia, but in 1974 Tito went a long way to putting that right, to giving us greater status for ourselves.'

Kemal shook his head. 'That was nothing. The Tito era was a

bad time, and that is what you must remember. His regime was a dictatorship, a dictatorship that was brutal and undemocratic. I read on the Internet that Tito's regime here in Yugoslavia was the eleventh worst in world history.'

I pressed him to explain. Was it eleventh in a league table of political assassinations or economic mismanagement or corrupt asset-stripping? All he kept repeating was that he 'read it on the Internet'. Muzafer mentioned that his brother had been jailed under Tito for political reasons, but again he could not remember exactly what those reasons were. By now Arnie was fuming, but he managed to control his anger to say this: 'Look at what we have seen since 1990 and the collapse of Yugoslavia. Surely that tells us Tito was special, by keeping the country together for forty years. Only now can we see what a miracle that was.'

The edginess of the exchange made it feel that it was time to say goodbye to our guests. Arnie was clearly cross at the way fellow Bosnian Muslims like Kemal and Muzafer could frame everything in terms of victimhood. I stood up and walked with our two guests to their car, Kemal's mobile phone pinging to announce the arrival of a message with a photograph attached. It was from a fishing buddy who had spent the day a few miles downstream from us and had sent a cheerful bragging photo of a large rainbow trout landed on a particularly tricky part of the river. The sparkle came back to Kemal's eyes. As any angler will tell you: better stick to fishing than politics.

Talk about the communist era brought to mind how the same land we were walking through had been the setting for Tito's rise to power through the Second World War. Indeed, for a brief period at the end of 1943, the potato-rich plain of Glamoč had been where an important series of events took place that was connected to the Allied decision to back the communist partisans led by Tito, a man at that time unknown beyond his inner circle. It was a strategic move that helped push Yugoslavia into the communist orbit once the war ended in 1945.

Yugoslavia, the country created in the Western Balkans after the First World War, had fallen to the advancing Nazis in 1941. The Germans were quick to deploy a 'divide and rule' strategy, chopping the territory into parcels that were run by Nazi-sympathising proxies. Hitler's occupation of the Western Balkans was as brutal as anywhere, with resistance sympathisers shot, Jewish communities destroyed and indigenous fascists given free rein. In one section of occupied Yugoslavia ultra-nationalist Croats were handed power, running a death-camp at a town called Jasenovac, where not only Jews and Gypsies, but rivals from within the local community, mostly Serbs, were put to death in huge numbers.

Initially, the Western powers believed local resistance to Nazi rule came from troops loyal to a commander named Draža Mihailović, a Serbian officer who had served in the 1930s Yugoslav army. As a result he enjoyed what little support the Allies could then offer: small-scale air drops of military supplies to his Serb-dominated resistance, fighters who proudly called themselves Chetniks. This low level of assistance was overseen by a series of middle-ranking British liaison officers smuggled into his underground headquarters. As these Allied operatives were constantly harassed by enemy patrols, their grasp of the complete military picture was sketchy.

Over time, suspicions emerged to change the way the Allies regarded the Chetniks. First, it became clear that another group of resistance fighters – communist partisans under a shadowy figure called Tito – might be inflicting more damage on occupying Axis forces. Second and even more important, in many places rivalry between partisans and Chetniks had erupted into full-blown combat, in effect civil war. Instead of fighting the occupiers, the two groups had begun to fight each other, cutting deals with German and Italian troops at the local level, and in some cases collaborating. The situation had got so bad in the early summer of 1943 that some Chetnik units fought alongside Italian troops in a joint operation that attempted to wipe out the partisans. The partisans, in turn, were accused elsewhere of making cosy arrangements with the occupiers.

To clarify this murky situation Winston Churchill demanded better intelligence, and this is where Glamoč enters the story. I had read extensively about the various Allied agents covertly deployed across the region. Some arrived by parachute, others by rubber dinghy launched at night from submarines operating off the Adriatic coast. It was exciting stuff. What intrigued me most was the way these accounts revealed the rivalries in the 1940s between local factions – partisans, Chetniks, fascists. The picture was a complex one, something that does not make for easy re-creation by storytellers. While many people are familiar with *The Guns of Navarone*, a wartime novel set in Greece by the British author Alistair MacLean, which was later turned into a popular film, his sequel failed to capture the public imagination. It was called *Force 10 from Navarone* and even though it would also be made into a feature film, with a full roster of stars including a young Harrison Ford, its popularity was nothing in comparison to its predecessor. It was set amidst the opaque factionalism, plotting and double-crossing of wartime Yugoslavia.

But while film-goers might demand the one-dimensional moral clarity of good against evil, I came to relish what I learned about Yugoslavia in the Second World War. Sliding moral values, human fallibility and cynical opportunism seemed much more real than Hollywood heroics. Eagerly I sought to untangle local history from the 1940s, not least because it seemed to mirror so well the complex war I wrote about fifty years later.

The most renowned British agent deployed to Yugoslavia was a namesake of the Navarone author, although no relation. Fitzroy Maclean, a Scottish warrior–diplomat, had been a founding member of the Special Air Service (the SAS) in the deserts of North Africa, a quixotic figure, tall and lean, often photographed in the kilt of his Scottish highland regiment uniform. The British press dubbed him the 'Kilted Pimpernel' and after his wartime exploits were publicised he came to symbolise the courageous, debonair secret agent. Ian Fleming was never able to dissuade the many people who believed that Maclean was the man on whom James Bond was based.

In the late summer of 1943 Maclean was summoned to meet Churchill to discuss Yugoslavia. In his wartime memoir, *Eastern Approaches*, Maclean recounted how he received his briefing from the British Prime Minister in the early hours of the morning, but not until a Mickey Mouse cartoon film had been forced on the assembled group of top brass. Churchill was famous for relaxing by watching films. In spite of lobbying by advisers who still favoured the Chetniks, the British Prime Minister already sensed that the partisans were a serious fighting force, writing a personal minute in July 1943 in which he described them as 'these hardy and hunted guerrillas'. When the potentially sensitive issue arose of which of the various Yugoslav factions were to receive British military support, Churchill gave simple and clear instructions. 'My task was simply to find out who was killing the most Germans and suggest means by which we could help them kill more,' Maclean wrote in his memoir.

After being dropped by parachute into central Bosnia, Maclean and his small team of Allied agents were led to the old fortress town of Jajce, briefly held by the communist resistance as its headquarters, and there he met their leader. He was named Josip Broz, but he would become known around the world by his partisan nom de guerre, Tito. What I found fascinating was how much Tito had in common with Princip. Born within two years of each other – Tito was the older – they were both southern Slavs brought up under colonial rule, both committing their lives to winning freedom for their people. Whereas Princip was born in 1894 in the Serb community of Bosnia, only recently absorbed within Austria–Hungary, Tito came from Croat and Slovene stock, born further north in Croatian land that had been under Austro-Hungarian rule for centuries. Where they differed was in their political vision. Princip focused no further than the short-term, on revolutionary acts intended to remove through assassination titular symbols of occupation. Tito looked further into the future, being a committed communist who saw the socialist model as the way not just to win freedom for all south Slavs, but to form a united country once the latest occupiers left.

Maclean spent several autumn weeks in 1943 with the partisans in Bosnia, dodging German patrols and seeking to build up as accurate an intelligence picture as possible of the resistance effort of the rival Chetnik and partisan formations. I tracked down his wartime diary with its colourful snapshots of life on the run deep in enemy territory: long treks, washing in rivers, being sniped at by Chetniks, daily language lessons, coming down with a 'gippy tummy'. The diary could have been written by many of the British soldiers who served here as UN peacekeepers fifty years after Maclean.

He was soon convinced that Tito's movement was the worthier recipient of British military support, writing a report that urged Churchill to switch from the Chetniks. It was a decision that still angers members of the Serb community, who grumble that the Chetniks were the victims of a dark plot by left-wing, communist sympathisers within British intelligence. In the 1990s I was once harangued by a Serbian petrol-pump attendant when I told him

I was from Britain. 'Fucking Winston Churchill, Fitzroy Maclean and all their commie friends,' the man shouted.

While it is true that there were communist supporters within British intelligence – this was the period before Kim Philby, Guy Burgess, Donald Maclean et al. were exposed as Moscow's agents – I don't believe their involvement settled the issue of where British support in Yugoslavia should go. Within the last few years it has been revealed that British code-breakers at Bletchley Park were able to decrypt German military communications emerging from the Balkans during the Second World War. These messages showed that the *Wehrmacht* took the threat from the partisans more seriously than that from any others.

What Maclean recommended, however, was a policy shift that would have a huge impact on the Balkans, a consequence that the warrior-diplomat was aware of at the time. By backing the partisans, Yugoslavia would be pushed firmly into the communist sphere then dominated by the Soviet Union. Maclean raised these concerns with Churchill who, as recorded in *Eastern Approaches*, had a typically direct response:

> The Prime Minister's reply resolved my doubts.
>
> 'Do you intend,' he asked, 'to make Yugoslavia your home after the war?'
>
> 'No, Sir,' I replied.
>
> 'Neither do I.'

Within a few weeks of Maclean's report being prepared, in December 1943 Winston Churchill, Franklin Roosevelt and Joseph Stalin put their initials to a memorandum spelling out the 'Military Conclusions' of the Tehran Conference. This was the first of the great meetings of the 'Big Three' Allied leaders, one at which the future of the post-war world was addressed. The first clause of the document, preceding the commitment to the D–Day landings in France, was the result of Maclean's work:

> The Conference agreed that the Partisans in Yugoslavia should be supported by supplies and equipment to the greatest possible extent, and also by commando operations.

The question then became how to deliver support at a time when Tito's troops were in control of only tiny parcels of territory. This is where Glamoč starts to be mentioned, as its wide valley floor offered the best site for the construction of a covert airstrip where Allied planes might be able to land. Maclean passed the task to a member of his mission, Major Linn Farish, an American combat engineer with pre-war experience of building aerodromes. Farish, an Anglophile Californian who won an Olympic gold medal for rugby union and preferred to go by the disarming first name of Slim, soon got to work, as described in *Eastern Approaches*:

> Farish, the expert airfield designer, found himself back at his peace-time occupation sooner than he had expected, helped in his work by the men, women and children of Glamoč who, under his direction, toiled away with pick and shovel, making the way smooth for the Dakotas which we fondly imagined would land there when all was ready . . . We signalled endless measurements and details to RAF Headquarters in the hope of overcoming the scepticism and distrust which in those early days they still displayed towards amateur-run improvised landing-strips. When not actually at work, Farish and his party carefully replaced the bushes that they had uprooted, so as to cover up their traces and thus avoid exciting the curiosity of passing enemy aircraft.

Eventually the order came to use the improvised strip to fly out a party of senior partisans so they could meet Churchill's military planners. The delegates gathered on the valley floor close to Glamoč in the chill of a November morning as the aircraft that was to fly them to Italy warmed up its engines, but disaster was to strike. Maclean described what happened:

> It was at this moment that, looking up, the little group round the aircraft saw, coming over the crest of the nearest hill, a small German observation plane. Before they could move, it was over them, only a few dozen feet above their heads, and, as they watched, fascinated, two small bombs came tumbling out.

The bombs exploded with devastating effect. They destroyed what was at the time the only aircraft in the partisan air force. More importantly, they killed two of Maclean's agents as well as Ivo-Lola Ribar, one of the partisan delegates, and wounded several others. For the partisans it was a huge blow. Ribar, a Croat and committed communist who enjoyed the full confidence of Tito, was young enough to be regarded as a potential successor as leader of the movement. He would later be venerated by the communist party of Yugoslavia as a national hero. A few days later Maclean made sure he was on board the RAF Dakota that touched down at the improvised strip near Glamoč, to pick up the wounded and a reassembled partisan delegation – the first successful Allied landing operation in occupied Yugoslavia. It was all very touch-and-go. Within a few weeks the Germans had overrun the area and the Allied air bridge was broken.

During the 1990s I had only been able to read about Glamoč, trying to picture the terrain where partisans, peasants and a rugby-playing American had worked so secretly. At that time the Bosnian

Serbs held the area, making it unreachable for a foreign journalist like me. But now the situation was different and I wanted to visit the spot where Britain's Second World War flirtation with the Balkans had momentarily been blown off-course. And when I reread Maclean's account I noticed a name that had a strong connection to Princip. Maclean recorded that among the wounded men collected by the Dakota was Vladimir Dedijer, a man Maclean reported as being in need of emergency surgery for a serious head wound. Dedijer, a former journalist who later became a renowned author, would survive the hardest years of wartime service with the communist resistance movement, fighting in some of the group's most important battles. With his own hands he had to bury his wife, Olga, killed on a remote hillside when the partisans came under attack by German forces. After the war Dedijer was to write the authoritative history of Princip's shooting of the Archduke, *The Road to Sarajevo*, which had been a foundation stone for researching my journey.

With help from Zdravko, the hotelier in Glamoč, I was able to find the Second World War-era airstrip where all this drama had played out. It was just a few miles outside town and as we approached in Zdravko's jeep Arnie began to nod in recognition at a stand of fir trees on the flat of the valley floor.

'I've been here before,' he began. 'Of course, I have. Of course, I have. How stupid not to remember. Back in my schooldays in the Eighties, when Yugoslavia was still communist, they brought us here for a day trip to see where the partisans had done secret things in the fight against the Germans. It was part of the glorification of all things red. I don't remember much about them mentioning British or Americans being involved in the air operations. They preferred to keep it simple and claim all the credit for the partisans.'

Arnie continued to nod as the trees came closer and closer. 'Yes,

yes, yes. They had an old Dakota on show. Must have been like the one you read about in Fitzroy Maclean's book. And I remember there was some sort of aerodrome tarmac, but that would have been built after the war had finished, I guess. I remember it as a modern airbase with the old memorial tucked on the side.' Zdravko had now turned off the main road and was following a track that took us in the direction of the copse. The terrain here was flat, unnaturally so, and clearly this was what Arnie remembered as the landscaped, communist-era airbase.

I was disappointed at how little was preserved from the partisan era and the bombing raid of November 1943. Zdravko turned along a lane that went through the trees, but all we could see were a few concrete plinths that had been stripped of memorial plaques and text. 'You are right, Arnie,' Zdravko said. 'There used to be a Dakota. It was parked somewhere around here.' He was now turning from side to side to peer under the trees, but he could find nothing. 'And the memorial to Ribar used to be well looked after. It was visited regularly during the communist period.'

'So what happened to it all?' I wanted to know.

'In the 1990s being communist no longer mattered,' Arnie piped up. 'Being Croat or Serb or Muslim was more important than being communist. All that commie stuff from the 1950s, 1960s and 1970s was seen as having been against the interests of the different groups. They did not just ignore the commie stuff, they deliberately destroyed it.'

Zdravko shrugged. 'Sure, the Dakota was scrapped and the Tito-era material destroyed. But to be honest, I cannot tell you if it was the Bosnian Serbs who got rid of it all when they were here, or the Bosnian Croat forces who drove them out. The point was we learned to look back on the communist period as bad for all of us.'

But I was not convinced. My conversations with Zdravko up

to that point had all been about the war of the 1990s, when honouring Bosnian Croat history had been so important. Ribar, the principal partisan victim of the 1943 raid, had been a proud Croat. I asked Zdravko for his feelings about the man. 'He might have been a Croat, but he was a communist more than he was a Croat,' Zdravko said, hauling on the steering wheel of the jeep so that we could turn back out onto the main road. 'And if you forget where you are from, then it is right that you are forgotten.'

Zdravko's indifference was a hollow epitaph for the men killed that wintry morning in 1943. Two Britons, named by Maclean as Robin Whetherly and Donald Knight, gave their lives here, but there is no memorial to their sacrifice.

As our walk progressed, we passed many houses destroyed in the war of the 1990s and still not rebuilt. But even these modern ruins sometimes had links back to the bitter fighting here in the 1940s. On some we saw the letter U daubed deep and capitalised on walls. It was the symbol of the Ustaše, the crypto-fascist, ultra-nationalist Croat group empowered by the Nazi occupiers during the Second World War. In this region the U symbol carries with it the same hateful charge as a swastika, yet in the 1990s it had been embraced enthusiastically by some of the Bosnian Croat forces.

Although small on the map, Bosnia felt at times as if it had a Tardis-like quality, a secret inner scale. Arnie and I slogged up hillsides, across plateaus and through woodland, our progress sometimes feeling as if it had stalled. Our conversation would inevitably turn to favourite foods that we would eat and drinks that we would enjoy when the hike was over. But my mind would also dwell on magic, on the power in this hilly land of myth clung to by communities huddling in unenlightened ignorance, unsure of what might be going on not just in far-off capitals like Vienna or Belgrade, but on the other side of the mountain, over the horizon. These days of walking showed me how much space there is in Bosnia for this type of projection, for the imagination to spin heroes and villains out of legends, for fear to ferment into prejudice. It felt not just understandable, but like the natural course for many nations. My own country – Britain – appears settled today, but as I grow older so I have learned how illusory this is. As Joseph Conrad's narrator, Charlie Marlow, says of Britain in the opening of *Heart of Darkness*: 'And this also has been one of the dark places of the earth.'

We rested for a day in Kupres, where yet more evidence emerged of Tito's links to this land. Arnie remembered the small mountain town as the place where his family always made a regular pit-stop on the annual summer holiday drive down to the Adriatic coast in the 1980s. 'We would be in T-shirts and shorts, but whenever we got to Kupres it was always bloody freezing,' he told me. So it was when we hobbled into town, a preternatural chill in a town where a massive new Catholic church, still framed by scaffolding, made clear that this was a town under Bosnian Croat rule. We both winced from blisters as we walked to a restaurant where Arnie ordered us large wooden bowls of a local speciality, a polenta-style dish called *pura*, made from locally milled maize that is served gooey with home-made cream cheese.

We sat with an elderly man called Ljupko Kuna, who told us of bear-hunting in nearby mountains. Aged eighty-four, he walked with a cane, his joints worn thin by decades of service as a hunting guide, and his vision had faded a little so he wore spectacles. But with blade-sharp recall he told us about his most famous bear-hunting client: Tito.

'I only shot with Tito for the last fifteen years of his life in the 1960s and 1970s, but for his age he was a good shot,' Ljupko said, pouring two sachets of sugar into his coffee. 'He was very precise as well, never shooting young animals and only going for them when they were trophy age, from twelve to fifteen years old. He never needed more than one shot for a kill. And that is not easy sometimes when the bear is in the wrong position or perhaps hidden by a branch.' Ljupko said Tito was so keen that he hunted every year, entertaining official guests, and although Ljupko remembered various heads of state fondly, he did not have a good word to say about the Libyan dictator, Muammar Gaddafi. 'That man shot at anything that moved,' Ljupko said. 'He was incapable of following any protocols when they stayed at the hunting lodge in Stinging Nettle Valley. It was built by the Austro–Hungarians.'

I had seen photographs of Tito hunting and was struck by how Austrian he looked. In one he stands over a slain bear, his hand holding the barrel of his rifle with its butt on the ground. His jacket is Tyrolean green, and the band around his brown felt hat is adorned with a feather, in the vogue of the European hunter. The photograph was almost identical to others I had seen of another keen hunter connected with this area, Archduke Franz Ferdinand. As the heir to the Austro–Hungarian Empire, he had rich opportunities to shoot at imperial hunting lodges, castles and estates spread across much of east and central Europe. The man who would be shot dead by Princip in Sarajevo logged every game animal, bird and trophy animal he shot during his lifetime, and had the numbers displayed on an ornate score chart that I had seen in Austria. The grand total came to 274,889.

'Tito really felt at home in these mountains,' Ljupko said. 'He fought around here during the Second World War at a time when he and the partisans were being hunted by the Germans. They always managed to escape, so he felt a special bond to this part of the country.' Ljupko was not the first to recognise Tito's close link to these hills. Fitzroy Maclean described in his war memoir how Tito appeared most at ease when living as a fugitive, dodging German patrols, in caves spread across Bosnia's mountains.

We emerged from the embrace of these same mountains on the last day of our walk to Bugojno, the gravel track firming into a suburban tarmac road, easing between comfortable family homes with jungle gyms in the gardens and modest cars parked out front. Then it grew yet further and connected to the main highway running into town from the south, and for the first time since Obljaj we had a proper pavement to walk along. I had covered the fall of the town to Bosnian Muslim forces in the summer of 1993 and for the first time on the hike I had reached a place I recognised – *terra* that for me was *cognita*.

There was no doubting which Bosnian community was in power. Just as new Catholic churches were the hallmark of today's Bosnian Croat authority over Glamoč and Kupres, so religious buildings in Bugojno told a story. In the town centre I walked by the seventeenth-century Sultan Ahmed Han II mosque, a building I had last seen as a wreck. My 1993 diary recorded that it had been struck by scores of artillery shells, and I had taken photographs of the gaping hole in the roof. All that was left of the minaret back then was a fibrous stump, the top section blown clean away by shelling from Bosnian Croat positions. Today the mosque is pristine, the main building restored to its pre-war condition, while the minaret has not just been rebuilt, but pumped up as if with steroids. The new column was roughly twice as tall as the original it replaced.

I found the supersized minaret unsightly. The traditional mosques of Bosnia, with their pincushion-domed roofs and needle-thin minarets, add so much to the landscape – a parcel of Europe where Muslims have worshipped for centuries. Rebecca West described them rapturously as 'among the most pleasing architectural gestures ever made by urbanity'. The new versions felt excessive, unworthy of the fine bridges and buildings left in Bosnia by 400 years of Ottoman occupation.

After roughly a hundred miles of walking from Obljaj, Arnie

and I searched out the old railway station where Princip and his father set off by train for Sarajevo in the summer of 1907. The Baedeker guide recorded the station here as the tip of a branch line on the outer fringe of the rail network built by the Austro-Hungarians. Primarily designed to haul timber felled in the region's thick forests, the line also ran occasional passenger trains. According to the old timetable recorded by Baedeker, the train used to take about five hours to reach Sarajevo from here, with several fiddly connections to get on and off the special locomotives needed to climb a particularly high mountain pass.

Arnie and I were too late to catch a train – about forty years too late. The last one left Bugojno in the 1970s when the line became so uneconomic that it was scrapped. The tracks had long gone, but we found the original station building, doubling now as the main offices for a bus terminus built where the trains used to run. The old station's paintwork was tatty, but at least someone bothered to tend the pot plants in their window boxes. With its tiled roof and three-storey symmetrical design, there was no mistaking its European origins. It would have looked perfectly at home next to a platform in the Tyrol.

Those early Austro-Hungarian railway surveyors had clearly known their business, for the road that today delivers you towards Sarajevo uses the exact same route as the original railway: down the valley of the Vrbas River, over the Komar pass into the Lašva River valley, finally joining the course of the Bosna River all the way to the capital. The slope at Komar was so steep that the train needed a special rack-and-pinion design to claw its way up the hillside. Ljupko, the bear-hunter from Kupres, had used the railway as a young man and told us that when it began to climb the pass most of the passengers would get off and walk, easily keeping up with the creaking locomotive.

Taking the bus would see us following the same route used by

Princip, so I bought two tickets towards Sarajevo and sat down
next to Arnie on a bench, happy at the thought that for the next
part of the trip I would not have to lug my heavy pack. The
summer sun was punishing and I was grateful for the shade from
the bus-station canopy. When Fitzroy Maclean arrived here on a
wartime locomotive 'belching flames, smoke and sparks', he
described conditions that could not have been more different.
'Under a cold, penetrating drizzle Bugojno station was bleak and
cheerless,' he wrote. As I contemplated the way history in Bosnia
so often runs over the same ground, another small coincidence
was offered up by the arrival of our bus. On its grille the maker's
name was spelled out in silver letters: Gräf & Stift. It was the
same company that built the limousine in which Archduke Franz
Ferdinand was being driven when he was shot by Princip.

CHAPTER 6

Rocking Bosnia

Rock band Franz Ferdinand performing in Bosnia

The author staying with Drago and Marija Taraba, Christmas 1993

The author visiting the couple nineteen years later

With the bus heading along the Vrbas valley, I sat back in my seat to rest, the window a screen on which a blissful summer scene scrolled past: river pools shaded by willows, recently mown pastures coned by hayricks, tanned children playing carefree in the dust. As Arnie gabbled away about never having had a hike to match the one we had just shared, I felt quietly relieved that we had made it safely on foot through some of Bosnia's more mine-contaminated backwoods. The walk had given me a sense of how far Gavrilo Princip had come when the 'weak boy' left home for the first time, not in terms of mileage, but more in terms of breaking with the only life he had ever known. He had left behind the closed rural society of Serbian serfdom and would encounter for the first time other Bosnians – Muslims and Croats – with their identifiers: religious buildings, clothes, food, traditions. It must have been bewildering for him as a thirteen-year-old to shift horizons so radically, to break away from the confines of a social system static for so long – one that had, in common with much of Europe, for centuries been framed by the strictures of hierarchy, feudalism and empire. To find out how Princip responded I would need to head on to Sarajevo, where he went to school.

Sadly I would have to do that without Arnie whose time away from his newspaper job in London was soon up. 'I am so sorry I cannot finish what we started,' he said. 'I have so many great memories to take from this trip. For a start, I had no idea this country was so stunning, so varied, so naturally rich, so incredibly beautiful and so bloody big. At times that walk could have killed me. But the best thing was the way the people we met could not have been more open, more friendly: the Princip family, the hotelier in Glamoč, the fishing mullahs. None of them gave a damn about my ethnicity. And yet we saw with our own eyes what the war has left behind: the oversized churches, the huge minarets, the land cut up by minefields, those ugly, ugly houses still burnt and not repaired.'

All societies have fault lines – rivalries, jealousies, suspicions – driven by the commonest of human frailties: self-pity and self-interest. The challenge is subsuming these fault lines and working towards a greater, collective good, one that draws a community of strangers to a shared project. To do that takes trust in a concept that is as modern as it is radical: the nation. So prevalent today is the idea of nation that one forgets how new it is. Much longer-established was order driven by obedience to a local superpower, whether it called itself baron or *beg*, king or emperor. The passage from coercion to cooperation, of people coming together because they choose to and not because they are forced to, is one of the greatest of human journeys. My encounters in Bosnia brought home how different countries are in different places on that journey.

A newspaper left on the bus carried an advert with a totally unexpected Princip link that caught my eye: Franz Ferdinand, a British band named after Princip's famous victim, was to perform in the north-Bosnian town of Banja Luka. To thank Arnie for all his efforts I suggested a short detour, a trip north so that I could treat him to some live music. A man who taught himself English from British music was not going to miss this chance, so instead of heading directly for Sarajevo we changed buses. First stop was the town of Jajce – somewhere I had always wanted to visit if only because, after being dropped by parachute, Fitzroy Maclean had met Tito there for the first time. With its relic of a medieval fort high on a hilltop overlooking the cascading confluence of two rivers, Jajce also had the reputation of being one of Bosnia's most beautiful towns. Rebecca West wrote that the town's name meant 'testicle', reflecting the round shape of the hill. During the war Jajce had been unreachable, so I had to make do with descriptions of its charms from other sources, such as this from Baedeker. 'A pavilion above the waterfall affords the best view; wraps are necessary.'

When the bus delivered us to Jajce, the town did not disappoint. Elegant houses spilled down a slope capped by the old fortress that had briefly housed Tito's guerrilla headquarters. The hill led all the way to an old town wall that skirted the left bank of a river called the Pliva. I could see skittish trout and knots of weed being worked by the current where the Pliva spread evenly across a shallow, ornamental pool leading to a weir. There a dramatic transformation took place. Once over the weir, the water tumbled seventy noisy, churning, globular feet straight down into the Vrbas below. In the summer heat I could not resist, stripping to my shorts and jumping into the upper pool, fish star-bursting away as I thrashed through the water towards the weir and dared myself to peek over the lip. It took just seconds to dry in the July sun, and Arnie then led me to the shade of an old hall on the river bank that he remembered well from his childhood. 'We were brought here all the time as a sort of school pilgrimage,' he reminisced. 'Back then it was an important national monument because it was in here in 1943 that the conference that founded communist Yugoslavia was held.'

Inside we found an elderly curator, dressed down in a replica shirt of the Dutch football team Ajax, who seemed delighted to have some visitors. He turned on the lights in the hall and shouted the old partisan wartime rallying cry: *smrt fašizmu*, 'death to fascism'. I was pleasantly surprised to find the museum so well looked after with its collection of Titoist memorabilia and

propaganda. In the communist era, when Arnie was marched
through here as a dutiful schoolboy in the 1980s, the museum had
been a place of almost religious devotion. Tito's star then still
dominated the national Yugoslav firmament. Events of the 1990s
had totally changed that, however, as militant nationalism let each
of Bosnia's rival groups dwell on how ill-used by communism they
believed they had been. The atmosphere in the museum when we
visited was no longer spiritual. It was more nostalgic, even comic,
like a teenager picking up a pair of granny's bloomers and
wondering how anyone ever wore such things.

From Jajce a two-hour drive along a mountain gorge cut by the
Vrbas delivered Arnie and me to Banja Luka where, sometime
after midnight, we found ourselves within the grounds of the
town's old Ottoman fortress, struggling against a scrummage of
young Bosnian Serbs and the abnormally high summer night's
temperature. For a moment all was darkness inside the compound.
There was just enough light from the night sky to make out the
high curtain walls and the hulk of a watchtower, which had the
same type of steeply pitched shingle roof as the old hovels back
in Obljaj. Then, with a blast of sound to wake the dead, a shock
of light came up on a stage, and all I could see was a thirty-foot-
high picture of Princip. For its first-ever gig in Bosnia the band
Franz Ferdinand was not going to miss the opportunity to flag up
the local boy who gave their name such impetus.

As the crowd surged towards the four musicians, I stared at the
massive backdrop of Princip's face. It would be the only time on
my entire trip through the Balkans that I would come across his
likeness displayed so publicly. I recognised it immediately as the
portrait taken while he was in Austro-Hungarian custody following
the assassination, the fire of his revolutionary zeal doused by
months of solitary confinement. His eyes are flat, moustache
meagre, hair mangy. When Princip scratched his initials on that

rock in the garden back in Obljaj and boasted to his friend 'one day people will know my name', could he ever have dreamed that the time would come when thousands of fellow countrymen would rock a summer's night away in front of a stage decorated with his portrait.

'The name came to me while I was watching horseracing on television,' Alex Kapranos, the band's lead singer, had confided earlier, after I managed to get past the security guards at the venue. They had thought I was a journalist and kept muttering 'no media, no media', but when I got a message through to the band that I was a British author researching Princip, the security cordon was lifted. 'Talking history with you makes a change from talking about sex and drugs all the time,' Alex said, shaking my hand.

'We had been playing together for some time and, to be honest, we didn't really have a name. It didn't feel important back then.' As Alex spoke he looked around for backing from the other band members, old friends mainly from college in Glasgow. Bob Hardy, the bassist, took up the story. 'It was when a poster was being designed for a concert and the designer said, "You guys really need a name or the poster just won't work",' he said.

'We wanted a name that people could make a connection with, that people could remember, maybe because it had a significance or an alliteration or certain phonetic characteristics,' Alex continued. 'Duran Duran is a name that somehow sticks in your head. It's hard to put your finger on exactly why but that's what we were looking for.

'So I was watching TV one afternoon, like a good student wasting my time with daytime television. And all of a sudden there was a horse running in a race and it was called The Archduke. It made me think of a name we all knew from school, and that's how we got to Franz Ferdinand. To be honest, I have no idea if the horse won.'

Later during the performance, at one of the breaks between

songs, Alex half-turned and swung his arm extravagantly as if to introduce Princip to the crowd, shouting into the microphone, 'And this next one is for old friends.' A cheer rose, but it was not a roar of recognition. It was more a rush of enthusiasm from the audience. Shouting to make myself heard, I asked all those standing near me in the crowd, but they had no idea who the man in the picture was.

Later as I struggled to sleep, my ears buzzing after the concert, my mind dwelt on why young Bosnian Serbs in Banja Luka did not know Princip. He is, without question, the Bosnian Serb with the greatest historical impact of all time and yet it was clear, from what I had heard, that a hundred years after the assassination he was not cherished, and was scarcely recognised, among his own people.

The issue of Bosnian Serb identity was horribly corrupted in the war years of 1992–5, no more so than in Banja Luka, the dark centre of it all. A once-mixed city was culturally flattened, made ethnically one-dimensional as extremist thugs from the Bosnian Serb community seized control and made it the de facto capital of territory under their control. Mosques were blown up and Catholic congregations attacked. It was a few miles north of Banja Luka that experimentation in extreme ethnic cleansing took place, when Bosnian Serb bullies probed the lassitude of the international community's diplomatic response, working out that in the late twentieth century they could still get away with murder on an institutional scale. Just up the road from the concert venue they established death-camps where Bosnian Serb forces bullied, killed, tortured, starved and raped Bosnian Muslims and Bosnian Croats.

Unjustifiable by any normal moral code, for Bosnian Serb apologists the cruelty had a perverse internal logic born of events here in the 1940s. While I had found exciting the wartime adventures of Fitzroy Maclean and his colleagues in the Balkans, the truth is that focusing on the experience of a few Allied agents does not do full justice to the reality of the Second World War in Bosnia. It was in Banja Luka that the fascistic Croat nationalists unleashed by the Nazis, the Ustaše, committed some of their worst atrocities. Hundreds of Bosnian Serbs were murdered in nearby villages, their religious leaders tortured, their places of worship destroyed, a brutality that gave dangerous new energy to Bosnia's cycle of victimhood and vengeance, contributing significantly to events fifty years later.

But what influence did Princip have over the racial cruelty of the 1940s and the 1990s? Very little, it was clear to me, which explained why young Bosnian Serbs today, brought up with the rhetoric and iconography of the recent war, have such limited knowledge of him. His rationale for shooting the Archduke must have been for a very different cause from that so viciously championed by Bosnian Serb extremists in the 1990s.

The next day Arnie and I continued on towards Sarajevo by road. Up to this point my mind had dwelled on the way Bosnia had influenced the world in the past, but as the road wound its way into the Lašva valley past the town of Travnik, I began to think of its much more contemporary impact, through the actions of young jihadists who were active in this area in the 1990s.

When the Bosnian War began in 1992 it attracted the interest of militant Islam, drawing in foreign fighters, mainly from Afghanistan and North Africa, who were willing to fight in defence of the Bosnian Muslim population. At that time the locals knew very little about these forces, referring to them simply as 'the Muj', a group that never numbered more than a few hundred, but soon gathered a rather sinister, bogeyman status, amorphous, ill-defined and threatening. I was one of many journalists working at the time in the area where 'the Muj' were active although they were highly secretive and hostile to approaches from reporters.

It was only after the attacks in America on 11 September 2001 that the role of the Bosnian War in radicalising Muslim militancy became clearer. The American government's official inquiry into the 9/11 attacks reported that Osama bin Laden's organisation funded pro-Muslim charities in Bosnia during the war of the 1990s. The report also said that Khalid Sheikh Mohammed, the man it identified as 'the principal architect of the 9/11 attacks', had spent time in Bosnia during the war. And it went on to say that two of the nineteen terrorists responsible for hijacking the planes on 9/11 had also been deployed to Bosnia in the 1990s – Khalid al Mihdhar and Nawaf al Hazmi.

The 'Muj' from Bosnia were highly secretive during the war, but while I was researching this book I made a breakthrough by tracking down one of the foreign Muslim fighters. It turned out that he grew up a few miles from my home town. Shahid Butt was just two years older than me, born in Birmingham to parents originally from Pakistan. Working as a reporter, I had first seen him in a Yemeni court in 1999 after he had been arrested and charged with terrorist activities committed in Aden, his Brummie accent being memorably out of place at the far edge of Arabia. It would be more than a decade before I was eventually able to sit and talk to him about Bosnia at a cake-shop serving Arabic tea and pastries in a Birmingham suburb with a particularly strong Islamic community.

'The thing you have to remember is that when I was growing up in Britain in the 1970s we had a difficult sense of our nationality,' he said. 'This was a time when the streets around my home would have walls painted with APL in huge letters. That stood for Anti-Paki League, and all through my teenage years people like me were being abused in the streets, getting beaten up, having dogs set on us, that sort of thing. Back then, just leaving your front door could get you into trouble.

'When I left school all I wanted to do was to serve as a soldier – I wanted to be a Royal Marine, right. It was the time of the Falklands War and the Royal Marines were the best of the best, all over the telly and in the papers. So I went into a recruitment office and asked to join the Royal Marines. You know what they said to me? They said, "We cannot have you because you're a fat Paki." So do you know what I did for the next year? I ran around the streets near my home in boots and with a rucksack full of bricks, and I went back to the recruitment office twelve months later and asked again to join the Royal Marines. This time do you know what they said? "Well, you're not a fat Paki any more but you are still a Paki."'

In the early 1990s he started to attend mosques where some of the first radical clerics were beginning to preach. It was around this time that the war in Bosnia began and he watched video cassettes showing Bosnian Muslim victims of the war. 'It was very confusing to begin with, to see these Muslims with blue eyes and blond hair. It was not like anything I had seen before. But it was very traumatic – overwhelming, you know – to learn that people were suffering like this just because they were Muslims.'

He joined an aid convoy arranged through his local mosque that sent out two coaches from Britain full of supplies intended for Bosnia, with the plan of bringing back refugees. It ended in chaos as the vehicle got no further than Zagreb in Croatia and was unable to cross the border into the war zone. 'There were all these guys who were meant to have organised this. I said to them, "You said you are going to do one thing but you end up doing another." We fell out. It was useless, so after some prayer I joined up with a guy from London who had a van full of supplies and we managed to drive into Bosnia. I had never been out of Birmingham, and there I was, all of a sudden in a war zone.

'We gave out the food. There were lines and lines of people and they took it all and that's where it came into my head. The media like to say a Muslim like me only fights because we are some sort of crazed psychotic, but it was not like that. I went to Bosnia to bring humanitarian help and, after the aid ran out, what other humanitarian help could I give apart from protecting them? These people could not protect themselves, so that is how I could help. I would fight.

'My mate with the van went crazy. "It's not like it is in the films," he said. "Are you for real? How are you going to fight? You don't know anyone here and you don't have any weapons." He went on and on trying to talk me out of it, but I had made up my mind. I wrote a letter to my wife, which he took with him, and then he was off in his van and I was sat there, six o'clock in the morning, the sun still rising, next to the road in a town called Travnik.'

I knew Travnik well. It was a few miles up the road from the farmhouse in Vitez next to the British peacekeeping base, where I had been stationed as a reporter.

'I prayed. What else could I do? And then a Nissan Patrol jeep turned up and a man stepped out, not a Bosnian, but a big foreign guy with a long beard wearing combats. He greeted me in Arabic, which is about all the Arabic I know, and we got talking in English. When I said I wanted to fight, he told me to get in the jeep, and that is how I got involved.'

He described several months of basic training alongside other foreign fighters: Arabs mostly, with only a sprinkling of European Muslims like himself. As a base they took over an old school a short distance outside Travnik and kept themselves separate from the regular Bosnian Muslim forces, an army that Shahid did not find impressive. 'These guys were fighting for their homeland, but mostly they just sat around drinking coffee and smoking. We were different, much more willing to take the offensive. We all had to have fighting names, so they called me Abu Hamza Britaniya, as I was one of the few guys from Britain,' he said. 'Sometimes I used to bump into British troops from the UN. The looks on their faces were classic when I spoke to them in a Birmingham accent. "All right mate, how ya doing?"

'Mostly it was training and training, but on a few occasions there was real fighting. I don't want to say I was a hero or anything, but at times I took part in attacks which were really heavy. Guys on either side of me getting hit, that sort of thing.'

By the time I met Shahid he was in his late forties, his hair greying, his waistline expanding. Now living back in Britain, he was anxious to emphasise the difference between the type of fighter he had hoped to be in Bosnia and the extremist jihadists responsible for suicide terror attacks.

'I saw myself as a traditional mujahideen. I was a fighter, sure, but I was fighting to help the oppressed, to protect them against an aggressor. It was a noble act, and one that I would do again. But these guys who take part in suicide attacks, they are not true mujahideen. They are killing innocent people, and for me it makes no sense at all, from any point of view. It makes no sense from a religious point of view, as it is not part of my religion. And it makes no sense from a military point of view, a strategic perspective. How are you going to win the hearts and minds of people if you kill people who are not involved?'

Bosnia's role in the evolution of modern jihad has largely been overlooked, but in Shahid I had found an example of what can happen when the anger of young people is ignored. Western politicians who stood by when the worst atrocities of the Bosnian War took place – ethnic cleansing, death-camps, genocide – inadvertently provided Islamic militants with a rallying cry used to justify later acts of terrorism.

With Arnie and me continuing along the road for Sarajevo, the terrain became steadily more familiar as we reached part of the Lašva valley where I spent many months in the 1990s. The view was of lush green countryside set against a blue summer sky, but in my memory the same scenery ran black and white: burnt buildings, a dead donkey rotting on the road, houses with planks leaning against the front as sniper shields, piles of dark earth where bodies had been hurriedly buried. The road took us through rolling farmland I recognised from the 1990s, hills nosing gently down to the wandering Lašva River, the fields peppered with the red-roofed houses of peasant farmers. Most were subsistence micro-systems largely unchanged from Princip's day: ricks of hay in the garden, stacks of wood to be burned against the winter cold and pens of livestock – a pig here, some sheep there.

The bus trundled past Ahmići, a tiny village, but a place name that became well known among prosecutors at the war-crimes tribunal in The Hague. It was here one spring morning in 1993 that Bosnian Croat thugs slaughtered Bosnian Muslim civilians, their henchmen going from door to door under cover of darkness to mark the homes of Bosnian Croat villagers with a Catholic cross. At first light those who emerged from unmarked doors, no matter their age or gender, were shot down like vermin. The village was so close to Arnie's house that his family stood on their balcony and watched in disbelief the smoke rising from the ruins of the shared community they had once believed in. A few miles later my bus passed a void left where a building had once stood. It felt appropriate that nobody had reoccupied the space. In late 1993 an A-framed villa stood here, one that I and my journalist colleagues had driven past unknowingly many times. What we were then not aware of was that it was being used by Bosnian Croat brutes as a rape-camp where Bosnian Muslim women were kept as sex slaves.

I was anxious to see what had happened to the farming family I had stayed with nearby, and from whom I bought the kilim that has followed my wanderings ever since. The feudalism that the Princip family knew at the start of the twentieth century might have ended, but the rural poverty my hosts endured at the end of the century would have been familiar to Princip. Between 1993 and 1995 my work as a reporter meant that I lived in this farmhouse more than in my flat in London, learning much about the relentless and repetitive rhythm of rural life in Bosnia.

I had found lodgings here because the house stood a few hundred yards from a school that was chosen as the main upcountry base for British troops deployed to Bosnia under the UN peacekeeping force. The school was on the outskirts of the town of Vitez, a name that translates as 'knight', a mixed community with large numbers of Bosnian Croat and Bosnian Muslim inhabitants. Just as the British troops arrived over the winter of 1992–3 fighting erupted between these two former allies, quite literally right outside the base. The presence of such a large British contingent drew journalists by the dozen to this tiny, turbulent community. War meant there was no mains power or water, no fuel in local petrol stations, no shops with any stock, so we rented rooms in local houses and survived on our wits and our Deutschmarks – back then the black marketeers' currency of choice.

Before the bus from Banja Luka delivered Arnie and me to Vitez, I pictured in my mind the sweep of the main road past the school, the house where the army press officers would brief us, the nearby bridge and the turning to the farmhouse where I lived. I thought I would recognise it all again instantly, but when we finally got there I struggled. Post-war reconstruction had been prodigious. 'It's all Croatian money round here,' Arnie explained. 'Ever since Dayton, this area is Bosnian Croat – hardcore Bosnian Croat – and since the war ended businesses from Croatia have flooded in.'

On the outskirts of Vitez I found what may be the largest

supermarket I have ever seen. This area had not just been empty fields during the war, but had been an active frontline, no-man's-land surrounded by torched houses and overlooked by a particularly persistent sniper. Today, the leviathan supermarket has parking for thousands of cars, and a restaurant and coffee shop where Bosnians who used to try to kill each other in the 1990s now talk into their mobile phones and blow the foam off cappuccinos. In the car park registration plates revealed cars from all over Europe: Germany, Belgium, Sweden, Switzerland, Holland and beyond. This did not mean Vitez had suddenly become a tourist destination. It simply reflected the reach of the Bosnian diaspora, dispersed by war just as Arnie had been, coming back from time to time to reconnect with their roots.

The layout along the main road might be new, but I found the changes ran only one building deep. All was familiar once I led Arnie on foot down the lane leading to the farmhouse. Here the buildings had not been renovated; it was the same collection of modest two-storey homes, many half-built like those back in Obljaj. There was the slight kink and dip in the lane that I walked many times when heading to the British base for briefings. A bullet once cracked straight over my head here, sending me jumping over a wall for cover. And then came the small orchard of plum trees. My old landlord had been a fan of plum brandy, a great fan. In the autumn of 1993 I had been staying at the farmhouse when the local distiller came round, a tradition keenly kept across this part of the Balkans. A roving artisan would arrive in a small rural community during plum harvest with a mobile still on a trailer. He would then light a large fire and distil fermenting plums to produce a year's supply of brandy. Before heading off to the next village he would receive payment: some of it in cash, some in bottles of hooch.

My host had been so keen on plum brandy that I had no expectation he would still be alive. Back in the early 1990s the farmer was a bewhiskered and rather befuddled old man, while his wife was already stooped and elderly. But when I turned the corner from the lane and shouted a greeting, there they both were, doing what I had left them doing all those years ago, swatting away horseflies and staring out over their barnyard. A stack of firewood stood in the same place where they had once set up a bucket shower for me so that I would wash myself amid an aroma of pine resin.

The couple invited me in, but with the same blend of suspicion and friendliness I had encountered from the Princip family back in Obljaj. The farmer, Drago Taraba, was now eighty-six and had no idea who I was. All he knew was that the arrival of a foreign visitor was reason enough to pour a round of brandy. Out came the shot glasses and down it went, my throat scrunching with the same fruity acid burn that I had got to rather like when I shivered through Christmas here in 1993. Drago then poured another, and out came the drinker's one-liners that I remembered hearing from him before. 'You came on two legs, so now you must have two drinks,' justified the second round. 'Those who drink alcohol will die, those who do not will die sooner' led to a third round. And so on.

The Taraba family is unmistakably Bosnian Croat, a crucifix on the wall marking clearly their Catholic faith, although I don't remember them being particularly observant. Drago's eyes were swimming, but when I asked him about the war they seemed to sharpen momentarily. 'They killed three members of my family right here,' he said, pointing to the wall of the barn outside. 'They shot them there, two of my brothers and my father. I was only sixteen at the time.' Drago was talking about the Second World War, not the war I had witnessed here. There is more than one way to park the trauma of war. Leaving for a new life overseas is one way, but plum brandy is another.

The recollection of his wife, Marija, eighty-four years of age, was altogether different. She was quieter and her eyesight was not perfect, but when I moved in close to show her photographs I had brought from the 1990s, she recognised me and her eyes filled with tears. 'You were the one who brought all that food, all that sugar and that oil,' she said. 'Your name is Tim, isn't it? There was even chocolate for the children that Christmas because of you. Thank the Lord.' The Bosnian war zone was then so low on supplies that I made a habit of filling my Land Rover with shopping from supermarkets in neighbouring Croatia before the long drive in. The booty would then be shared around friends trapped within the war zone. On the occasion in 1994 when I crashed on ice, I remember groggily coming round after the vehicle finally stopped rolling and being momentarily bewildered by the sight of torn sacks of sanitary towels being blown by the wind through the debris of my vehicle spread across a snowy field. For women trapped in central Bosnia such items were priceless.

'Tell me about your family?' Marija asked. 'Did you marry Tamara? Such a nice girl that Tamara.' She was referring to another wonderful translator I had worked with during the war, a language student from Croatia called Tamara Levak. Momentarily disappointed to learn we had only ever been friends, Marija then clucked over the photographs of my children that I keep in my wallet. 'Just like you, just like Marinko,' she said, pointing at the grinning face of my blond six-year-old son, Kit. Marinko was Marija's youngest child, a fair-haired boy who in the 1990s had just been old enough to be pressed into service as a soldier by the Bosnian Croat forces. Back then Marija would weep whenever his name came up, mumbling tearfully that I reminded her of Marinko, who was off serving in the trenches.

'He survived the war,' she beamed, when I asked after him. 'He works as a policeman now in Sarajevo. Special police. He guards the American Embassy.'

Before leaving I asked about her weaving, and reminded her of the beautiful kilim she sold me all those years ago. 'That was a fine piece,' she said. 'All that wool was from our sheep. I combed it and spun it and dyed it. And then I did all the weaving. It must have taken me years.' Bosnia's knotted ethnic history meant there was nothing odd in a Catholic farmer's wife meticulously creating a rug using designs and techniques from the Orient. 'But the young ones today, they do not want to learn the old skills,' she continued. 'In the end I became too old, my fingers could not do the work. So I gave the loom to my sister-in-law. That's her in the photo over there.' As she pointed, her sleeve moved and I caught a glimpse of a blue blemish on the skin at the back of her hand. It was a tiny tattoo, something I remembered her showing to me one winter's night in 1993, an inky echo of this land's turbulent heritage. To deter Ottoman lords from stealing their young women, a tradition developed here among Bosnian Croats of tattooing the girls, deliberately giving them blemishes, in the hope this meant they would not be whisked away under *droit de seigneur*.

As Arnie and I stood up to leave, Drago became animated once more. 'Now one more for the road,' he said, slopping brandy around rather than into our shot glasses. I stood up and took in the house properly. It was utterly unchanged from the wartime years: the same furniture arranged around the same wood-burning stove; the same hob where Drago would kindly warm me a pan of water to wash with before dawn; the smell of the same unrefined detergent; thick blankets folded on the same sofas that doubled as beds in winter when everyone gathered around the stove.

My time with Arnie was coming to an end. I would continue on to Sarajevo while he would spend a day with his father, who still lives in Vitez, before heading back to London. Before reaching his old home he spoke to me with emotion that he had never previously expressed.

'I could never come back and live here,' he said. I was a little shocked; I hadn't expected this. 'I mean, it's beautiful and everything. Beyond beautiful. Just think about all we saw on our hike. But I would worry about people like Zdravko, the hotelier back in Glamoč.'

Now I was confused. What had Zdravko done to threaten us? He could not have been friendlier. But that turned out to be precisely Arnie's point.

'You saw how kind he was to us, right? He could not have done more. He opened up the little hotel, he took us around town, he made sure we had food and drink. He did everything possible to help.'

I was still baffled. 'So how do you get from that to saying you could never come back here to live?'

'It's because the good and the bad live so close by each other – the light and the dark, the love and the loathing,' he replied. 'The Zdravko we got to know is exactly the sort of man I was brought up next door to. My family are Bosnian Muslim, but back when I was growing up that did not mean anything, because we were all communists, right? We weren't green, we were red. All one nation, all Yugoslavs. There were some from our community who went to the mosque, but for most of us it was more important to be Yugoslav. Being Muslim was part of our yesterdays, our history. We had no greater say over it than we do over the genes that give us blond hair or brown eyes. Being Muslim was no longer part of my today. We had more important things to worry about than religion – things like family, school and getting a job.

'Where we lived in Vitez, if you were able to save money and build your own house, you did so up on the hill. The view was great, it was cool in the summer and you were above the freezing mists that come down in the winter. You could look out over the valley and down beneath you were the workers' apartment blocks. If you moved up the hill, it meant you had made it.

'Well, after many years' saving and saving, we finally had enough to build a house up on the hill and move away from our tiny flat down with all the others. Everything we had went into this new house. For its day, it was seriously cool. I mean I had a bedroom all of my own, after living in a small flat, all of us on top of each other. Can you imagine what a big deal that was, for a teenager?

'Our neighbours, mostly Bosnian Croats, were fine. I mean they were just neighbours: some friendly, some strange, some nosy – just normal. Basically they were fundamentally good people. People like Zdravko.

'And then all this shit comes along in the 1990s. Suddenly it matters if you were a Muslim or a Croat. That stuff had been parked for years, for decades. Those people who said, "These people have always hated each other" were just being lazy. In my own life I saw people from different communities work together, live together, get married even. There was nothing inevitable about what happened in the 1990s. It was just that a few – the extremists, the elite, the greedy – saw nationalism as a way to grab what they wanted.

'When it all erupted we were in the shit, as there were so many Bosnian Croats around us. We were stuck out there all alone, the only Muslims on the hill. I can remember the day the bad guys came to our door – it was April 1993. I mean these people were our neighbours, right? People my mother and father had known for years. My mum went to answer the door and I was standing behind her. I had my dad's old army pistol in my hand, but I did not know what to do with it. We were scared shitless.

'Suddenly they shot through the door. Right there, into our house – the house we had built, that one my family had saved for, had sacrificed so much for. I mean, you English and your houses, they are your castles, right? The bloody bullet-hole is still there in the doorframe after all these years. We cannot bring ourselves to fix it. We need to be reminded. Thank God nobody was hit, but the message was clear and we had to move out quick; our lives changed for ever.

'And the point is this: I know the people who did it and they are no different from Zdravko. He is kind and he is generous and he is helpful. We saw that for ourselves. But I know in my heart that, when it comes down to it here, ethnicity can be toxic – it can count more than whether it is in your nature to be kind and generous.

'What will you do when the shit really hits the fan? It's the question that would always be on my mind if I came to live here again. That's why I cannot come back.'

We had worked together for years during the war, but never had Arnie opened up to me like this. Our relationship had always had a degree of stratification to it. I was the foreign correspondent, the employer with the Deutschmarks in my pocket, and he was the polyglot, the local gatekeeper, the employee, seeking to earn those Deutschmarks. When he turned up as a teenager at the UN base outside Vitez, I had known nothing about his background and he had volunteered nothing. I naively thought he had chosen to come and work with people like me. I had no idea that there was little sense of volition. He had come – at considerable personal risk – because he had to, because if he didn't his family would go hungry, they would freeze in the winter, their lives would falter.

His words moved me. Learning not to love is so difficult. A brother who falls out with a brother has to learn something totally unnatural: he must learn not to love. I know this to be a difficult, heartbreaking pain. For Arnie, being forced to learn not to love his home had been just as traumatic – a lonely journey of cutting links that were part of his essence. It is a journey that countless Bosnians have been forced to take by the events of the 1990s, fleeing their country in search of a new home they can try to love. Andrić, the novelist, wrote a fictional letter from a person leaving Bosnia, trying to explain to a friend his decision to go. Although written in the 1940s and influenced by the ethnic violence encouraged by Nazi occupation, to my mind it captures the raw feelings of the many Bosnians, like Arnie, driven away by the trauma of the 1990s war:

> Bosnia is a wonderful country, fascinating, with nothing ordinary in the habitat or people. And just as there are mineral riches under the earth in Bosnia, so undoubtedly are Bosnians rich in hidden moral values. But, you see, there's one thing that the people of Bosnia, at least people of your kind, must realise and never lose sight of – Bosnia is a country of hatred and fear . . . The fatal characteristic of this hatred is that the Bosnian man is unaware of the hatred that lives in him, shrinks from analyzing it and hates everyone who tries to do so. And yet it's a fact that in Bosnia there are more people ready in fits of this subconscious hatred to kill and be killed, for different reasons, and under different pretexts, than in other lands.

My understanding of Arnie was changed for ever by what he said. I came to see him as belonging to the quiet majority in Bosnia: those who did not give in to the toxicity of ethnic nationalism, but who were nevertheless its victim. In him there was no sense of self-pity, more an honest commitment to go in search of what is good, sustainable and lasting. Often he repeated that he did not want 'to make a fuss', to complain about what his family had been through, because the suffering of those who had died had been so much greater. Yet he was a man in search of a home. The same fault lines Arnie described were there in the early twentieth century when Princip journeyed through this land away from his own, insular Bosnian Serb community, and yet I was still unclear how he responded to them. Did he belong to the few identified by Arnie who exploited nationalism for their own ends, or did he withstand the toxicity and work for something higher?

Leaving Arnie and carrying on alone to Sarajevo felt sad, but strangely appropriate. After passing by Vitez on the train in 1907, Princip was dropped in Sarajevo by his father and had to make his way by himself. So, after hugging my friend farewell at the bus station in Vitez, a short walk from his family home, the one with the bullet-hole from 1993 still in the doorframe, I continued on my journey. On the outskirts of town I saw a poster advertising a local sporting event, a Bosnian bullfight or *korida*. Unlike Spanish bullfighting, which involves man against beast, this Balkan version pits beast against beast in a sort of push-of-war. Two animals compete at a time, locking horns and then seeking to muscle each other out of the way. The winner is the one that dominates the other, although both animals inevitably end up drained of strength. I can think of no better symbol for the occasionally brutish, thick-headed, nobody-really-wins-we-all-lose clashes between the people of this region.

With the bus now barrelling along the highway towards Sarajevo, the avalanche of memory threatened to bury me: road bridges that I remembered having been primed with explosives; the turning to the village where I found three girls with their throats cut; signboards with place names still so charged that my stomach tightened when I read them. I decided to get off the bus a few miles outside the city in the small town of Hadžići, where Princip's older brother, Jovo, had once lived and worked as a woodsman. It lies at the bottom of the massif of Mount Igman, one of the most fought-over pieces of territory in the war of the 1990s and a place where I had once felt more crazily alive than at any time in my entire life. Walking over the mountain into Sarajevo felt like the most appropriate way to reacquaint myself properly with the city.

It was a perfect summer morning. A nectarine bought from a roadside stall was so ripe it had me half-sucking, half-chewing, the juice running off my chin, as I looked for the road that zigzagged its way up the mountain. I began the climb, the tap of my hazel stick on tarmac lonely without the accompaniment of Arnie's. A car stopped almost immediately and the driver offered me a lift, warning that the way ahead was steep. I declined, keen to explore this mountain at leisure, free of the tension that I had known back in the 1990s.

Mount Igman was the saviour of Sarajevo in the war, the reason the besieged city never fully fell. For years the mountain provided the city's solitary lifeline to the outside world. The geography of Sarajevo back then was brutally straightforward, with the city surrounded by hostile Bosnian Serb forces on all sides except for the airport, with its mile or so of tarmac runway, which was in the hands of UN peacekeepers. Mount Igman overlooks the airport, so if Bosnian Muslim forces could hold the mountain, they could maybe reach the airport and perhaps connect to the city beyond. The UN force's precarious neutrality meant that it could not allow combatants to transit the aerodrome, so instead a tunnel was dug by hand right under the tarmac – a fact that was kept secret for years from outsiders, including the many journalists like me who occasionally drove over the mountain to get into Sarajevo. Hostility to foreign reporters meant that we were rarely allowed through the Bosnian Serb checkpoints ringing the city, so we either flew in on UN flights or drove over Mount Igman where, as non-combatant reporters, we were allowed safe passage across the runway by UN guards.

For the Bosnian citizens of Sarajevo the tunnel provided the city's umbilical cord. Food, ammunition and fuel were all dragged through it into the city, along with troops deploying to and fro as fighting shifted between frontlines. As the seasons passed, plans for the tunnel became more ambitious, and by the end of the war electricity cables and phone lines ran through it, all of which had to be strung across the open vastness of Mount Igman. It was an incredible story of survival through ingenuity and determination, but it came at a high price, with near-constant combat along active and bloody frontlines that ranged right around much of the mountain. For the Bosnian Muslim forces the loss of Mount Igman was simply not an option.

As I walked slowly up the road I passed a number of shrines to Bosnian Muslim soldiers who died in this struggle. The importance of this tiny mountain trail was officially recognised some years after the war when it was renamed Freedom Road. The intensity of the combat was clear from the number of mine-warning signs I walked past, nailed to trees on either side of the road. One shrine from the 1990s lay next to one from the 1940s commemorating partisans who died fighting for the same strategic spot during the Second World War.

I thought of Princip making this same climb as a sixteen-year-old schoolboy on a summer night in 1911. An adolescent, angst-filled essay attributed to him was found long after he died, written on a page of a mountain-lodge guestbook. It was dated 25 June 1911 and signed 'Princip, Fifth Grade':

We left Hadžići at sunset when the western sun was blazing in purple splendour, when the numberless rays of the blood-red sun filled the whole sky and when the whole nature was preparing to sleep through the beautiful, dreamy summer evening in the magic peace – that beloved, ideal night of the

poet . . . We could go no further. We ate our frugal supper.
We built a fire – the best sight I ever saw. No poet has ever
described it well enough. Oh, if you could have seen what
beautiful and ever-changing scenes were made by the lively
red and black, and hellish darkness, the whispering of the
tall, black fir trees, and this hideous Night, the protector of
hell and its sons; it seemed to me like the whisperings of
bedevilled giants and nymphs, as if we were hearing the song
of the four sirens and the sad Aeolian harp or divine Orpheus.

I too had been young, aged twenty-seven, and anxious when I
crossed Mount Igman after nightfall during the war, an episode
so vivid it still comes to me in acute detail. It was June 1995 and
the situation inside Sarajevo had worsened dramatically, with the
Bosnian Serbs restarting their artillery assault on the city. The
fighting had got so bad that for many weeks even the Mount Igman
road was closed, adding to the sense of claustrophobia and desper-
ation within the city. I had been ordered to pull out by my editor,
but had not been able to leave, part of a growing group of journalists and foreign aid workers going increasingly stir-crazy. At one
point I went to investigate reports of a hospital being shelled,
arriving in a ward to find the body of a headless male patient who
had been lying there. The man had been decapitated by a Bosnian
Serb shell smashing through the wall. By this stage my emotional
frame was askew, and I remember responding with manic giggles
when I saw the victim. He was headless, but completely covered
in what looked like pink talcum powder. The explosion had atomised the brick wall, creating a rouge dust that coated absolutely
everything in the room: beds, medical equipment, furniture, floor,
corpse. My coping mechanism was to find this comic.

One Friday afternoon word went round that the Mount Igman
road would be opened for a few hours that evening. Desperate not

to miss the chance to get out, I skittered around gathering my gear, begging fuel and loading my Land Rover. Other journalists needed a ride, so just before twilight we set off, with me at the wheel next to two colleagues, a man and a woman, squished into a driving compartment designed for two, creeping across the runway of Sarajevo airport and along the potholed, cratered lanes that led to the mountain trail snaking to safety over Mount Igman. We knew that the Bosnian Serbs could shoot at vehicles on the road – we all remembered the British soldier killed there a year or so earlier at the wheel of a supply truck – but if we timed it right there would be enough light to make it safely across. We were out of luck.

By the time we got to the bottom of the trail, all up-traffic had been stopped. We were told the road was too narrow and too hazardous to allow two-way traffic, so a cyclical one-way system had been imposed: for an hour only upward vehicles were allowed, after which the flow was switched to downward. We had just missed the upward flow, so would have to wait an hour for our turn to go. This meant it would be completely dark by the time we set off – a worry, given that we were not allowed to use lights. To turn on a headlight was to give the Bosnian Serb gunners a target, so all lights had to be disconnected. I had even taken off a panel from underneath the dashboard of the vehicle and removed the fuse, so that my brake lights would not show when my foot touched the brake pedal.

When our turn eventually came, I remember being so wired with adrenalin that I was in a transcendental state. It was pitch-black, a moonless, cloudy night, but my senses were so alive that I managed to coach the vehicle through the darkness up what would become known as 'The Most Dangerous Road in Europe'. This disturbing soubriquet was bestowed by Richard Holbrooke, the lead American diplomat responsible for eventually bringing

an end to the war in Bosnia. During his negotiations he got to
know all about the dangers of the Mount Igman road. Some months
after I drove it, Mr Holbrooke was in a convoy on the track when
a vehicle carrying three of his close colleagues got too close to the
edge. The hillside gave way and the vehicle tumbled down the
forested slope, killing all three Americans.

As I drove that Land Rover up the trail, my two journalist friends
responded in very different ways as we sat crammed shoulder-to-
shoulder in the driving compartment. The man, an American, was
utterly silent, while my British colleague talked non-stop. It made
no difference. I did not care. I was too alive, too fixed on staying
so. Night on Mount Igman was 'hideous' for Princip, but for me
it was something quite different, a life-affirming thrill.

After crossing the mountain into safe territory we drove through
the small hours to reach a hotel down on the Croatian coast, where
I fell into a delicious sleep. When I woke I turned on the television
to witness an event of great significance to the country I now call
home: South Africa's victory in the 1995 Rugby World Cup. It
was a moment made magical by Nelson Mandela's grand gesture
of forgiveness. Rugby had long been associated with South Africa's
white community, the dominant minority that had so cruelly
exploited the black majority, yet there was Mandela willing on the
Springboks, even wearing a Springbok shirt. It was a rare but
inspiring example of past hatreds being buried, people looking to
tomorrow and letting go of yesterday, breaking the cycle of victimhood and vengeance.

The memory of that life-affirming drive kept me going as I
explored the mountain on foot seventeen years later. As if guided
by a vapour trail of 1995 adrenalin, I made the correct turnings
in the forest and chose the right way from a maze of footpaths
and trails that star-burst across the hilly plateau. Every so often
I was passed by a carload of holidaymakers exploring the mountain

and the old sporting facilities dating from the Sarajevo 1984 Winter Olympics, when Mount Igman hosted several of the main events. At one point mountain-bikers whooshed past me. I came to an old mountain lodge, where the housekeeper made me tea brewed with leaves picked from mountain bushes. He kept a loaded rifle near the door, but it was for bears, not combat. This is how a mountain should be used, I thought, for recreation, not as a desperate battle-ground for control of Europe's most perilous road. At one point a car of Bosnians stopped and the driver asked me the way to Hadžići. After two weeks' hiking, improving my Bosnian language skills and getting to know the layout of the country at peace, I was rather proud to be able to direct him.

The track I was on finally began its descent, eventually making a sharp hairpin that I remembered well. I was near the bottom of the trail, once the most dangerous part of the most dangerous road. It was near here that the three diplomats fell to their deaths and the British soldier was killed by Bosnian Serbs. All of a sudden the trees parted and a view opened up in front of me. There in the near distance was the airport, and beyond that rose the bar-graph of skyscrapers from the city's modern suburbs. I had reached Sarajevo.

CHAPTER 7

The Fall of Gabriel

First school report for Princip at the Merchants' School in Sarajevo,
student Number 32, his first name given as Gavro

Tourist postcards of central Sarajevo, circa 1910

From the foot of the mountain I took a tram into the centre of Sarajevo, a twenty-minute journey that reminded me of perhaps the most surprising feature of a city that has had such an impact on global history: it is tiny. Passing strata of architecture gave clues as to the development of Sarajevo through the ages. First, there were buildings constructed since the war of the 1990s: brightly lit shopping centres set amid dense residential areas, some large, modernist mosques and one particularly striking new land-mark, a twisted tower of mirrored glass that dominates the skyline of the city not far from the site of the old railway station, where Gavrilo Princip would have arrived. Then there were the massed ranks of buildings I recognised from the war: bland apartment buildings constructed during the communist era, still with a smat-tering of tinny, locally made Yugo cars parked outside. As the valley narrowed, we came to the first structures that would have been familiar to Princip: neo-colonial constructions from the Austro-Hungarian period of occupation, solid European-looking office blocks adorned with carved stuccowork on their façades and hefty wooden doorways. And finally I saw buildings dating back hundreds of years from the Ottoman occupation: bridges, minarets and storerooms roofed with turtle-shell domes.

Sarajevo was founded where a narrow gorge cut by a small mountain river called the Miljacka blooms into a full valley protected by steeply sided slopes. The oldest part – dwellings, mosques, hammams, shops and hostels ensnared by a web of alleyways – grew where the valley was still at its tightest, easiest to control from fortresses built on high bluffs that to this day still define the city's easternmost limits. As the centuries have passed Sarajevo has crept both down the river and up the hillsides to create a city bowl snug within the contours of its highland setting.

When the Ottoman Empire swallowed Bosnia in the late fifteenth century this defensible valley was the strategic site chosen by its commanders for their new capital. It led to a golden age of construction in the first half of the sixteenth century, when some of Europe's most elegant mosques were built and the Miljacka was laced with fine stone bridges. 'The Bosnian countryman gapes with as much wonderment at the domes of the two chief mosques as an English rustic at the first sight of St Paul's,' wrote Arthur Evans when he trekked here in 1875 at the end of Ottoman rule. Established as a hub on trade routes across the Balkan Peninsula, Sarajevo grew quickly through commerce, with one seventeenth-century visitor reporting that the population had already reached 80,000, making it a true metropolis for that era, one of the largest cities in the Balkans. It was a city then dominated by Islam, the faith both of the Ottoman colonial outsiders deployed to Bosnia and of the growing cohort of local Slavs who converted to the religion of the occupier. Evans echoed others when he noted that Sarajevo's ethnic heritage was writ in 'a skyline of a hundred minarets'.

As the city's commercial power grew, so Sarajevo drew many from beyond the Islamic world, earning a name for inter-ethnic tolerance. Local Catholics (forerunners of today's Bosnian Croats) and Orthodox Christians (the original Bosnian Serbs) established sizeable minorities in a city that became so mixed it was known as the 'Damascus of the North'. One of the oldest Ottoman structures spanning the Miljacka was named the Latin Bridge, because it linked the small Catholic district where the Latin liturgy was observed on the south bank of the river to the main body of the city over on the north. There was also a significant community of Sephardic Jews, who made their home here after being expelled from Spain in the late fifteenth century. The city's original Jewish cemetery was one of the most fought-over pieces of land during the war of the 1990s, with trenches that burrowed between bulky, trunk-shaped gravestones used by local Jewry for hundreds of years. I once listened as soldiers from the two sides shouted abuse at each other, separated in places by only a few feet of no-man's-land.

The racial egalitarianism seen in Sarajevo was typical of Ottoman pragmatism, the most efficient way to develop an imperial outpost in land heavily populated by 'non-believers', although this period was not without friction. The Sultan's regular feuds with his always reactionary and occasionally mutinous military elite, the Janissaries, sometimes spread from Istanbul to Sarajevo, just as it did to other cities in the empire. Furthermore, leaders of the Bosnian Muslim community in Sarajevo grew so wealthy and powerful that they came to clash with the Pasha, the Sultan's representative sent from Istanbul. After winning exemption for Sarajevo from imperial taxes, the increasingly haughty Slav elite grew ever more dismissive of the authority of the Sublime Porte. Friction with the Pasha became so acute that he was effectively ousted, and for many years around 1800 he was not welcome in the city, being obliged to move his capital elsewhere in Bosnia. Tradition had it that the Pasha could visit Sarajevo safely for just one night, but beyond that his security could not be guaranteed. Such an arrangement was never going to last, and the Turkish commanders who eventually arrived to put the upstart Slav Muslims back in their place did so bloodily and ruthlessly. Wider Ottoman military ambitions also cost Sarajevo dear, with raids by the empire's traditional enemies from Hungary and Austria that saw large parts of the city burned to the ground.

With the Ottoman Empire ailing through the nineteenth century – 'the sick man of Europe' – so Sarajevo declined, and by the time Austria–Hungary sent its troops to occupy Bosnia in 1878 the population had roughly halved from its peak. When Arthur Evans arrived on foot he described it as 'dark, fanatical and backward', noting that there was not a single bookshop in the entire city. His description of street sanitation was particularly base, recording that it was not safe to go out on the streets at night because by then they belonged to rough, lawless, malodorous gangs of cleaners, sweepers and human-waste collectors. A city map from 1908 shows that even though Sarajevo was 400 years old, it still only nosed about a mile or so westwards down the valley. Beyond lay open country, although here the map showed grand colonial plans for a large development zone marked as 'New Sarajevo'. At the time of the map's publication this huge plot remained empty except for the railway station and a vast military barracks, both newly built on orders from Vienna.

Within the city limits of Sarajevo proper, the Austro-Hungarian occupiers had sought to project order on the muddle left by the decaying Ottoman Empire. While the new authorities left alone the main bazaar quarter, they laid out an ambitious grid of government offices, courthouses, colleges, museums, theatres and other more Western buildings. In 1895 Sarajevo became the first city in central Europe with an electric tram system, technology so cutting-edge it would be replicated in the network eventually installed on the streets of the imperial capital, Vienna.

The Miljacka was not spared the attention of the Habsburg urban planners. A Sarajevo city map from 1880 shows the river meandering past gravel reaches and islets between uneven muddy banks lined by a higgledy-piggledy assortment of gardens and houses. The Austro-Hungarians moved to impose order on the Miljacka and after several years' work it ran, as it does today, ramrod-straight through the city centre, apart from two faint kinks. A stepped series of weirs still keeps the water shallow and slow-moving, canalised between masonry-lined banks with buildings on the entire length of the northern side, separated from the river bank by a wide, busy boulevard named Appel Quay by the Austro-Hungarian colonial authorities.

On occasion the clash of styles could grate between classical Ottoman and expansionist Habsburg designs. Indeed, Rebecca West described witheringly the faux-Moorish town hall that went up next to the old bazaar soon after the Austro-Hungarians arrived in Sarajevo. 'The minaret of the mosque beside it has the air of a cat that watches a dog making a fool of itself,' she wrote. In 1914 the town hall would be the last building Archduke Franz Ferdinand would enter alive.

In spite of all this work, the city's mostly Muslim population lived at the start of the twentieth century as they always had, in dwellings of medieval simplicity that lapped up the steep valley sides, with none of the modernist rigour enforced downtown. To reach them you climbed narrowing alleys of cobblestones that snaked ever upwards, speckling the city's contoured surrounds with grey shingle roofs and the occasional splash of headstone-white from tumbledown Muslim graveyards. 'The numerous minarets and the little houses standing in gardens give the town a very picturesque appearance,' enthused the 1905 Baedeker. A less benign description of the city comes from John Gunther, an American author writing in the 1930s. He wrote of Sarajevo as a 'mud-caked primitive village'.

Princip was a little jumpy when he arrived here as a thirteen-year-old after his long journey on foot and by train. The trip had already extended his cultural horizons through exposure to other ethnic groups beyond the dirt-poor community of Bosnian Serb serfs where he had grown up. Reaching the city must have

accelerated that process dramatically. Although small on the scale
of twentieth-century Europe, Sarajevo was large enough to have
been giddy-making for a boy from the rural hinterland. Vladimir
Dedijer, the freedom-fighting author who was flown out wounded
from Glamoč in 1943, collated anecdotes in his book, *The Road
to Sarajevo*, about Princip's early life. According to one, the young
boy refused outright to stay in one guesthouse because it was run
by a Bosnian Muslim innkeeper wearing the traditional costume
of his community. 'I do not wish to sleep there. They are Turks,'
the boy cried as he fled.

Lodging was eventually found for the young boy in the house
of a Bosnian Serb widow, Stoja Ilić, who took in tenants at her
home on Oprkanj Street. It was a lane on the edge of the city's
old bazaar quarter – narrow, twisting and just a stroll from where
tinsmiths, carpet sellers, jewellers, saddle makers, coffee grinders,
spice merchants and a slew of other traders had been noisily and
fragrantly going about their business for hundreds of years. It
would have been a thrilling place to explore for any new arrival:
getting to know shortcuts through the network of alleyways;
friendly traders offering a cheap treat, and grumpy ones to be
avoided; the best spots to fish down on the river. And it would
also have allowed the boy from an isolated Bosnian Serb community to feel the ethnic weave both of the city and of the wider
country it represented, as he wandered lanes where the familiar
Bosnian smell of meaty *ćevapčići* nuggets grilling over coals merged
with the exotic aroma of flavoured tobacco from the Middle East
being smoked through *nargileh* water-pipes.

Sarajevo's merchants at the time faithfully reflected the city's
diversity, with Muslims, Catholics, Orthodox Christians and Jews
all firmly rooted in the trading community. Baedeker warned
foreign visitors about the difficulties of price negotiations in the
bazaar, saying 'purchases cannot well be made without an

interpreter'. To avoid the holy days observed by such a spread of faiths, Wednesday was kept as the official weekly market day; and early twentieth-century photographs, taken at roughly the time Princip was first nosing around, capture the bazaar thronged with sellers and buyers from outlying rural communities. The pictures show market alleys lined with walnut-faced farmers, their skin tempered by the extremes of weather, crouching in the dust next to sacks of fruit, herbs and other farm produce, as primitive weighing scales are hoisted shoulder-high to measure purchases.

Prices for dearer items such as gold might be negotiated in more discreet wooden jewellers' booths erected as small shops running alongside the fronts of large stone storerooms dating from the early Ottoman era. The timberwork was often burned, destroyed and replaced during Sarajevo's more turbulent spasms – a fate that would be repeated during the shelling of the 1990s – yet the substantial masonry warehouses behind were sturdy enough to survive. As I studied the photographs, my imagination projected a soundtrack of bells on a market caught between Europe and Asia Minor: tinkling bells from traditional Ottoman-style water sellers proffering drinks in polished metal cups holstered on their belts, and from modern trams announcing their departure back towards the railway terminus.

A few Western suits and modern hats are visible in the pictures, but traditional outfits from Bosnia's three main ethnic groups dominate, lending an air of Eastern exoticism to what is geographically a European city. These costumes were not rare subjects that visiting photographers chose to highlight; but appeared standard for that time. Indeed as recently as 1937, when Rebecca West passed through Sarajevo on her first visit, she described seeing the same outfits: men from mountain communities in felt leggings, embroidered waistcoats and baggy trousers, their heads topped with an Ottoman-style fez or maybe a woollen cap or a swirl of

cloth twisted into a turban. Dress was then used as a cultural
indicator, and the different ethnic groups of Bosnia visiting the
city clung proudly to the sartorial signature passed down from
earlier generations. Women from Bosnian Muslim communities
were pictured wearing veils over their heads, but many also had
their faces covered completely by black cloth, without even a slit
for eyes, nose or mouth. In the mid-1870s Arthur Evans recorded
that, although Bosnia was the Ottoman Empire's most distant
western province, its public displays of adherence to Islam were
so strong as to appear fanatical. 'In Bosnia, in general, women are
veiled and secluded as they are veiled and secluded nowhere else
in Europe.'

The search for an education had drawn Princip to Sarajevo, and
within a few days of his arrival he was taken by his older brother,
Jovo, to enrol at school. The original newspaper notice that his
brother spotted had promised places at the city's Austro-Hungarian
Military Academy and this is where the young boy would have
started his education, had not a shopkeeper apparently intervened.
According to Dedijer, Jovo had stopped to buy his younger brother
fresh underwear and shirts, when the merchant told Jovo, 'Do not
give the child to an institution in which he will be uprooted and
become an executioner of his own people.' Only through the last-
minute intervention of a politically minded shopkeeper did the
young man who would bring down the Habsburgs avoid being
indoctrinated as one of their imperial cadets. At the suggestion of
the outfitter, Jovo looked elsewhere, arranging a place for his
younger brother at the Merchants' School, one of the many buildings on the city-centre grid so recently constructed by the Austro-
Hungarians. The 1908 map places it close to the prominent
Catholic Cathedral of the Sacred Heart, which itself had only been
completed a few years before – a political statement by the city's
new Catholic occupiers: Western Christian bell-towers were to

take their place on the Sarajevo skyline alongside those famous minarets. The first term of the school year did not start until September, so Princip had a few weeks in which to get to know the city that one day would be for ever linked to his name.

With the 1914 assassination having been the subject of intense scrutiny over the last hundred years, I had not expected to find new Princip material when I humped my gear off the tram that ran me into the city centre. Not only had generations of historians hunted the same quarry, but I was sensitive that many in the city might retain an uninterested, even hostile attitude towards the assassin. This seemed to explain the response I received the first morning after arriving, when I approached the board of the museum that stands next to the spot where the assassination took place.

They could not have been less interested. Phone calls went unreturned, messages ignored. I eventually managed to track down the chairman, but when I asked about the Merchants' School he shrugged his shoulders. He did not know where in the city it had been located, had no interest in finding its records, and no, he did not have any ideas about any aspect of Princip's life, beyond the few details on display in the museum. If I wanted to contact the museum again, I was to write formally in advance and wait until I was informed that my approach had been officially approved. Follow-up emails all went unanswered. It was very disappointing. A tour around the museum showed up errors in what little Princip material it held. Perhaps I would be better off looking elsewhere anyway.

The museum's attitude chimed with a warning given to me by my oldest friend from Sarajevo, Amela Filipović. She is a lawyer whose life, like that of the entire city, had been put on hold by the turbulence of the war. To survive she had worked with foreign journalists as a translator, for a long time enduring the ghastly commute past snipers and mortar barrages to the Holiday Inn hotel, which for several years was Sarajevo's journalistic hub. Even though it had been so long since we had last met, when I contacted her again she was kind enough to invite me to stay in her flat in the Skenderija district of central Sarajevo.

With her career now firmly back on track, running her own successful city-centre legal practice, Amela was about to take her daughter for a summer holiday down on the Adriatic coast, and I was welcome to use the guestroom. I had only visited her flat once during the war, at a time when her father, invalided through a stroke, was still living there – a particularly painful time for a family struggling for dignity and normality within the failing body of a besieged city. The surrounding slopes that had offered the city protection in the Ottoman era had become a source of menace, occupied by hostile Bosnian Serb forces and their artillery pieces; and nowhere more so than in Skenderija, which lies right at the foot of Mount Trebević, one of Sarajevo's most dramatic peaks and one that was in the hands of Bosnian Serb forces for the duration of the war.

After greeting Amela warmly and looking around the beautifully refurbished apartment, among the reminiscences welling up between us was her recollection of my single visit here. 'I remember it so well,' she said. 'It was the summer of 1994 and you brought us all supplies in your Land Rover. In particular, I will never forget the flowers that you gave us. You made a lot of people happy that day.'

It took hours to catch up properly, to hear about her father's death, the troubled rebirth of the city following the Dayton peace treaty and all the resulting turns in her life. We took a stroll near her flat, and I complained about the problems I was having exploring the back-story of Princip. She tried to console me. 'This is a city which does not look after its history properly. The city authorities are too focused on its politics now to care about anything in the past. Just look at that,' she said, pointing at a muddled assortment of masonry fragments scattered across an abandoned piece of land that we were walking past. They were clearly ages old. 'We have plenty of rich history here, but nobody bothers to look after it. Can you imagine this sort of thing in Britain? If these sorts of artefacts were in London, they would be displayed behind a fence with a sign explaining where they come from, not left like a rubbish dump.'

Determined to keep looking, and hoping that I might yet find new flotsam from Princip missed by earlier historians, I trooped between the many museums and archives that still exist in Sarajevo: the National Archive, the National Museum, the Museum of History, the Jewish Museum, the National Gallery, the Historical Archives and various sub-departments of the History Faculty at the city's main university. It was a frustrating and, at times, disheartening experience. The librarian at the National Museum told me how the whole establishment was facing imminent closure because of a budgetary row along ethnic lines, between the complex governmental structures born in Bosnia out of the Dayton peace accord. When she showed me into the library the main door still had shrapnel damage from the 1990s, when mortar rounds detonated outside. Within a few weeks of my visit the museum's doors would be closed; the librarian was owed a year's salary.

My breakthrough finally came at the much smaller Historical Archives, a modest building I must have passed unknowingly many times during the war. It stands on the main road that led up to where the UN military headquarters had been located, although back in the 1990s the archive was as non-operational as the broken traffic lights a short walk away outside Bosnia's presidency building. I remembered them hanging forlornly over a major junction, ignored by the occasional vehicle with enough fuel to be out on the roads. The archive director, Haris Zaimović, was a young man and I immediately warmed to his curiosity and enthusiasm. His positive response to my approach could not have been more different from that of the museum authorities I had been tangling with to date. When he told me that in the archive's holdings were many of the original report books from the main Sarajevo schools set up during the Austro-Hungarian colonial period, I worked out the exact dates of Princip's school years and, between us, we began a focused search. Within a short time we had retrieved the entire paper record of Princip's secondary education in Bosnia.

Dedijer, the author whose work from the 1960s still dominates the received history of Princip, paints his early years in Sarajevo as ones of stability, both at school and where he lodged. Dedijer has him performing consistently in the classroom and staying in Sarajevo only with the widow, Ilić. 'The first three years in the Merchants' School were rather uneventful for Gavrilo,' he wrote in *The Road to Sarajevo*. A different picture emerged from the original school reports that I found.

Hidden for more than a hundred years within Sarajevo's shifting and sometimes arcane network of officialdom, the reports catalogue in meticulous detail a student going off the rails. The fall of this Gabriel begins after he performed brilliantly in his first school year in Sarajevo, an exemplary A-grade student, but one for whom stability was clearly lacking. The documents show his address changing six times in four years as he roamed rootless and often penniless, supported by a scholarship for only part of one of his four completed school years. By the time Princip finally left school in Sarajevo, the student whose first-year performance was given a First Class Diploma with Honours (the highest possible ranking allowed for by the Austro-Hungarian education system) was now rated D in most subjects. His absenteeism surged to 199 lessons missed, and he was obliged to resit that year's final examination in Latin. These rediscovered school reports provided the clearest evidence of the teenage transformation undergone by Princip.

After so much research filtered through books by others, it was electrifying to have in front of me the 1907–8 school-year report for pupil number 32 of Class Ib of *Trgovačka Škola u Sarajevu*, the First Grade of the city's Merchants' School. The file had been glued inside a marbled ledger, the cover page bearing an official stamp in purpling ink from the headmaster's office. On a grid the class's ten teachers had each written down the subjects they taught and had signed their names in swirly, occasionally blotchy ink from a fountain pen. The maths teacher, Mr I. Kurtović, had got into a muddle and signed his name twice, the second version imperfectly erased. Maths would clearly be useful at a school for students intending careers in commerce, but the spread of subjects taught to Princip in this first year of secondary school went way beyond standard business matters.

Along with religious instruction in the faith of the Habsburg Empire – Catholicism – students also received instruction in Orthodox Christianity, Islam and Judaism. Clearly the view was that to do business in Bosnia, trainee merchants must have knowledge of the country's different ethnic groups, and to do that you needed to know something about their religion. History was not one of the subjects on offer to the class in this first year, although language was taken very seriously. As well as the language of the occupier – German – the pupils had lessons in their native language. I was intrigued to see that the same sensitivities that I came across in the twenty-first century had applied a hundred years earlier. In the language box on the form the printed term 'Bosnian' had been scrawled through by someone with red ink and replaced with the handwritten term 'Serbo-Croatian'. Use of the term 'Bosnian' implied the existence of a Bosnian national identity, an issue clearly of some sensitivity even at the start of the twentieth century.

Inside the folder, Princip's name was recorded in a flourish of copperplate manuscript, his first name abbreviated to Gavro, just as his descendants had referred to him affectionately when I had listened to the family history back at the start of the journey in Obljaj. The section for recording any bursary or scholarship showed that he received nothing, and his address in Sarajevo was given as 4 Oprkanj Street.

His date of birth was correctly recorded except for the month, which was entered as June, not July as official records have it back in Obljaj – a divergence that came close to costing him his life following the assassination of the Archduke. Under the Austro-Hungarian criminal code, a prisoner guilty of a capital crime could only be executed if aged twenty or older on the day of the offence. Had he been born on 13 June 1894 he would have hanged, as that would have made him twenty when the Archduke was shot on 28 June 1914. After a long investigation – not helped when his own mother, Marija, got into a muddle over exactly when her son had been born – the best legal minds available in Austria–Hungary settled on 13 July 1894 as his actual date of birth, saving him from the death sentence by a matter of days.

The report then graded his performance through the academic year, which was divided into two long terms, each several months in duration. Although he had arrived in the city with nothing more than a rural primary-school education behind him, Princip really shone. The normal starting age for secondary education was eleven, making the thirteen-year-old new boy a little old for his first year, although the class records indicated a wide spread of ages among classmates and he was not necessarily the oldest. Such an age range was to be expected in a country with a poorly developed education system. Under Ottoman rule, schooling had been almost non-existent, something that was changing only slowly under the Austro-Hungarians. Interestingly, all the Bosnian schools Princip studied at were open to students from any of the country's ethnic groups and there was no dogma that insisted on the reports being kept in the Western, Latin script used by the Habsburgs. Some of the reports were written in Latin script, but several others were in Cyrillic. The register for his class recorded names of Bosnian Serbs like himself alongside Jewish students, Bosnian Croats and Bosnian Muslims. The boy who ran away in fright when he saw a Sarajevan innkeeper from the Bosnian Muslim community was now living and learning alongside young people from across the ethnic spectrum.

Princip's descendants in Obljaj had told me that he had done well at school, but the marks I found in his early school reports were extraordinary. He scored highly across all subjects and improved as the year progressed, ending with the highest possible overall grade. Maths was his best academic subject, German his worst, although here he still scored far above the average in the class. In terms of behaviour, he scored almost perfect marks for conduct and did not miss a single lesson. Princip was clearly yet to develop his troublemaking streak.

His report for the following academic year, from autumn 1908 to summer 1909, showed that he followed the standard trajectory by going up a year to Class IIb, the Second Grade. His scholarship remained nil and his address was unchanged at 4 Oprkanj, along with the same incorrectly recorded month of birth. But now his scores began to dip, his rating for behaviour being much worse, his grade for maths slipping and twenty lessons being missed across the year. The school then changed its name to the Professional Merchants' School, and when Princip went back in autumn 1909 the Third Grade that he joined was named Class I Professional. The school

report showed that this year he was the recipient of a scholarship
worth 150 crowns from *Prosvjeta*, a Serbian cultural group, and
suggested that he had moved from Oprkanj Street, recording two
addresses in the city for that year: one on Franz Joseph Street, the
other on Upper Bjelava Street. Another unpublished document that
I came across at the Sarajevo Historical Archives, the official records
of an Austro-Hungarian census carried out across their Bosnian
colony on 18 April 1910, had Princip lodging at a further address,
this time on Jezero Street with old family friends originally from the
Obljaj area, Ačim Bozić and his wife, Staka.

His academic marks were now in free fall, with absenteeism
rocketing to sixty-eight lessons missed in the first term alone of
the 1909–10 year. Princip's commitment to the Professional
Merchants' School had clearly gone, and he did not make it through
to the end of the academic year. Notes in red ink recorded that on
11 May 1910 he left the Merchants' School 'with the permission
of his parents', although he was not giving up on school, transferring instead from the commercial school to the grammar system.

Princip's family members in Obljaj had said that from an early
age he was so bookish that he sometimes overlooked his shepherding duties, and here was proof that this bookishness had led
to more academic ambitions. After an early taste of secondary
education in Sarajevo through the trade school, he wanted to
complete all eight grades and perhaps even go on to university
– a rarity for Bosnian students at the time, when official figures
for 1902 stated that only thirty locals had a university education.
Princip's aim of completing all eight grades would be impossible
to fulfil if he stayed where he was at the Professional Merchants'
School, an institution designed to produce shopkeepers and traders
and which did not go all the way up to the eighth grade. To be
able to complete the full secondary-education cycle he would have
to enter the grammar-school system.

Dedijer suggested there was another reason for Princip's 1910 switch, claiming that the fifteen-year-old's awareness of politics meant he now viewed the mercantile interests of the Merchants' School as too bourgeois. Although Dedijer gives no evidence, this account chimed with the reports I had found. Whatever the motive for the switch, Princip was clearly determined to make it happen, even though it meant leaving Sarajevo temporarily and first moving to a grammar school in Tuzla, a provincial city in the north of Bosnia, for the start of the 1910–11 school year. Again, I was able to find the school report from Tuzla, although it recorded simply that Princip studied there for only the first month of the year, attending as a boarder and without any of the scholarship he had enjoyed the year before. The report recorded that no sooner had term begun than Princip left Tuzla on 7 October 1910, transferring back to Sarajevo, where a place had become available at the most prestigious school in the land, the High Gymnasium.

The founding of this showpiece institution was one of the first acts by the Austro-Hungarians when they occupied Sarajevo. After so many centuries of Ottoman rule in Bosnia, routinely described by Westerners as unenlightened, the establishment of a modern education system was another statement of political intent by the new colonists. The school network they set up was piecemeal, thinly covering the whole country, but it benefited many young Bosnians who would otherwise have had no meaningful education. Among them were Princip and many other activists who would work to bring down the same empire that had made possible their education.

By the time Princip came to study at the High Gymnasium in the late autumn of 1910 it was housed in a prominent, purpose-built colonial building set just back from the Appel Quay boulevard, which was created through the straightening of the Miljacka. The school is of such historical importance that its image has appeared on Bosnian postcards and postage stamps, and lists have been published of its star alumni, including luminaries such as Ivo Andrić. Princip's name does not make it onto those lists.

The 1910–11 school year would be the last Princip would complete in Bosnia. His report notes that he arrived at the start of the year from Tuzla, records that he had no scholarship and gives him yet another city address, this time on Mjedenica Street. After such a stellar performance in his first year at the Merchants' School, the end-of-year grades for pupil number 21 of the High Gymnasium's Class IVb, the Fourth Grade, make dismal reading. His highest score was a B in gymnastics and most of his other grades were D. The report says his Latin exam was retaken in the summer holiday, on 18 August 1911, some weeks after he had trekked up Mount Igman and written his doom-laden description of the forest by night. The report shows he scraped a D in the resit, still enough to allow him to go up to the next grade: Class Vb, the Fifth Grade. He would attend only the first few months of the new academic year and his Fifth Grade school report, which places him at a new address (this time on Hadji Suleyman Street), contains no performance grades. He did not attend enough classes to earn a rank as his Bosnian school career petered out, the end being marked by a teacher's note that said simply: 'failed to attend exam, Sarajevo, 28 Feb 1912'. Dedijer wrote that Princip was expelled for taking part in demonstrations against the Austro-Hungarian authorities, but the school records make no mention of this.

At the trial following the assassination Princip claimed, under cross-examination, that he left school in Sarajevo after falling ill and resolving to continue his studies in Belgrade – the capital of what was then the small but growing nation of Serbia, Bosnia's independent neighbour to the east. When asked why he wanted to do this, he answered obliquely, saying, 'That is my private affair.'

The best clue explaining how this clearly capable student with academic ambitions came to abandon schooling in his homeland comes not from the personal report for his final year, but instead from the High Gymnasium's yearbook for 1911–12. Under the list of Fifth Grade students who dropped out that year there are thirteen names. Princip is one of them, but among the others are Trifko Grabež and Lazar Djukić. All three would be dead within a few years, sacrificing their lives to the cause of fighting Austro-Hungarian rule in Bosnia. This was just one grade at one Bosnian school, and yet three of that year's dropouts would become revolutionaries of the most militant stamp. It was a pattern repeated across the country in the early twentieth century as the education system became Bosnia's primary breeding ground for radicalism, a Petri dish in which political plots could morph like multiplying bacteria into thoughts of change, direct action, even assassination.

CHAPTER 8

Fin-de-siècle Chat Rooms

Princip posing with older brother, Jovo, left,
and younger brother, Nikola, right, circa 1910

Postcard written by Princip to a female relative,
Persa, back in Obljaj, circa 1913

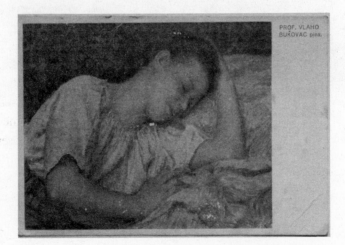

The school reports I had found gave new life to my mental picture of the adolescent Gavrilo Princip. He would still be in his teens when he assassinated the Archduke, so these formative years of education were of real significance. Here was evidence of an outlier student who began by defying a provincial childhood of extreme poverty to outperform fellow students from much richer, more sophisticated families in the capital city. At first he could not stop himself from doing the conventional thing by studying hard and obeying the teachers – no more so than could those members of the Princip family back in Obljaj who over the generations had worked as border guards and policemen for the colonial authorities, first Ottoman, more recently Austro-Hungarian.

The earliest photograph of Princip, one I retrieved from an archive in Belgrade, dates from this early period of his schooling, a souvenir family portrait taken in a professional studio with all three Princip brothers as its centrepiece. They appear rather self-conscious, stiff even, determined both to look away from the camera and to show publicly that they had broken with their peasant serf roots. The oldest brother, Jovo, sits to one side, fashionable flat cap on his head, cigarette in his left hand. Over on the other side Nikola, the youngest, maybe not yet in his teens, rests on a fake balustrade, with his arms tightly crossed in front of a painted backdrop showing a very un-Bosnian scene, an ornate, landscaped garden. Gavrilo has been given the most prominent position, right in the middle.

The photograph is not dated, but it would appear to have been taken in Sarajevo around the time of the 1910 census. The official form I found for the population count showed that Gavrilo, aged fifteen, was not the only Princip boy then lodging at Jezero Street with the Bozić family. Nikola, aged twelve, was recorded as living at the same address, having also come to the 'big city' to receive an education. All other pictures of Princip, which date from around the time of the assassination in 1914, show him with a rather hunted, even haunted appearance: face drawn, eyes sunken. But in this early photograph alongside his brothers we see a very different boy. His face is full and healthy, the shaped chin that is so characteristic of the Princip family is clearly visible and his hair is neatly parted. He wears a smart three-piece suit over a collared shirt and tie, while for footwear peasant clogs have been replaced by lace-up leather shoes. In his hands he holds a book: the very image of the dutiful, hard-working, successful scholar.

And yet this A-grade student turned. To understand why, I would have to search out other sources. He had kept no diary, and only a few scraps of his own writing survive along with a handful of photographs, so I was drawn instead to the extensive legal and medical records from the Austro-Hungarian authorities that arose following the assassination. Under cross-examination during the trial that followed the shooting and as part of the police investigation, he answered numerous questions about his background and schooling. Other clues come from the records of an Austrian psychiatrist, Dr Martin Pappenheim, who was allowed to visit him four times during his imprisonment. Dr Pappenheim, a professor from the University of Vienna, asked a wide range of questions, probing not just the 1914 assassination, but also the life experiences and intellectual development that led up to the event. These clinical notes were published verbatim in 1926 by an Austrian publisher in German, and in English by an American magazine the following year.

The dominant theme that emerges from these sources is a growing anger, one that drove a young man to kick back against a way of life imposed from above. The rage was directed against the Austro-Hungarian colonial occupier of Bosnia, but in essence it was no different from that felt in the same period by the Russian serf struggling against tsarist exploitation, or the British worker still without a representative political party in Parliament, or the peasantry calling for home rule in other parts of the Balkans such as modern-day Macedonia or Slovenia or Croatia. The history of these many struggles is rich and involved, but in essence it has one common feature: the rage of the oppressed.

What marks out Princip's anger is that it grew to consume him, knocking off-course the dutiful student and ultimately leading to direct action. This was a young man who, as his family told me so proudly, could not help himself doing whatever was necessary to protect victims of bullying, whether it was hitting a primary-school teacher with a pencil case or getting into a fight with an abusive imperial gendarme. And what I found intriguing was how it all began with his first journey to Sarajevo – an experience which showed him that the poverty he experienced growing up was the same across the country, through all of Bosnia's south-Slav communities. The dire conditions that killed six of his siblings in infancy applied all over a territory where an impoverished peasantry was still by far the largest single social cohort. And as he spent more time in the capital city, events took place that spread his anger to the older generation of his own people, local leaders from the south-Slav communities grown docile under the rule of Austria–Hungary. To bring about meaningful change, the older generations could not be relied upon.

The politics of change had been mobilising the young across Europe from far back in the nineteenth century. From 1848, the year when so much of Europe flirted with revolution, to the Paris Commune in 1870s France, the 1881 assassination of the Russian Tsar, Alexander II, and the Young Turk rebellion of 1908 that hastened the end of the Ottoman Empire, a central role was played by younger generations. As the twentieth century began, the forces of reaction were holding on, but calls for change were growing all over Europe, especially among the young. When these went unheeded, support grew for more radical change. Britain today might enjoy a reputation for stability, but it was not immune. Emily Davison, a campaigner who called for nothing more radical than the right for women to vote, was in her thirties when she left the following rallying cry on the wall of a prison cell in 1909: 'Rebellion against tyrants is obedience to God.' Four years later she would die after throwing herself in front of the King's horse at the Derby.

The exact same forces found purchase among the younger generations in Bosnia, so much so that a movement grew up that they would later call Mlada Bosna or Young Bosnia. That is not to say it was a single, disciplined party with a coherent structure, leadership or set of internal rules. It would be more accurate to describe it as an amorphous grouping of diverse young people from across Bosnia's ethnic and social spectrum, coalescing around one shared aim: the removal of Habsburg colonial rule. Ideas about how this would be achieved and what type of regime would come in its place did not enjoy the same unanimity. These questions remained unsettled, subject to fierce debate and bitter disagreement. But what stands out to me – as someone who saw Bosnia pull itself to pieces in the 1990s over ethnicity – is that the group was not called Young Serbs or Young Croats or Young Muslims. By using the name Young Bosnia, there was a deliberate attempt to achieve inclusivity, a common purpose between all those living in Bosnia that was not limited by ethnicity and religion.

In the eyes of many observers, Bosnia's geographical position on the south-east Balkan periphery of Europe served to distance it fundamentally from the rest of the continent. When the 1990s war was raging, Western politicians sought to decouple their world from Bosnia. John Major, then the British Prime Minister, implied that it was a place unlinked to the West when he spoke of conflict driven by 'ancient hatreds'. It was perhaps John Gunther, the American author, who best captured this sharp and rather resentful presumption of disconnect between the Balkans and the rest of the world. He wrote in *Inside Europe*:

> It is an intolerable affront to human and political nature that these wretched and unhappy little countries in the Balkan peninsula can, and do, have quarrels that cause world war. Some hundred and fifty thousand young Americans died because of an event in 1914 in a mud-caked primitive village, Sarajevo.

Yet the more I read about the country at the time when Princip was losing his way at school, the more I saw it as fully joined up with European political thinking at the time. The Mlada Bosna movement reflected perfectly the spectrum of political debate occupying minds throughout Edwardian Europe: the gradualism of social democracy, the theoretical promise of revolutionary socialism, the turmoil of anarchism, and all points between. The same political tracts that stirred so much revolutionary thinking elsewhere in Europe were steadily becoming available, smuggled into Bosnia under the noses of the Austro-Hungarian censors – every publication that made it through being a gesture of defiance against the foreign occupier.

The works of Bakunin, Kropotkin, Marx, Gorky, Dostoyevsky and others were handed around like forbidden scripture to be parsed, analysed, discussed, memorised, copied and distributed. As they did for the downtrodden all over Europe, these thinkers raised in the minds of radical young Bosnians the possibility of changing a stratified, feudal social order that had altered little in hundreds of years. The young might not have had the Internet chat rooms of the twenty-first century, but they did have school libraries, youth clubs and coffee houses, and it was here that the merits of socialism, anarchism and nationalism were all boisterously debated. Secret societies emerged, sometimes modelled along the strict need-to-know basis of Russian revolutionary cells, protected by oaths and passwords and under constant attack by spies in the pay of the Austro-Hungarian authorities. Some of the student activities in Sarajevo were so low-level as to be almost harmless: a campaign to deface signs printed in German, the language of the occupier; another to pull down flags showing emblems associated with the Austro-Hungarian authorities. Graffiti would appear denouncing the foreign rulers or *Schwaben*, as they were pejoratively referred to by young Bosnians. But with assassination an already established reality of early-twentieth-century politics, one that had claimed the lives of prime ministers, plenipotentiaries and presidents from France, to Russia, the United States and beyond, the potential impact of secret student groups could not be ignored.

The Austro-Hungarian occupiers were fully aware that young Bosnians were experimenting with political ideas that clashed with the fundamentals of traditional imperial rule, and made great efforts to suppress them. Student societies were outlawed and anyone caught violating this rule faced expulsion. The high school in Mostar was a particular hot zone for Mlada Bosna, so much so that in 1913 the whole school was shut by the colonial authorities. In the same year 141 secondary-school students were arrested across Bosnia and tried for membership of groups hostile to the state.

But try as they might to close off this seam of angry young people, the Austro-Hungarians failed – in many ways victims of their own success at empire-building. Bosnia was, after all, a component part of the Habsburg Empire at the start of the twentieth century. Its population, including any student sufficiently rich and qualified to seek out further education, could travel easily to Vienna and other nexuses of political thought across Europe. As citizens of the empire, Bosnians needed no passport to travel across its vast territory and their only obligation was to register at the police station of any town or city they reached. At his trial Princip recounted how, as he became older, he had travelled extensively through the empire, visiting Zagreb, capital of today's independent country of Croatia, and other cities outside Bosnia on the Adriatic coastline.

Leon Trotsky, then based alongside so many other would-be revolutionaries in the political hothouse that was early-twentieth-century Vienna, would take a close interest in Mlada Bosna. On a number of occasions he met several of its senior figures, influencing some of its internal ideological discussions, not least on the old trope of whether socialist revolution was possible in a rural, peasant society such as Bosnia, which had no significant industrial proletariat. Other young Bosnian schemers made pilgrimages to Zurich to meet leading Russian revolutionaries within the circle of Lenin, himself a longtime exile in Switzerland. Links would reach right across Europe, with Edith Sitwell, the *avant-garde* English poet, later falling under the influence of the mystic and poet Dimitrije Mitrinović, who was born in Herzegovina and was one of the earliest Mlada Bosna pioneers. He had been among the first wave of student troublemakers at Mostar high school, where he had set up a secret library to exchange revolutionary texts. Bosnia was fully linked up with contemporary political debate and, although it might be geographically on the edge of Europe, in many ways this made it all the more important. History teaches us that it is on the margins that the greatest change often happens.

From the moment in 1907 when Princip was lodged in Sarajevo at the house of the widow Ilić, there was no chance he could avoid exposure to Bosnian youth politics. The person he shared a room with at Oprkanj Street was already a keen admirer of all that Mlada Bosna stood for. Danilo Ilić, the landlady's son, was four years older than the thirteen-year-old boy from the provinces given the spare bed in his room. An unsettled young man, Danilo had a life that was typical of those young Bosnians experimenting with politics at the time. After qualifying as a teacher, he failed to settle down to a career in education, wandering instead between jobs as a bank clerk, proofreader and journalist writing columns critical of the Austro-Hungarians, but unsure how best to serve the goal of taking on the occupiers of his homeland.

Princip soon became friends with the older boy, who showed him how to find his way in Sarajevo, starting with the teeming bazaar so close to the front door. But their relationship would soon reach beyond ways to survive in the big city. Ilić was already caught up in underground youth politics, so much so that he would later travel to Switzerland and beyond, meeting revolutionaries and carrying back to Sarajevo their latest publications. His journeying would become so extensive that, according to Dedijer, Danilo Ilić became known by other young Bosnians in Sarajevo as Hadji – as if he were a pilgrim bringing back life's inner secrets from Mecca.

Princip turned out to be a slow-burn revolutionary, only gradually embracing the radical politics that drew in his room-mate so fully. When he arrived in Sarajevo he was already a keen reader and for these early years in the city, when his school performance was still so good, he was remembered by schoolmates as a solitary, private individual who preferred to surround himself with books.

In these early days he read nothing more inflammatory than the work of Alexandre Dumas, Oscar Wilde and Walter Scott, while joining the many Sarajevans who eagerly devoured the Sherlock Holmes whodunits serialised in popular local news-sheets. Dr Pappenheim's clinical notes were consistent with the school reports I found:

> No diseases in the family . . . Always has been healthy . . . Always an 'excellent student' up to the fifth grade . . . Was not much with other schoolboys, always alone. Was always quiet, sentimental child. Always earnest with books, pictures, &c. Even as a child was not particularly religious.

As he matured, Princip sought to express himself through poetry, scribbling away for hours and sharing the results with friends. They were not impressed. At one point he tried to summon the courage to submit one of his compositions to Ivo Andrić, only a few years his senior, but already a young man with a reputation as one of Sarajevo's finest literary talents. Princip could not overcome his nerves and chickened out in the end. His failure calls to mind another would-be artist struggling to survive at exactly the same time in another Austro-Hungarian city. In around 1910 Adolf Hitler was trying to make it as a painter in Vienna. He too failed and was forced to direct his energies elsewhere.

Numerous friends reported that the young Princip did not drink and he did not chase members of the opposite sex. There was one girl he did have a special bond with, according to the psychiatrist, Dr Pappenheim, although it was a chaste, unconsummated relationship that he did not want to discuss. 'Relates he knew her in the fourth class,' the doctor's notes stated. 'Ideal love; never kissed; in this connection will reveal no more of himself.'

Dedijer named the girl as Vukosava, the younger sister of one of Princip's associates in Sarajevo, although the passion got little further than him giving her a copy of his favourite Oscar Wilde stories. There is a legend that Princip wrote Vukosava many letters and poems, opening his heart and expressing to her his innermost feelings and thoughts. But as with the original court transcript and much else connected with Princip, these letters – if they ever existed – went missing. The story went that Vukosava buried them in a village out in the Bosnian countryside during the First World War, but somehow in all the turmoil they were never retrieved. This did not stop acquaintances of the young couple recomposing some of the text of these love-letters and publishing them in the years after the First World War. By then the interest in Princip was of such intensity that many friends, contemporaries and acquaintances wrote books and memoirs about their time with the young assassin. I rather fear the desire to be published overcame adherence to the truth.

Princip's retiring, solitary nature did not necessarily win him friends, with some of his contemporaries regarding this behaviour as superior and boastful. Dobroslav Jevdjević gave a rather damning character reference for him in a sworn statement that was read out at the trial following the assassination: 'Gavro Princip stood out . . . He pretended that no one was better than he, especially in his knowledge of literature and he used to say that he was the best among us.' Dedijer described the two as 'intimate friends', something I found strange. The whole tone of Jevdjević's testimony was very negative regarding Princip, and when the statement had been read out the defendant objected fiercely that many of Jevdjević's assertions were wrong. 'It is true that I had a conflict with him,' Princip announced to the court.

A key event took place in 1908, a year after Princip started school: a political and diplomatic crisis that was centred right there in Sarajevo, but soon spread far beyond Bosnia. It would change fundamentally the character of Bosnian youth politics, launching quiet students like Princip on a much more radical path. It would also give final proof that the country's remote geographical location did not stop it from playing a role in high European diplomacy. The Bosnian dispute was so serious it almost led to a European war and can be regarded today as a dress rehearsal for 1914: it was the formal annexation of Bosnia by Austria–Hungary.

When Bosnia was occupied by the Habsburgs in 1878 through the settlement agreed at the Congress of Berlin, the diplomatic rubric insisted that the Ottoman rulers nevertheless retained nominal control or suzerainty over the land. While this did not limit in any meaningful way how Austria–Hungary set about administering and exploiting its new Bosnian dominion, the words retained a certain diplomatic potency, one that only became truly apparent once Vienna pushed through formal annexation in October 1908, claiming for itself full sovereign rights over Bosnia for the first time.

The move was a pre-emptive strike by the Austro-Hungarians to deal with murmurings of discontent within their already large population of south Slavs, made up of Serbs, Croats and Slovenes spread across the empire's long-established territories in the North Balkans. The emergence during the nineteenth century of an independent nation of Serbia further south had given the south Slavs within the Habsburg Empire an example to aspire to. They had not known meaningful self-rule since the Middle Ages, yet they watched closely as fellow south Slavs in Serbia showed that in the modern age it was possible to rule themselves. In order to put Serbia back in its place, so the thinking went in Vienna, Bosnia would be formally annexed, thus shifting the centre of gravity for all south Slavs away from Serbia.

The upgrading of occupation to annexation in a small corner of the Balkans might today sound arcane, but it had dire implications in the context of early-twentieth-century diplomacy when the balance of power was as painstakingly and delicately constructed as a house of cards. For several months around the winter of 1908/9, Bosnia was the epicentre of a portentous international debate, as European statesmen struggled to deal with Vienna's unilateral violation of the treaty agreed at Berlin. If the annexation represented a diplomatic gain for Vienna, which of the other Great Powers would stomach a loss? For many months the name of Bosnia, the layout of its borders and the details of its administration occupied the attention of the greatest diplomats from London to Rome, St Petersburg to Berlin, desperate both to save face and restore order. That these statesmen were successful in managing to avoid a European war has meant that the importance of the Bosnian annexation crisis is today rarely recognised. But what I found particularly striking in my research was that so many of the diplo-politico linkages that would lead the world to war in 1914 were in play during this earlier crisis: Serbian attempts to draw in Russian support; Germany's willingness to back Austria–Hungary; Britain's sweeper-role monitoring the impact on Europe's balance of power; secret talks, ultimatums. In the end it was Russia's reluctance to offer military support to Serbia that defused the situation, eventually leading to Serbia's grudging acceptance of the annexation. By the spring of 1909 the Berlin treaty had been amended, the annexation was complete and the house of cards still stood.

Princip had only just started his second year of the Merchants' School when the crisis began in 1908. But what he witnessed on the streets of the capital city was the impact of the annexation: deeper entrenchment of Austro-Hungarian colonial rule, emergency powers granted to imperial governors, new waves of non-Slav immigration from elsewhere in the Habsburg Empire, growing resentment among fellow Slavs who grumbled that advancement was being monopolised by foreigners. The 1910 census illustrated the population shift clearly, recording a city population of 52,000, with the Muslim and Orthodox communities relatively static. In contrast, the Catholics, consisting mostly of arrivals from elsewhere in the Habsburg Empire, had ballooned in just three decades from 700, when Bosnia had first been occupied by Austria–Hungary, to 17,000.

This was when Princip's simmering anger towards the foreigner began to strengthen into rage. During these early years in Sarajevo he endured a meagre existence, spending what little money he had on books. Friends said he would rather go hungry than sell from his beloved library, surviving mostly on loans advanced against the promise that his older brother would pay off the debt. While Jovo did everything he could to support Gavrilo, there were occasions when he was not good for the money, forcing his younger sibling to change digs – hence the many addresses I found on Princip's school records. 'I did not have the means to maintain myself here,' he said at his trial. 'I always lived on credit.' He found himself exactly where his serf forebears had been, anchored to the bottom of a social order imposed by a foreign power. The anger only got worse when he went home on school holidays. Land reform had been one of the promises made by the Habsburgs, and yet whenever he travelled to Obljaj – such as in 1909, when he scratched his initials on the wall in the garden of the family home-stead – he saw that Bosnian peasants like his own family were no better off under the Austro-Hungarians than they had been under the Ottomans.

This mounting fury towards Vienna seeps through Princip's testimony at his trial. He accused Austria of 'doing evil to the south-Slav people', 'imposing torments upon the people' and 'behaving badly to our people'. There are several references to his 'hatred' of the occupier and to his desire for 'revenge' against injustices forced on the south-Slav citizens of Bosnia. 'If I could, I would destroy Austria completely,' he declared towards the close of proceedings.

But there was also a sense in which his anger metastasised. It was not just the foreign occupier that he hated. He also came to distrust those leaders of his own south-Slav community who accommodated the Austro-Hungarians. These were local councillors, businessmen and politicians who took the view that working for change from within the occupation was wiser than fighting against it. They were derided as *Mamelukes*, an Ottoman euphemism for slaves, by young Bosnian zealots then poring over their revolutionary texts. The Serbian government's decision, albeit under intense diplomatic pressure, to accept the annexation of Bosnia by Austria–Hungary was the clearest proof that the older generation of south Slavs could not be relied upon to bring about change. Their gradualism would never deliver true freedom, so something more radical was needed. Dr Pappenheim's notes capture Princip's attitude:

> Our old generation was mostly conservative, but in the people as a whole existed the wish for national liberation. The older generation was of a different opinion from the younger as to how to bring it about. In the year 1878 many Serb leaders and generals prayed for liberation from the Turks. The older generation wanted to secure liberty from Austria in a legal way; we do not believe in such a liberty.

As an underground movement Mlada Bosna did not have any formal membership process, so there is no paper trail tracking Princip's links with the group. But it was in the aftermath of the annexation that, still only fifteen years of age, he began to associate with its members in Sarajevo and to embrace its ideals of taking on the imperial occupier. Again his evolution was far from head-strong. Princip did not rush into radicalism, exploring instead a wide range of options, from the peaceful utopianism of William Morris – after his death a copy of Morris's *News from Nowhere* was found with Princip's signature inside – to the more turbulent radicalism of the Russian revolutionaries. 'I read Krapotkin and the Russian socialist literature,' he said during his trial.

Princip remained a very private individual, an introvert, at his happiest keeping himself to himself. As he dabbled with politics in an environment rife with Austro-Hungarian spies, he learned the true value of discretion. One of the books in his growing library was an obscure series of short stories written in German – *Wenn Landsleute sich begegnen*, by Jassy Torrund. As well as having his signature within the covers, it was found that he had picked out and transcribed a few portentous lines from the text:

> What your enemy should not know,
> You shouldn't tell your friend.
> If I don't tell the secret, then it is my slave,
> If I do, then I am its slave.

Up until the annexation in 1908, the dominant voices within Mlada Bosna were moderate, but after the crisis such restraint was thrown off. Sarajevo – like so many other cities, not just in the Austro-Hungarian Empire but across all of Europe – simmered with the injustice felt by the masses. It led to pressure for direct action, a force that built and built. With only sham democracy in place, one that allowed for a local parliament to be elected, but without the power to challenge the colonial occupier, there was no safety valve to release this pressure. Eventually revolutionary thoughts in Sarajevo turned to calls for political assassination.

An account of life in Sarajevo at the time from a young boy

who would go on to become one of Austria's most renowned artists gives a wonderful counterpoint perspective on this febrile atmosphere. Hans Fronius was a perfect example of the Austro-Hungarian colonial immigrant class that had flooded into Bosnia. His father was a doctor who served as a state physician based in Sarajevo, and his grandfather had been one of the early train engineers who built Bosnia's narrow-gauge railway network for the Habsburgs. Describing the childhood he enjoyed in Sarajevo around the time of the annexation crisis, Hans Fronius wrote:

> We Schwabians, the incoming Austrians, lived in the Balkans like colonialists and enjoyed a high standard of living. I was a quiet child and drew a lot. But despite all I did to cut myself off, I nevertheless could feel that not everything was in order in this peaceful world. There were workers' strikes, as well as parades against the threat of war and attempted assassinations on the governor. Unforgettable was the following mental image: my father still agitated as he talked about an attempted assassination, removing his bloody shirt cuffs while washing his hands.

Amid all the growing political tension that was born of the annexation one episode stands out. In June 1910 a young man called Bogdan Žerajić – a Bosnian Serb from Herzegovina, just like Princip, and also a supporter of Mlada Bosna – took a pistol and fired five times at the Austro-Hungarian governor of Bosnia, General Marijan Varešanin, as he was being driven by coach over one of the old Ottoman bridges across the Miljacka in Sarajevo. The General had just taken part in a high-profile event, the state opening of Bosnia's quisling parliament – one that was brought into existence as a result of the annexation eighteen months earlier. In Žerajić's eyes, the parliament was nothing but a council of *Mameluke* lackeys, south-Slav elders complicit in the oppression of Bosnia's population by the Habsburg outsider. The time had come for action.

Žerajić was standing about halfway across the Emperor's Bridge when his target drove past. It was a narrow bridge, so the General would have been only a few feet away from him when Žerajić pulled out the gun and fired. He missed his target with all five bullets. But the gunman then did something that marked out his assassination bid as different from others. With his sixth bullet he shot himself dead – a martyr in the eyes of Mlada Bosna supporters; a cowardly suicide terrorist in the view of Austria–Hungary. The way his body was then treated added to his legend. Some sources said that General Varešanin got out of his coach, walked over to the body and kicked it. Others said he spat on the body. What is not disputed is that the gunman's head was cut off and his skull ostentatiously used as an inkpot, *pour encourager les autres*, by one of Sarajevo's more brutal colonial police investigators.

The legend of Žerajić grew in tribute poems and essays written by fellow Mlada Bosna members and the whole incident had a great impact on Princip. For young political activists like him, this was not the highbrow theorising of philosophical debate or the strategic-level calculus of international diplomacy. This was politics at its most real: direct action by a student only a few years older than himself – Žerajić was in his mid-twenties when he died – from exactly the same background, for a political cause that he shared, and right there, in his own neighbourhood. The bridge where it happened lies a few minutes' walk from where Princip attended school and he must have passed the spot often, each time being reminded that the fight against the foreign occupier could demand the ultimate sacrifice.

At Princip's trial in 1914 the ghost of Bogdan Žerajić was ever-present. When mention was made of a poem, 'Death of a Hero', that praised the failed assassin, Princip shouted out, 'May Žerajić rest in peace!' It was an outburst that incensed the Austro-Hungarian judge and led to proceedings being suspended. Earlier, when the name of Žerajić came up, Princip was candid in his explanation of how highly he regarded him: 'He was my role model. At night I used to go to his grave and vow that I would do the same as he . . . The grave was neglected and we put it in order.'

Princip was only fifteen when Žerajić died in 1910. It would take time for the slow-burn revolutionary to complete his own journey from schoolboy dreamer to assassin. Dr Pappenheim's clinical notes recorded how that journey started shortly after the failed assassination attempt by Žerajić, when Princip began an episode of sleepwalking. His schoolwork, as indicated by the worsening grades of his school reports, no longer mattered as much as politics. He found himself increasingly caught up in student demonstrations and agitation against Austro-Hungarian rule. The young man told his psychiatrist that the year following the Žerajić shooting was 'critical':

Left the school in Sarajevo in 1911. At that time nationalistic demonstrations were taking place . . . Was in the first lines of students. Was badly treated by the professors. Read many anarchistic, socialistic, nationalistic pamphlets, *belles lettres* and everything. Bought books himself; did not speak about these things.

The Žerajić shooting started Princip on the path that would lead to the assassination of the Archduke. In this country, where history so often trips over itself, the 1914 assassination would take place in Sarajevo just a hundred yards away from where Žerajić shot his pistol on the Emperor's Bridge four years earlier. But as Princip told Dr Pappenheim, he was 'not yet ripe and independent enough' to be able to consider such direct action. For Princip to complete his own transformation to radical assassin, he had one more important journey still to make.

Across the Drina River, which forms Bosnia's eastern frontier, lay Serbia, the south-Slav nation that had recently won independence. It was small, with borders yet to satisfy the territorial ambitions of its rulers. It was new, with official recognition coming only in 1878 at the Berlin Congress following decades of rebellion, insurgency and uprising against Ottoman occupiers. It was also unstable, with a rivalry between royal houses so intense that in 1903 the King and his wife were murdered by mutinous army officers, attacked in their palace in Belgrade, their bodies disembowelled and defenestrated. But Serbia was free from foreign occupation, and that was what made it so important for Princip and millions of other south Slavs still under foreign occupation in the Balkans.

Princip – intense, secretive and private – told the trial that while he had started off reading Russian revolutionary texts, it was nationalism, specifically south-Slav nationalism, that he came to focus on. Serbia was the place where nationalism had delivered self-rule and so, after withdrawing from the Bosnian school system, Princip joined the growing stream of young Bosnians and others drawn there from across the Balkans. The Bosnian Serb boy from Herzegovina, who had been brought up listening to renditions around the fire of epic poems about medieval Serb heroics, set off in early 1912 to his 'homeland' for the first time, hitch-hiking, walking and taking public transport all the way to Belgrade. There he would complete not just his formal education, but his transition to full-blown assassin.

Before following Princip to Belgrade, I set out with my 1908 Sarajevo map to try and picture the city as he would have known it during his four years there as a schoolboy. Even though I was

staying in the centre, the provincial character of this city meant
that when I walked out onto the streets just before dawn I could
hear cockerels crowing from smallholdings up the nearby flank of
Mount Trebević. In the 1990s very different sounds came from the
same mountain: the reports of Bosnian Serb artillery pieces firing
into the city, although my diary reminded me that not all gunfire
was life-threatening. During the football World Cup in 1994,
soldiers on both sides fired their guns in the air in wild celebration
when Germany, the nation that occupied Bosnia in the Second
World War, was beaten by a fellow Balkan country, Bulgaria.

During the post-Second World War communist period in
Sarajevo, tower blocks and apartment buildings bloomed where
the valley widens into the zone ambitiously demarcated by the
Austro-Hungarians as 'New Sarajevo'. But with its steeply sided
setting constraining its growth, the heart of the city remains
remarkably unchanged. The skyline of twenty-first-century
Sarajevo would be perfectly recognisable to one of Arthur Evans's
open-mouthed Bosnian bumpkins from the nineteenth century.
Princip would certainly know his way around.

To reach Oprkanj Street, where Princip's Sarajevo life had begun,
I walked through the old bazaar quarter. The late-nineteenth-
century decision by the Austro-Hungarian colonial planners to
leave it alone, while modernising the rest of downtown Sarajevo,
is a blessing for the modern city, providing a natural draw for
visitors, whether local or foreign. The layout of the boulevards,
the course of the river, the shape of the city's hills all serve to
funnel people towards Baščaršija, the Turkish name by which the
market area is still known.

The mosques, with their ancient fountains, tombs and ritual
fittings, are still very much in use, and as I explored I saw, within
their precincts, groups of Bosnian Muslims going about their
devotions just as earlier generations had. The older men passing

through the gates were recognisable by the dark berets they wore on their heads, a last remnant of the days when costume was an ethnic identifier. In the women's sections I could only snatch glimpses through open doors and latticework screens, but it was interesting to note that while I saw plenty of headscarfs, there were only a few full face-covering veils. Yet the market area's main attraction was not religion, but what it has always been: the business of living. The baggy-trousered traders with sacks of spices might have gone, but the same web of alleyways remains, lined by stalls selling mobile-phone air time, memory sticks, football shirts, flip-flops and all the other bric-a-brac of modern life.

I had only known the market area when it was battered by shelling, its shops battened down and its stockrooms emptied by the Bosnian Serb siege that choked off supplies. Over the centuries the market has endured fire, plague, invasion and other crises, so back then the shop owners did what their forefathers had always done – they waited. In the summer of 1994 I was taken to one of the booths that was owned by the family of an Albanian jeweller. The shutters were down and it was closed, dank, dark and dusty, but there I was entrusted with a mission that spoke of an earlier age: smuggling a tiny package of gold out over Mount Igman for delivery to a family member who had managed to escape from Sarajevo to London.

The waiting game had clearly paid off, as Baščaršija was now heaving once more, youngsters with tattoos barging out of crowded bars, tables choking the alleys where the flagstones were freshly polished by the footfall of shoppers laden with purchases. And as throughout the city's long history, Sarajevo wore well its Janus-like duality. Slices of pizza were being hawked loudly next to eateries selling *burek*, traditional Bosnian stuffed-pastry tubes prepared in vast, swirling spirals that Rebecca West described as 'cartwheel tarts'.

While a few people, tourists mostly, sat on low cushioned benches smoking *nargileh*, my ear picked up a very un-Balkan sound. It was 'Waka Waka', the anthem of the 2010 football World Cup played in South Africa, spilling out of a bar nearby. A friend in Cape Town played bass on the track, so I took out my phone to send him a recording of his African beat being played in an un-African setting. As I fiddled with the buttons, the device buzzed to say it had picked up a wireless Internet network from the Hotel Europe, a name that I immediately recognised. During the siege it was a huge, burnt-out wreck memorable for the unfeasible number of refugees crammed within and for the busted ATM machine outside. It was the only one I ever found in Sarajevo, its fading VISA sign then a symbol of a city cut adrift from modernity. Now my mobile phone was like a compass guiding me to a new age, as I turned and looked up to find towering above me a very different Hotel Europe, completely refurbished, its façade partially clad in elegant glass, flags of various nations hanging ostentatiously above the portico. Sarajevo was about to host an international film festival, and the hotel staff were in a flap of final preparation for the arrival of their VVVIP guest, Angelina Jolie. I went inside and would have taken a drink on the terrace that was deliberately built with a view of the ancient Ottoman bazaar, only my filthy trekking gear felt rather inappropriate for the setting.

At the trial that followed the 1914 assassination Princip described Oprkanj as a 'back street', a description that still holds today. While visitors to Sarajevo's old town flock to take photographs of the raised, latticed kiosk that caps the ornate Sebilj fountain in Pigeon Square, few ever wander up the crooked little lane one block to the east. It has none of the cafés and booths so prominent elsewhere in Baščaršija, just a few old houses and a boutique hotel with a rather cheesy name, the Villa Orient. A museum to Princip was once opened on this street, and I was able to find an old photograph of the bedroom that had been mocked up in the museum to display how Princip had once shared a room here with Danilo Ilić. In the picture you can see a single bed, a table to work on and kilims spread on the floor and hanging on the wall. There is also a large religious painting in the style of an Orthodox Christian icon – a strange choice for the room of a young man who under cross-examination at the trial described himself as 'an atheist'. Today there is no trace of the museum. It was closed without fanfare decades ago.

You can take a tram from the top of Oprkanj Street, but to reach the site of the Merchants' School there really is no need. The old centre of Sarajevo is so small that it took me only ten minutes to pick my way through the crowded bazaar and out along Ferhadija, the main pedestrian thoroughfare that connects the market with the street-grid laid out by the Austro-Hungarians. After a few hundred yards the school building was on my left, although no longer in use for education, the Merchants' School having been rehoused elsewhere in the city long ago, rebranded as more of a business school.

It was a very tight stage on which the drama of Princip's city life had played out, Sarajevo then reaching scarcely ten blocks at its longest point and only a few blocks across at its widest, all within the hilly frame of the Miljacka valley. With the street names retrieved from his school reports, I made a tour on foot. It took less than an hour to walk between all the addresses Princip was registered as using during his years in Sarajevo: Oprkanj, Franz Joseph, Upper Bjelava, Jezero, Mjedenica and Hadji Suleyman streets. Many of the buildings had been modernised, but all the roads were still there and I could picture Princip's wanderings among them. The student who started out doing so well at school, posing so conventionally in his family portrait, walked these same lanes, smelled the same oily aroma of frying *burek*, dodged trams running along the same routes and watched the level of the Miljacka River chart, as it still does, the season's passing from winter rage to summer's slack water. And it was in Sarajevo's school libraries, reading rooms and coffee houses that his growing anger against the Austro-Hungarian occupier slowly took form, from the dreamy utopianism of William Morris to the direct action of Bogdan Žerajić, who shot himself dead on a bridge over the river.

The most striking feature of my tour was that there was nothing to tell the visitor that Princip had ever been there. He was the Bosnian with the greatest impact on world history, and yet in today's Bosnia there were no plaques or signs, nothing to record his many years living in the city before he headed to Belgrade.

CHAPTER 9

A Mystical Journey

Bosnian Muslim fighters who made it out alive when Srebrenica
fell to the Bosnian Serbs, July 1995

Each anniversary of Srebrenica's fall, newly-recovered remains of Bosnian Muslim victims are interred. In 2012, 520 were buried.

There is no record of the exact route through eastern Bosnia that Gavrilo Princip took in 1912 on his first journey to the Serbian capital of Belgrade, a distance from Sarajevo of roughly 120 miles. The rugged Bosnian terrain was then serviced by a few rough roads and a narrow-gauge railway, one the schoolboy artist Hans Fronius remembered his colonial grandfather building with 'a hundred tunnels'. Although it is now closed, it was still functioning when Rebecca West travelled here in 1937, so she was able to take a train all the way to where the Drina River acts as the border between Bosnia and Serbia. In *Black Lamb and Grey Falcon* she described dozing in and out of sleep, the train moving in and out of daylight as it huffed its way through a 'Swiss country of alps and pinewoods'.

When Princip was interviewed by the police in 1914 he used the word 'mystical' to describe his journey through this region. For centuries, stories of magic and spiritualism had been spun here, tales of superstition, the evil eye and individuals with powers beyond explanation. Princip's mind, as he recounted during the trial, was then churning with the ideals of nationalism. In those early years of the twentieth century, nationalism still had about it a moral purity, an innate pride shared by peoples reclaiming a birthright long denied by foreign usurpers. It was such romantic thinking that underwrote the creation of the unified states of Germany and Italy in the late nineteenth century, a romanticism that had yet to morph into extremes of fascism with all its resulting horrors.

My mind was occupied by the sinister ways in which nationalism can be twisted, during my bus journey from Sarajevo to the north-Bosnian city of Tuzla just a few hours away. There I began the most emotional hike I have ever made. The route passed through exactly the same mountains Princip crossed, yet it was intimately connected to the brutal endgame of the war of the 1990s. It led to a place that will for ever be associated with nationalism contorted into its most toxic form. Three days of walking and camping took me to the town of Srebrenica.

Ore deposits rich with silver, or *srebro* as the locals call it, had been discovered hundreds of years earlier up a remote hilly valley in eastern Bosnia. It led to the founding of the town named after the precious metal sometime in the late Middle Ages. For centuries mining grew little beyond the artisanal level, although under Austro-Hungarian rule efforts were made to develop the industry properly. Foreign investors arrived in Srebrenica, changing the town name briefly to Edelbauer – a German name that translates as 'Noble farmer' – with colonial entrepreneurs setting up there one of the spa hotels so popular across the Habsburg Empire, where visitors could enjoy the medicinal effects of local waters laden with minerals. Investment fell away when the Austro-Hungarians left, and by the end of the twentieth century Srebrenica was a provincial town typical of eastern Bosnia, a bit rundown and tatty, but still large enough to be the focus of a substantial population based mostly in villages sprinkled over a landscape of forested valleys and high mountains. Unlike the three-way tug of war I had seen in towns like Glamoč in the west of Bosnia, eastern Bosnia had no meaningful Bosnian Croat population, making it a community shared by Bosnian Muslims and Bosnian Serbs. The skyline of Srebrenica reflected clearly enough which side dominated, with the bell-tower from a single Serbian Orthodox church set alongside several minarets.

The town's remote position was its saviour at the start of the war in early 1992. Bosnian Serb forces swept through only briefly and then pulled out, focusing their military efforts instead on their attempt to take Sarajevo, and on the ethnic cleansing of territory they regarded as more strategically important, adjacent to Serbia on the western side of the Drina River. It was here that Bosnian Muslim communities fell victim to the extreme nationalism espoused by the political leadership of Slobodan Milošević in Belgrade: houses torched, women raped, men murdered. Srebrenica lies some distance away from the main roads that the Bosnian Serb forces needed for their military operations, so after their departure it was soon retaken by the Bosnian Muslim side. Largely cut off from the shrinking area of central Bosnia controlled by Bosnian Muslim forces, the people of Srebrenica ended 1992 surviving on food gathered in from outlying villages. People went hungry, but they did not starve.

With the hardening of winter the situation deteriorated, as the town's population was swollen by thousands of Bosnian Muslim civilian refugees forced out of their homes by the intensified systematic cleansing of the Drina valley by Bosnian Serb forces. Srebrenica had now become the closest town of any size still in the hands of the Bosnian Muslim authorities, so there they streamed on foot and on carts hauled by tractors, horses and donkeys, traumatised by the cruelty they had witnessed and forced to cram themselves into houses, apartments, rooms and any other viable space, eking out what little food was available.

Bosnian Muslim soldiers grew ever more desperate for supplies, launching raids from what had become a pocket of Bosnian Muslim territory centred on Srebrenica, surrounded by land controlled by Bosnian Serb forces. In a war characterised less by the clash of soldiers against soldiers and more by soldiers committing atrocities against civilians, there were a number of attacks on Bosnian

Serb towns and villages that led to civilian casualties on the Bosnian Serb side. In the propaganda battle, the Bosnian Serbs emphasised these fatalities more than any suffering endured by their enemies. The Bosnian Muslim forces lacked artillery and tanks, fighting with whatever pistols, machine guns and hunting rifles they could muster, but local knowledge of the mountain terrain made them at times a potent military threat. Over the winter months of 1992 they broke out of the pocket several times, even succeeding in blocking the main road needed by the Bosnian Serbs to resupply their forces around Sarajevo. No longer could Bosnian Serb commanders afford to ignore Srebrenica.

Early in spring 1993 Bosnian Serb forces moved to deal with the growing military threat from the Srebrenica pocket. Infantry supported by tanks, armoured vehicles and artillery pounded the area, attacking outlying villages, killing large numbers of civilians and driving the survivors into an already crowded town centre gripped by hunger, panic and fear. The assault eventually failed, in part because of piecemeal intervention by UN peacekeepers struggling to protect the civilian population. With casualties rising on both sides, an uneasy stand-off was eventually reached after Srebrenica was given special status, designated in April 1993 a 'United Nations Safe Area' to be protected by UN peacekeepers. The UN commander, a French general called Philippe Morillon, had made a brief and chaotic visit to the pocket, at one point being blocked from leaving by a mob of desperate Bosnian Muslim civilians. The people of Srebrenica remember little about his visit, apart from what he said at a heaving public meeting where the atmosphere was jumpy and tense. The UN's most senior general in Bosnia gave them a personal assurance that he would not abandon them.

Srebrenica spent the next two years in a zombie-like state, its men growing thinner and more malnourished as they desperately manned the defences, its women and children clinging to life on

aid supplies begrudgingly allowed in by the besieging Bosnian
Serbs. A few hundred UN peacekeepers nominally guaranteed
Srebrenica's Safe Area status, although in truth the pocket was
defended by a Dad's Army militia of ill-equipped Bosnian Muslim
forces. Relations between the UN soldiers and Bosnian Muslim
forces were strained, not least because under the rules of the Safe
Area arrangement all local soldiers were supposed to be disarmed,
entrusting their weapons to the UN. Stuck in Sarajevo, I would
stare at the map showing Srebrenica's unreachable island of
Bosnian Muslim territory adrift in a sea controlled by the Bosnian
Serbs. Occasionally there would emerge accounts of starvation
among the besieged, accusations of atrocities by the besiegers,
mysterious military resupply flights by unmarked helicopters, and
stories of smuggling deals cut by local Bosnian Muslim thugs with
Bosnian Serb opportunists. As so often in the Balkans, the stories
would circulate wildly, but would rarely harden.

The end came in July 1995, when Bosnian Serb forces launched
a final assault to deal with the pocket once and for all. The combat
lasted only a matter of days as Bosnian Serb tanks and armoured
personnel carriers swept past the primitive defences. It was what
happened next that will for ever taint the name of Srebrenica.
Thousands of male prisoners were exterminated by the dominant
Bosnian Serb forces, with the best estimates suggesting a death-
toll of around 8,000. The exact number remains unclear, although
human remains are still being exhumed from mass graves all these
years later. What is clear is that the Srebrenica killings represent
the worst genocidal war crime in Europe since the Holocaust.

The assault on Srebrenica would prove to be the beginning of
the end of the Bosnian War. After three years of standing by on
the sidelines, the international community was shamed into finally
taking determined action. NATO – a military alliance that had
spent four decades in the Cold War preparing for combat, but

never actually fighting – came of age. It was in Bosnia in the late summer of 1995 that NATO forces launched large-scale attacks for the first time in its history, their artillery and war planes pounding Bosnian Serb positions. A military machine equipped, trained and motivated to take on the Cold War's perceived enemy from the Soviet Union found itself fighting not Russian soldiers, but Bosnian Serbs. The United States went one step further by using its air power to support Bosnian Muslim and Bosnian Croat forces on the ground as they attacked a Bosnian Serb enemy that had been so dominant throughout the entire Bosnian War.

Srebrenica changed everything. Within a matter of months the Bosnian Serb forces were routed, the political leadership of Slobodan Milošević in Belgrade forced to come to the negotiating table. The peace accords that ended the war were agreed in November 1995. A war that had drifted on for three years was over, the borders of the country unchanged, the former enemies agreeing to live alongside each other in a single country, albeit one where the three ethnic groups fiercely guard their own devolved authority. Of great importance was the way in which this relatively confined war in Bosnia would come to influence future global events. In 1914 events in Bosnia had had global consequences, and so it proved once more eighty years later. The events surrounding the fall of Srebrenica changed fundamentally the attitude of the international community towards military intervention. In the years that have followed, world powers have repeatedly shown a greater willingness to deploy ground troops, whether in Kosovo, Afghanistan, Iraq or elsewhere.

At the strategic level I had charted all this as a war correspondent for the *Telegraph* in the late 1990s and 2000s, but it took the hike through the mountains of eastern Bosnia to give me a fuller under-standing of the horrors that had such monumental impact.

*

The route I took after arriving by bus in Tuzla was the main one used by the few thousand Bosnian Muslim men who made it out alive from Srebrenica in July 1995. When Bosnian Serb forces launched their attack on the pocket, the defenders faced the grimmest of choices as the UN's public undertaking to protect the Safe Area collapsed to nothing. A Dutch peacekeeping detachment with a few dozen combat troops was in the pocket at the time of the assault, hopelessly under-equipped to stop the Bosnian Serb forces, and haplessly commanded by officers tactless enough to be filmed engaging with the attackers, drinking toasts and accepting gifts. As the situation became more chaotic, several peacekeepers were taken prisoner by advancing Bosnian Serb forces and many were disarmed. One was shot dead by the Bosnian Muslim side as he tried to withdraw from an observation post. The Dutch did eventually make requests for NATO war planes to attack, but they were lost in the UN chain of command. With the situation on the ground unclear, a small group of British special forces was deployed by helicopter on the hilltops, but they were under orders simply to observe and not intervene. The political leadership of the international community was yet to be shamed into decisiveness. Precisely what the French general had assured the people of Srebrenica would never happen *was* happening – they were being abandoned.

The population of the pocket was then estimated to stand at roughly 30,000, the majority of whom were non-combatant civilians. To begin with, the Bosnian Serb commanders made repeated promises that anyone who surrendered would be treated properly. They would be taken by bus and delivered safely to Bosnian Muslim-held territory a few hours' drive to the west. While the locals could be confident that the Bosnian Serbs would deliver on their promise to allow free passage to women and children, they were not so sure that men of fighting age would receive the same treatment. Every single person inside the pocket knew how the Bosnian Serbs had routinely maltreated male civilian prisoners earlier in the war. By this point most of the pocket's population were themselves the victims of ethnic cleansing, forced to flee here from their homes closer to the Drina River, and many knew from first-hand experience how casually murderous Bosnian Serb militiamen could be. Some of these militia were not trained soldiers, but common criminals and thugs; some were loutish football fans recruited from the rougher end of the terraces, who were given uniforms, weapons and licence to persecute non-Serbs. The men of Srebrenica had to decide whether to hand themselves over to this type of militia or try and make it out by themselves.

The men who trusted the Bosnian Serbs were to become victims of genocide. They were separated from the women and children, sometimes dragged off buses in front of their families, taken away and executed. A group of ten was led away within clear sight of Dutch peacekeepers, their corpses found the next morning, shot in cold blood within walking distance of the UN base. Much larger numbers of men, estimated to total several thousand, were corralled by the Bosnian Serbs for three days in buildings a few miles north of Srebrenica, before the order was given for their extermination. Driven by bus to remote rural locations, they were shot at close range, often being made to kneel and told derisively to 'pray to Allah'. Buried initially in mass graves, some of which the victims themselves were forced to dig, they would subsequently be disinterred and dispersed to a number of other smaller mass graves, as part of a deliberate attempt at concealment by the Bosnian Serbs. Sometimes the bus drivers were given orders to shoot at least one prisoner as a disincentive ever to speak about what happened.

All of this came out in eyewitness testimonies that would be given at war-crimes trials years after the event. What has never fully emerged is the story of the men who did not trust the Bosnian

Serbs; those who refused to give themselves up, embarking instead on an extraordinary forced march which, like so many epic Balkan stories, is both heroic and tragic. Of the 13,000 men who started this march, it is believed a little over half survived.

Srebrenica might have been surrounded by Bosnian Serb forces since the war began in April 1992, but the truth was that the pocket was never hermetically sealed. The Bosnian Serbs blocked all the roads that fed in and out of the area, laid minefields and put observation posts on strategic heights, but the terrain of eastern Bosnia defied them. Lumpy with mountains, pleated with valleys and patched all over with thick deciduous and conifer forests, it gave enough cover for small, inconspicuous groups of Bosnian Muslim defenders to smuggle themselves occasionally in and out of Srebrenica. It was via this route that modest ammunition stocks inside the pocket were maintained.

The closest territory in central Bosnia controlled by friendly forces – the Bosnian Muslim army – lay about twenty miles west of the pocket. Instead of taking this direct route, which was heavily defended by the Bosnian Serbs, the smugglers used one that was longer but safer: a fifty-mile overland trek running north-west from the pocket. Particular care had to be taken when passing the occasional main road and around minefields planted near bridges that cross small mountain streams that feed the Drina River, but much of the route ran through remote countryside, none more so than the massif of a mountain called Udrč. With stealth and courage it was possible to trek under cover of darkness all the way from Srebrenica to territory close to Tuzla, the largest city in the north of Bosnia held continuously during the war by the Bosnian Muslim side.

Throughout the war a small patch of land just east of Tuzla was among the most heavily fought over in all of north Bosnia. It would become known as the 'Sapna Thumb' because of the

thumb-like shape on the map of land fiercely defended by Bosnian
Muslim forces, surrounded on three sides by Bosnian Serbs and
tipped by a small town called Sapna. Princip would pass through
here when he was making his way back to Sarajevo for the assassination, although when I first went there in 1994 I was more
focused on the modern war.

My diary reminds me of an anxious encounter when I made it
to Sapna. Conditions in the area were bleak, with Bosnian Muslim
villagers clinging on to their homes under constant threat of mortar
and artillery attack from the Bosnian Serbs while being defended
by Bosnian Muslim forces. A teenage boy told me the attackers
had been using cluster bombs, a breach of international convention, and offered to show me some evidence. I agreed, thinking
he would show me one or two of the devices – dangerously unstable
bomblets that are armed and primed to go off any time after landing
on the ground. Bomb-disposal experts despise cluster bombs
because they are so unpredictable and volatile, set to explode at
the slightest movement or even a change of temperature. Direct
sunlight can be enough to cause a detonation. The boy led me to
a bucket in which he had tossed about thirty bomblets, casually
collected from the surrounding countryside. I took a photograph
and backed away very slowly and carefully, making sure not to cast
a shadow across them. What I did not know when I first went to
Sapna was its secret. This was where Srebrenica's lifeline began.
If the Sapna Thumb fell, then the smuggling route in and out of
Srebrenica would be closed.

The secret was kept and the lifeline remained open, right up
to the fall of Srebrenica in July 1995, so it was the obvious route
for the escape column to attempt. The route had worked for years,
so it made sense to use it to save as many people as possible. But
the smugglers had only ever travelled in small groups, with never
more than a few dozen individuals, which were relatively easy to

conceal. With Bosnian Serb forces descending rapidly on the pocket, the escape column gathering for the off had already grown to well over 10,000, mostly men, but with a scattering of female medical staff tending the wounded and the occasional woman desperate not to be split up from her menfolk. It would take twelve hours after the head of the column left the pocket for the tail to begin marching. What happened next has entered legend, being commemorated each July by the *Marš Mira*, or Peace March, when several thousand young Bosnians walk the lifeline route in reverse, from the Sapna Thumb back to Srebrenica. I was in time to join the *Marš Mira* of 2012.

The walk combined the youthful enthusiasm of a music rock festival with an undertow of horror reminiscent of an Auschwitz memorial service. Cheerful groups of young Bosnian men and women lugged rucksacks crammed with camping gear and food, their cooking pots clanking as they swung from strings knotted to the outside. Flags were borne proudly by some of the groups, bearing memorial messages for the victims of Srebrenica, the task of carrying the poles being rotated among the walkers. The occasional ghetto-blaster boomed raucous tracks of Balkan turbo-folk and all the time the mood was contagious in its spirit of focused determination.

The three-day route took us through countryside every bit as beautiful as the terrain I had crossed in the earlier part of my journey through western Bosnia. We crossed the occasional asphalt road, but for the most part the trail followed footpaths and farm tracks through landscape that in many places was just as wild as the wolf country I had already visited. There were pastures where the grass had been scythed and gathered up into ricks as tall as houses. There were mountain streams where my fishing radar twitched, glistening reaches of clear water rich in the promise of wild trout. There were forest glades offering shade against the strong summer sun, and moments when the tree cover broke to give tumbling views of hills growing ever paler as they fell away to the Drina River valley far off to the east. There were climbs so steep that in places we had to grab onto tree trunks to stop ourselves sliding back down on sledges of muddy, matted leaves.

Every few miles we would come to another mountain village. These were Bosnian Muslim homes, but they were indistinguishable from Bosnian Serb and Bosnian Croat farmhouses I had already visited on my journey. In the spirit of the London marathon, locals set up tables of water cups for the marchers and, in one memorable instance of history's loop, a group of aid workers from Austria – the modern remnant of the Austro-Hungarian Empire – enthusiastically handed out bananas from crates they had arranged to be driven to the summit of one of the longer climbs. With so many people taking part in the march, police vans, ambulances and other emergency vehicles were deployed here and there. A fire engine caught my eye, donated from Britain, the name of the East Sussex Fire Brigade still stencilled on its side.

Snapshots from Bosnia's history littered the trail. In one section of forest we passed a *stećak*, one of the medieval box-like Bosnian tombstones that date from the era when the various eastern and western forms of Christianity struggled for supremacy among the south Slavs living here before the arrival of the Ottomans in the fifteenth century. The centuries had knocked it askew, but the surface of the grey rock bore circular repetitive carvings, hallmarks of an ancient south-Slav culture that is still the focus of academic study. Later I saw something that needed no explanation, a *Wehrmacht* steel helmet dating from the German occupation of Yugoslavia. It was rusted to a wafer and nailed to the top of a fence post, but the shape was easily recognisable from the long schoolboy hours I had spent playing with Second World War models.

At the end of each day we stopped en masse at a pre-arranged location, the marchers dispersing into nearby villages, settling down for the night in barns and outhouses, where blistered feet received attention, food was prepared and bedrolls were spread out. Farmers' wives gave me *burek* prepared not quite in the same vast cartwheels as Sarajevo's restaurants, but in more modest swirls the size of a baking tray. I ate contentedly, cross-legged on the ground, flakes of thin pastry drifting onto my lap, eagerly wolfing down the cheese-and-spinach stuffing to restock my energy levels. It was the raspberry season, and several times I was able to pick fruit from farmers' gardens before a thimble of coffee was proffered as a digestif. Tired enough to fall asleep quickly each night in my tent, I was woken early in the morning by the Muslim call to prayer from mosques rebuilt after the war. Throughout the walk there was joshing and high spirits, with one particular farmer's wife reminding me of a word learned earlier on my journey when she insisted jokingly that I leave her my *šator* as a gift. On another occasion when a local man, a shopkeeper called Mirza, found out I was British, he looked me straight in the eye and said in south-London-accented English: 'Next year we are going to be millionaires, Rodney.' He was a great fan of the British sitcom *Only Fools and Horses*, which is so popular across the Balkans that it is repeated endlessly on local television. The name of the show here is *Mućke*, a word that translates as 'wheeler-dealers', a concept that resonates strongly with Bosnians from all three ethnic groups.

These should be my dominant memories from the walk: natural beauty, local generosity and rural simplicity. But they are not. My overwhelming memory is that I was dancing on graves.

The route followed by the escape column from Srebrenica is today shown not by normal road signs. Instead it is marked by mass graves, one after another: the smaller ones where half a dozen bodies were uncovered, the larger ones found to contain more than

500 corpses. Over the three days of walking I recorded passing twenty mass graves, although there were some points where I was so exhausted that I might have missed a few, my eyesight not what it should have been because of sweat in my eyes. Each of the mass graves I did see had a sign that gave the name of the site and the coding used by the war-crimes investigators who have spent the years since 1995 exhuming bodies, gathering evidence and arranging for the remains to be moved to a proper graveyard near Srebrenica itself. And each had a photograph: one showing an investigator's gloved hand holding a skull; another showing a skeleton's hands still tied with wire; another an identity card displaying a man's sober-faced passport photograph peering out through a smear of mud. Many of the bodies in the graves lay exactly where they had been killed during the escape. Others were brought from where they had been hurriedly buried elsewhere after execution, then were driven here and hidden among the woods in what war-crimes investigators called 'Secondary Graves' – places so far off the beaten track that the Bosnian Serb author- ities hoped they would never be found.

The spirit of the march was at once respectful towards these sites and yet businesslike. For many of these young people a fifty- mile hike represented the greatest physical challenge they had ever attempted, so while acknowledging the mass graves, they did not dawdle, pressing on instead with the next section of the challenge. Next to one of the mass graves that we passed on the first day an ice-cream stall had been set up by a local man – one that did great business.

Over the days it took me to walk the hills into Srebrenica I built up a picture of what had happened from one of the survivors of the escape column. It took some time to win the confidence of Džile Omerović, a bearded, barrel-chested bear of a man in his mid-thirties who had ended up as a refugee in Switzerland after making it out from Srebrenica alive. Each evening we would chat in French, and to begin with he displayed the same survivor's guilt as Arnie – a reluctance to make a 'fuss', to highlight his own plight when death denied so many others the chance to voice properly their suffering. But after spending some time together he began to let go, offering up threads of his story.

Džile was born of farming stock in the village of Pobudje, a Bosnian Muslim hamlet about a day's walk north of Srebrenica. He was seventeen when the war began, eagerly joining a community defence force that was commanded by his father, Musa, the headman of the village.

'To begin with, in that first summer, we were well organised and the Serbs left us alone,' he said. 'There were shelters for the children and we had enough food as a community to survive. My father was in charge and things were peaceful enough here, even though the main road the Serbs were using was just two miles down the hill at the bottom of the valley. At one point an order came to try and block the road, so one night the guys went down there to try and blow up the bridge where the road crosses a river. All of us know the area, so we waited for a misty night and then we dragged down gas canisters to use as explosives – the tanks of gas you use for a welding torch. They stuffed them under the bridge and blew them up. There was a great big flash and a lot of smoke, but it did not make any bloody difference. The bridge was still there in the morning.'

A wry smile crept across his face at the recollection of these early amateur attempts at warfare and then, looking earnest once again, he said something with echoes of Princip's young life. 'My great love was reading, and in that first year the thing I missed most was books. All I wanted was books. Anything to read, anything to keep my mind going. I knew nothing about the world, so it was through books like Henry Miller's *Tropic of Capricorn* that I was able to escape. I was only a teenager then, and that book is all about the thing teenagers are most interested in – sex.

'I took part in another raid and found myself down in the valley near a school. It was night-time, and when I saw a window had been left open I climbed inside. I had no idea if there might be any Serbs there, but all I wanted to do was find some books. I crept up the stairs in the dark and found a lot of places where intravenous drips had been set up. They had been using it as a field hospital to treat their wounded, right there in the school library.

'I grabbed as many books as I could carry and then spotted a typewriter. God knows why I did this, but I sat down, grabbed a piece of paper and typed out really carefully DO NOT BURN. The typewriter was one of those fancy ones with three colours, so I made sure the letters were as visible as possible. It made no difference. Some stupid guy from my side then came in and torched the place. He was carrying a bottle of brandy and was half-drunk, one of those stupid Bosnians from the old joke, the one where one guy says to the other, "Would you like to buy a book?" and the other says, "No thank you, I already own one."'

When the Serbs launched their operation to neutralise the threat from the Srebrenica pocket in spring 1993, Džile's village found itself on the frontline. Its proximity to the main road made it a target for the standard Bosnian Serb tactic, which was to shell an area intensively for days in the hope of driving out the population and then send in their ground troops. 'It was Henry Miller who saved my life. I had gone to my grandfather's house, so I could read my book in peace when the shelling began. The first blast landed right next to the house I was in and the wall was blown open. Luckily there was a large cupboard that took the blast and I was saved. But then a second shell landed right next door near where my family lived, and I heard the voices screaming. "Musa is dead, Musa is dead." We buried my father on the hill behind the house.'

It was no longer safe to stay in the village, so the surviving members of the Omerović family trekked on foot into Srebrenica, part of the refugee influx that threatened to overwhelm the town. Džile's mother and sister were allowed to leave on convoys arranged by the UN, but men of fighting age like him, then eighteen, had to stay. He spent the next two years surviving as best he could.

'I remember going to the library in Srebrenica and asking if I could borrow some books. Do you know what they said? They said I was not originally from Srebrenica district and so I must go to the library in my home district. Bloody idiots! My district town was in the hands of the Serbs. That's the only time in my life I stole a book.'

Over the years since the war ended some have sought to project an image of undiluted heroism on Srebrenica during this period, a picture of stalwart defence by courageous fighters of the highest moral purity. Džile's account was much more honest. The scenario he described was one closer to rats trapped in a sack, occasionally turning on each other to survive. 'There are some things that are difficult to think about even now after all these years,' he said. 'Things like soldiers from our side caught dealing with the other side. There was a guy I know about who was caught doing this in a village out near where I am from. The commanders had him marched back into Srebrenica, but somehow on the way back before he got to the town he was shot dead. Did he know too much? Were there senior officers who were in on the smuggling deals who wanted him silenced? I don't know. But I do know that while most of us went hungry, there were some inside the pocket who made money. Those guys made me sick.'

Our conversation moved on to what Džile viewed as firmer moral ground when we talked about the crisis of July 1995 and the final advance of the Bosnian Serbs. He was one of the 13,000 who refused to hand themselves over to the enemy and took part in the escape column. 'It was all down to a man called Senad,' he said. 'Now there is a true hero, a true patriot. He's not some guy who shoots a gun four times in the air and is promoted to Brigadier; no, he is the reason any of us got out alive. Did he ask for any recognition? Of course not. All he wanted to do was to go back to a life growing vegetables in his market garden.

'It was Senad who opened up the route from here all the way to Tuzla. Udrč mountain is enormous, but he knew every stream and every gully like the back of his hand. Twenty-seven times during the war he led small groups of guys to bring in ammunition along that route. More than anyone else, he kept the pocket alive.

'So when the crisis came and the Serbs were advancing, it was Senad who led the head of the convoy. You've got to remember, if you stretch out 13,000 people in a line, that line will reach for miles and miles, so the decision was taken to put the best fighters at the front with Senad, the guys with the best guns, the guys with at least some ammunition. But you have got to remember these are all hungry men, people who have not eaten properly for years, who are wearing civilian clothes because their uniforms have become rags, whose guns might not even work. Many did not have boots. It was not a column of American troops from the 101st Airborne. By that time I was wearing scraps of clothes, some of which were bits of uniform stolen on raids into Bosnian Serb territory. I had with me only a pistol and a grenade, and I was ordered to the back of the column to protect the civilians.'

After days of attacks the pocket of Srebrenica fell to the Serbs on 11 July 1995, when their forces swept up the main roads leading into the town from the south and the north. Unknown to them, the escape column was that same day mustering in the village of

Šušnjari, which lay a few miles away from the main roads over to the west.

'It was around midnight on the eleventh that the column began to move. Silence was imperative, so the order was given for no one to speak as they set off in the dark heading north, to begin with over the hills towards my village of Pobudje. For those first few hours the guys at the front were able to move quite quickly and they even got across the main road near my house. But then the Serbs discovered what was happening and they sent everything they had to stop us.

'By the time we got to the top of Bulim mountain, which comes before Pobudje, the Serb shells were landing among us. It was chaos. I carried a wounded man up to where I thought we would be safe, but then we saw Serbs coming up the hill and we fled and hid in the trees.

'It was like being trapped in hell,' he said, 'I know no other word for it.' He quietly repeated the word 'hell'. This was where his survivor's guilt comes from: the knowledge that many did not make it out alive, the nagging worry that he might have done more to save others.

A few thousand men fought their way all the way up to the Sapna Thumb, led by Senad past minefields and booby-trapped bridges, through ambushes set up by the Bosnian Serbs. I met a few of these men just after they arrived, their faces cadaverously thin, their feet bloody with blisters, their gaze unnervingly distant. They were reluctant to speak to reporters, fully aware that those further back in the column were still stumbling through the woods like hunted prey. On several occasions large numbers of Bosnian Muslim men in the escape column surrendered, after finding themselves trapped. The Bosnian Serbs disarmed them, drove them by truck to remote locations and executed them. Some were shot where they were found, among the same trees that all these years later gave me and my fellow marchers the sanctuary of shade on the *Marš Mira*.

In 1996, a year after the pocket fell, I returned to the area. At that time the Bosnian Serb side still denied that any atrocities had occurred, sticking to the story that the only killings that took place were the result of regular combat. I was about ten miles north of Srebrenica when I turned off the main road and drove down a track that first crossed a small stream and then climbed up a hillside. A clearing in the forest opened out, and suddenly I found myself driving through a field of human bones. I stopped the car and got out. All around lay skulls, vertebrae, femurs, rotting scraps of clothes, footwear and a few personal possessions. So thick lay the bones on the ground that, when I turned the jeep, I remember the back wheels lurching over a ribcage. I took photographs, but from nowhere a man appeared carrying a shotgun and told me to leave. I still feel guilty for panicking that day, for fleeing that crime scene, relying on the presumption that it would one day be found by war-crimes investigators and the human remains properly identified.

That field turned out to be a mile or so from Džile's home.

'All around here there was killing,' he said as we walked. 'There were moments when I saw the Serb forces coming through the woods as if they were out hunting birds – a long line of them, all carrying weapons and sweeping through the grass to kill whatever they could find. I hid in a tree and they passed close by, without looking up. I could hear words relayed by loudspeaker, with messages like "Give Yourselves Up" and "You Will be Treated Properly".'

The situation he described was one of worsening chaos and feral survival. Moving only at night, he soon got lost as the rear column splintered, and he would walk in circles for hours through the forests and fields, terrified every time he bumped into other shadowy figures, for he could not be certain if they were friend or foe. 'One man I came across was completely naked, shouting and shouting into the darkness. I begged him to be quiet, but he had lost his mind. I would hear shooting down in the valley or over on the other side of a hill and I would run in the opposite direction. When morning came, I did not know where I was.

'At one point I came across ten men in uniform with guns. First, I thought they were Serbs as they ordered me to come forward. I can remember the sound of them cocking their weapons as I approached, my hand behind my back holding my pistol, ready to shoot myself if they turned out to be the enemy. Then I saw several of them wore nothing but wool socks on their feet. They were our side. But they did not know who I was, and when they saw that some of my uniform was Serb they demanded proof. They made me drop my trousers to show I was circumcised.'

The hours turned into nights, and the nights into weeks, and the weeks into months. In all Džile spent two months surviving in the forests of eastern Bosnia, eating snails for sustenance, drinking from mountain streams and moving only at night. On 11 September 1995 he finally made it to friendly territory – a dirty, bearded, half-starved scarecrow staggering out of the woods.

The *Marš Mira* hike is timed so that participants can attend the commemoration service held for the dead of Srebrenica each year on 11 July, the anniversary of the day the pocket fell. It takes place not in the town itself, but at a huge graveyard laid out a few miles to the south, next to the disused factory where the UN peacekeepers had their base. The scale of the killings was such that even after all these years, the service allows for the burial of human remains newly identified by war-crimes investigators sifting through evidence recovered from mass graves. With my rucksack on my back and my clothes still mucky with sweat, I joined mourners visiting the old factory where the caskets of those to be buried at the service of 2012 were laid out. There were 520 of them.

Each casket was made of wood, but had been covered in green cloth trimmed with gold, and shaped to the same elegant fluted design that was a little smaller than a normal coffin. The passing of the years had left at most a skeleton, perhaps some scraps of clothing, a wristwatch or other non-perishable recognisable possessions, so a narrow casket was all that was needed for that load to be borne. The cold science of war-crimes investigation allows for the DNA of human remains to be matched against that of surviving family members. So it was with scientific certainty that the relatives of the 520 were summoned to the cemetery for a service that allowed some sort of closure for a trauma reaching back seventeen years.

More than 20,000 people gathered for the lengthy service. Speeches were made by local Muslim clerics and Bosnian politicians. The ambassador corps from Sarajevo attended in strength, and a rabbi from New York gave an oration in which he compared the genocide endured at Srebrenica to the depravity of the Holocaust. It was a cloudless summer day of ferocious heat, yet my arms dimpled with goosebumps as the names of those to be finally buried were read out. Families wept as the caskets were hoisted head-high and processed through the crowd, a scattering of green flotsam on a sea of grief. Within minutes the whole scene was smoky with dust thrown up by family members wielding shovels to fill in the graves newly dug alongside those of thousands of other victims buried in earlier years. Each headstone bore the same epitaph:

> And don't say for those
> Who died on the road of Allah:
> 'They are dead.'
> No, they live on
> Even if you cannot see them.

I let the crowds disperse and then walked along footpaths looping past row upon row of graves, thinking about the 'Known unto God' epitaph I had seen on graves from the First World War.

Reporting on the Bosnian War has left me troubled by a persistent sense of shame. It cannot be dignified by being described in the same terms as the survivor's guilt felt by genuine victims such as Džile. It is more a feeling of being ashamed at witnessing a war voyeuristically, unable to influence events, powerless to do anything more than passively report the atrocities. And for me, the fall of Srebrenica is the strongest source of that shame.

I got as close as any reporter to the pocket when it fell, rushing to the city of Tuzla, which was under Bosnian Muslim control, the fields outside its airport overrun by Srebrenica survivors: women, pensioners and infants so beat that they had passed the night on the ground curled up against the hedgerows. Most were still sleeping when I got there at dawn, but a young boy caught my attention and beckoned me over to a nearby stand of trees. From a distance it looked like a bundle of rags caught in the branches, but close up I found myself looking at a woman who had hanged herself with her Muslim headscarf. So tormented was she by what the enemy did to her husband in Srebrenica that she stole away in the night, abandoned two young children and took her own life.

The image of her purpling face, unflinching as flies settled on lifeless lips moist with dew, troubles my sleep still. It became my symbol of private shame for bearing journalistic witness to – but not being able to influence – a conflict, my totem of personal failure. Within days the treadmill of news drew us off elsewhere: to Mount Igman, where NATO artillery units were about to attack Bosnian Serb forces for the first time; to the area around Obljaj, where the army from Croatia was preparing to launch its decisive coup, Operation Storm. And yet, at the time when our attention was being drawn away, men like Džile were still struggling for their lives in the woods around Srebrenica.

Seventeen years later, as the memorial service wound up, I walked through the cemetery to where the names of those known to have died in the Srebrenica killings have been carved on tablets of granite. There are thousands of them, ordered alphabetically on tabletops of stone that are arranged around a huge circle. My heartbeat surged when I found a name that I had written down in my notebook all those years ago: Selman Osmanović. The body I had found hanging in the tree was that of his wife, Ferida.

Before leaving Srebrenica I asked Džile what he felt about Princip. 'He was the Serbian guy who shot the Archduke in Sarajevo, right?' he checked, before giving his answer. 'Well, if he had anything to do with the sort of Serbs who attacked Srebrenica, then I would say I have to hate him. But did he have anything to do with the guys who attacked Srebrenica?'

It remained the key question, and one that I could only answer if I continued along Princip's trail to Belgrade. Džile gave me a lift down to the main road below his house, the one that was the scene of so much skirmishing back in 1992, and left me to make my way onwards to Serbia. He shook my hand and, with a cheerful wave, drove back to the farm where his father lies buried on the hill and where the fields were so recently sown with the bones of the dead.

CHAPTER 10

Arming the Trigger

The only known photograph of Princip, right,
during his time in Belgrade, 1914

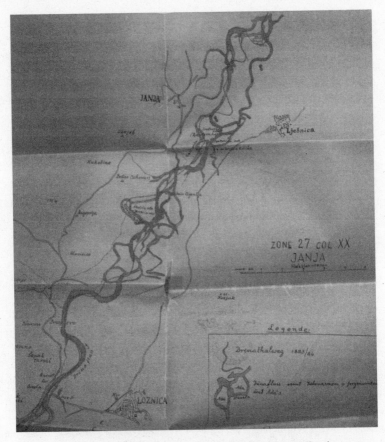

Police sketch of the Drina River crossing used by the assassination team
covertly entering Bosnia from Serbia, May-June 1914

Two days of hitch-hiking took me across the Drina River frontier from Bosnia into Serbia, the landscape easing all the time as the mountains on the western side of the river gave way to a plain that was tabletop-flat reaching east all the way to Belgrade. Travellers in the early twentieth century knew from afar when they were approaching the city from the sight of the great fortress built on the high rocky promontory that towers over the junction of the Sava and Danube Rivers. It would have been visible from miles away, dominating unchallenged what was otherwise a classic central-European flatland of forest, field and marsh.

The urban sprawl of modern Belgrade, with its ranks of electricity pylons, tower blocks and red-and-white-chequered factory chimneys, rather diffused the sense of drama when my last lift dropped me in the city. But soon enough I was back on the trail of my quarry, as the road I found myself walking up near Belgrade's railway station was named Gavrilo Princip Street.

The capital city reached by Princip in 1912 was new and still very small, although growing rapidly in a rush of nationalist awakening. The rebirth of Serbia, a nation that had not known independence since the Middle Ages, had been a slow and bloody process that lasted almost the entire nineteenth century. Rebellions against Ottoman occupiers that began as far back as 1804 had eventually led, through a series of brutal reprisals and counterattacks, to the establishment of a new Serbian state around a capital city that for centuries had consisted of little more than the hilltop

Turkish fortress above the river junction, and a modest local community serving the needs of its garrison. In 1838 the population of Belgrade stood at just 13,000, and by the time Serbia's independent status was formally recognised at the Congress of Berlin in 1878 it was not much larger.

As the twentieth century began, Serbia was still a work in progress, its rulers deeply divided over how to deal with their powerful neighbours, not least Austria–Hungary, which controlled both Bosnia to the west of Serbia and a section of territory that reached all the way to the opposite banks of the rivers just across from Belgrade. With a pair of binoculars it was then possible to see from the fortress the black-and-yellow imperial standard bearing the Habsburg eagle flying a few hundred yards away over the water – a chastening reality for Serbian rulers unsure of how to preserve the long-term security of their infant country. While many insisted that Austria–Hungary was an enemy to be confronted, others accepted the rationale of accommodating such a strong, martial neighbour – a difference of opinion that led to fierce disagreement within the Serbian ruling classes. When the Serbian king was murdered by officers of the Serbian army in 1903, part of the motivation for the attackers was his perceived willingness to develop closer links to Vienna. Unanimity among Serbia's leaders was proving to be a myth, with plots, coups and political assassination now routine.

As Serbia grew, so did the confidence of the hardliners, peaking with the annexation crisis of 1908 when Austria–Hungary formalised its occupation of Bosnia and declared it sovereign Habsburg territory. Ardent nationalists in Serbia, many of whom belonged to the army's officer corps, demanded military action as crowds of young men took to the streets of Belgrade vowing to use force to take on the Austro-Hungarians in order to win freedom for the significant population of fellow Serbs in Bosnia. Serbian paramilitary groups were set up with the explicit purpose of fomenting nationalist uprisings in Bosnia, and secret smuggling channels were established to move agents, propaganda material and weapons across the Drina River.

When it became clear in early 1909 that Russia was not at that time willing to send its forces to support Serbia in a war with Austria–Hungary, the Belgrade government had no choice other than to accept the annexation. It was too weak to fight an offensive war by itself, so the crowds on the streets were dispersed and the order given for the paramilitary groups to be disbanded. It was an instance of bitter realpolitik, one that would leave deep scars in political opinion, with nationalist hardliners incensed by what they regarded as a betrayal of the Serbian cause by traitorous elements within their own government. Throughout the twentieth century the same divisions would return, not least at the end of the Bosnian War when Slobodan Milošević would be accused by hardliners of betrayal for eventually signing the Dayton peace treaty in 1995.

Following the annexation, the diehards were driven underground, covertly maintaining their ambition for military action in the name of the Serbian national cause. One such small but powerful secret group, which had been closely involved in the killing of the monarch in 1903, vowed to keep up the fight for the Serbian national cause. It was called Ujedinjenje ili Smrt, which translates as 'Union or Death', its members sworn to secrecy through the making of a blood-oath, its literature adorned with the skull-and-crossbones motif of Serbian freedom fighters. The group would play an important role in the run-up to the 1914 assassination and is better known by its shorthand name of *Crna Ruka*, or 'Black Hand'.

By the time Princip arrived in 1912, a new focus was opening up for Serb nationalism, a frontline to the south, against the old enemy that had been confronted in the nineteenth century, the Ottomans. The independent country of Serbia recognised in 1878 had been established in only a small portion of territory claimed by the Serbs. Across its southern border, in land still occupied by the Ottomans, lay what nationalists in Belgrade referred to as Old Serbia, an area with many of the oldest religious sites venerated by the Serbian Orthodox Church dating from the Middle Ages and a large local Serbian population. The drums of war were beating again in Belgrade, and this time gradualism would not restrain them. The Ottoman enemy was then a weakened and friendless imperial power, confronted not just by Serbia, but by several other Balkan nations willing to fight. Greece, Bulgaria and Montenegro all had territorial ambitions to win back what they regarded as their own territory, which had been occupied by the Ottomans for centuries. The four nations formed an alliance and in October 1912 the First Balkan War began. It took only a few months to drive the Turks out of Europe once and for all.

This was the febrile atmosphere that Princip encountered when he reached Belgrade for the first time. The slight seventeen-year-old, whose anger against the Austro-Hungarian occupiers of his homeland had been turned to fury by the suicide of the failed assassin Bogdan Žerajić, was able to watch close up as fellow south Slavs took action to push back an occupier. Clutching his bundle of books, he made a rushed attempt in June 1912 to pass the Fifth Grade exams at the First Male Gymnasium in Belgrade. He failed, his mind elsewhere, as other young Bosnians streamed through Belgrade to enlist in the Serbian army and paramilitary groups about to attack the Ottomans. After turning eighteen Princip tried to join them, but after taking part in basic training his application was turned down. Under cross-examination at his trial in 1914 he said he was rejected because he had fallen ill, but he was more candid when later interviewed in his cell by the psychiatrist.

'Wanted to go into the Balkan War, but was found too weak,' Dr Pappenheim recorded in his notes.

How it must have hurt the young dreamer to be told that he was not man enough for the fight. The would-be activist who, as a schoolboy in Sarajevo, had found his escape through books grew ever more brooding and withdrawn. 'Many who have spoken with him think he is a child,' wrote Dr Pappenheim, 'think that he was inspired by others, only because he cannot express himself sufficiently, is not generally gifted as a talker. Always a reader and always alone, not often engaging in debates.'

Princip spent much of the next two years milling around Belgrade living on the breadline, sleeping in dosshouses frequented by other young Bosnians who had migrated to Serbia, all of whom were resentful about the continuing occupation of their homeland. They would gather around Green Wreath Square, an open area of the city on the hillside leading up to the fortress, easy walking distance from the railway station, which was laid out along the bank of the Sava. The square took its name from the Green Wreath Hotel, but all around were other hostels, coffee houses and soup kitchens, modest establishments with similarly lyrical names, such as the Golden Sturgeon, the Acorn Wreath, Café America and the Theatre Café. The Sarajevo trial would hear from one witness who described the area as the sort of place where 'only lower-class people used to go'. Here a cheap meal could be had and ideas exchanged on how to earn money to pay for the next one. A few hundred yards below lay Belgrade's main harbour for the large barges plying the Sava and Danube, a place where piecemeal work as a stevedore was sometimes on offer. When times were particularly hard, young Bosnians such as Princip would present themselves at Belgrade's larger churches and monastic communities to beg for alms. Dedijer wrote that many of these young Bosnians were in effect vagrants willing to spend the night sleeping in a kennel.

The area was so thick with south-Slav immigrants from the Austro-Hungarian Empire that one of the main thoroughfares just down from the square was named Bosnia Street. Its flophouses were places where crowds would gather to hear Bosnian folk songs being performed and stanzas declaimed from epic poems learned in childhood back in the *zadrugas* of home. Most were Bosnian Serbs, but among them was a small number of Bosnian Croats and Bosnian Muslims, driven to Belgrade by the ongoing occupation of their homeland. Young men who fought as guerrillas in the Balkan Wars of 1912 and 1913 were frequent customers, for the price of a drink being willing to tell tall war stories to an audience of young Bosnians keen to hear how the Ottoman occupier had been driven out. Over their tiny cups of 'Bosnian coffee' and plates of *ćevapčići* and *burek*, the young men would listen closely, brooding and plotting about how freedom might one day be won for Bosnia. At a time when the Serbian government was still led by those who opposed confrontation with Austria–Hungary, the young men dreaming of liberating their homeland had to be ever on the lookout for spies. Care had to be taken not just against informers in the pay of Austria–Hungary, but also against others loyal to these moderate elements from within Serbia itself.

Throughout his time in Belgrade Princip was constantly on the move, staying at a number of modest addresses around Bosnia Street, where he was forced to share rooms with others as he worked on his studies. In spite of his failure at the Fifth Grade examination in June 1912 he still had ambitions to complete his secondary education. Surviving on modest stipends sent every so often by his brother Jovo, he would head back overland to Bosnia towards the end of each year when the money ran out and spent the winters of 1912 and 1913 back with his parents in Obljaj or at his brother's home in Hadžići, driving Jovo's wife mad because of the time he spent with his books rather than helping around the house.

By the summer of 1913 Princip was back in Belgrade and in a matter of a few months managed to pass the examinations for three school grades, the Fifth, Sixth and Seventh. At the Belgrade Historical Archives I found his school reports for this period and saw that his academic performance was now back to the high levels of his early schooling in Sarajevo, graded Very Good in several subjects. Interestingly, the 'weak boy' was ranked as Excellent at gymnastics. Hand-written notes on the report sheets indicated he passed special grade exams authorised by the Serbian Minister of Education, a procedure that appears to have been a standard requirement for foreign students from the neighbouring country of Bosnia. At his trial Austro-Hungarian prosecutors mocked the education system of Serbia, where three school years could be tested in such a short period of time. 'It would never happen in a serious education system such as ours,' they sneered. After another winter with his books back in Bosnia, Princip returned to Belgrade in March 1914 with plans to take the final secondary-school exams, the Eighth Grade, in the late summer of that year.

He would never take the exam. An opportunity arose in the early summer of 1914 for the young man, now nineteen years of age, to prove wrong those who had judged him too frail to make a freedom fighter. 'Wherever I went,' he later told Austro-Hungarian police investigators, 'people took me for a weakling, indeed, for a man who would be completely ruined by immoderate study of literature. And I pretended that I was a weak person, even though I was not.'

Of the original Green Wreath Square, little was left when I set about exploring the city. The initial artillery barrages of the First World War were launched against Belgrade by Austro-Hungarian forces from positions dug in just across the river at the end of July 1914, and many of the square's buildings were damaged. It was eventually redeveloped as a bus station, one that today retains a tatty, rundown air, a hangout for vagrants, drug addicts and prostitutes, the flophouses replaced by tattoo parlours, fast-food outlets and slot-machine arcades. I found its underpasses being used by twenty-first-century descendants of those Bosnian wanderers: Roma Gypsies scraping a living by selling cheap clothes, phone-chargers and other tat from unlicensed stalls. When I approached the bus terminal for the first time I found all the subway hall lined with Roma hawkers, their wares laid out on flattened cardboard boxes spread across the tiled floor. As I walked in, a shout went up and, as one, the traders scooped up their sandwich-board shops and made a run for it. Two policemen walked in just behind me and arrested one of the Roma who was too slow off the mark.

Just down the slope stood one of the few nineteenth-century buildings to survive the redevelopment, the original Golden Sturgeon café where Princip often went to eat. Today it is the Luo Wang Fa discount shop, where cold-eyed Chinese shop assistants follow customers down the aisles to make sure they do not shop-lift the cheap crockery, household goods and other items on the shelves. The plaster on the building's façade is dark and patchy with disrepair, but the original outline of the building remains intact, the windows still there on the roofline, opening into attic rooms where Bosnian vagrants would have been packed a century ago. I asked the shopkeepers inside if any of them had heard of Princip, but they shook their heads, looking over my shoulder to make sure my questions were not a ploy to distract them while they were being robbed.

On the graffiti-covered wall outside I found a plaque dating from the building's heyday as a busy café. It recorded that crowds gathered here in 1906 for the official founding of the *Jedinstvo* workers' singing society. I wondered if their performances had ever been listened to by Princip, the student who had read so keenly about socialist workers' rights. A few doors down stood a shop selling erotic lingerie. Walking up the slope from the busy four-lane highway that feeds the bus station took me to a much more upmarket part of Belgrade, the pedestrian street of Knez Mihailova, which is lined by elegant nineteenth-century buildings with façades that have not been allowed to fall into disrepair, a long run of expensive boutiques, restaurants and cafés crowded with people. It follows the ridgeline of the promontory, a thread connecting the old Turkish fortress of Belgrade with the modern city that came into existence through Serbia's rush for a new identity after winning independence.

The fortress that for so many centuries was such a strategic asset, commanding the flat plain that stretches north towards modern-day Hungary, sits today within the leafy confines of Kalemegdan Park, a large recreational space of lawns and tree-covered gravel walkways. Youngsters play tennis on courts chalked out below the old fortress walls, and the former barracks today house the National Military Museum, a file of redundant artillery pieces on permanent display outside, an eclectic collection born of Serbia's long martial history of clashes with the Ottomans, Austrians, Hungarians, Germans and, most recently, NATO. The battlements that used to have such key military value are crawled over by children licking ice-creams and tourists taking photos of the spot where the Sava and Danube Rivers merge serenely down below. On Friday nights in the summer the battlements throng with youngsters dancing to music arranged by Serbia's hippest DJs. With independence, a surge of Serbian national pride sought to erase all traces of foreign rule in what had for so long been an Ottoman settlement. Scores of mosques were deliberately demolished, yet within the precincts of the old castle

I saw a relic from an era that lasted four centuries – an ancient Turkish *turbe* or shrine, identical to others that I came across in Sarajevo.

Princip would often visit Kalemegdan with his compatriots, walking its tree-shaded footpaths and brooding over what might be done to strike back against the Austro-Hungarian occupiers of their homeland. But as I went in search of his trail, the park I wanted to find was elsewhere: a small triangle of grass lined with trees just a block down from Knez Mihailova. Only one photograph of Princip survives from his time in Belgrade, one taken on a bench in what is today a park named after Vojvoda Vuk, the title won by a Serbian freedom fighter, Vojin Popović, who died in the First World War. A hundred years ago it would have been a quiet place for three young Bosnian immigrants to pose for a photograph. It was taken just a few years after the family souvenir snapped in Sarajevo, but the Princip framed by the camera this time is a very different person. He sits on a bench, his face now lean, malnourished even, his top lip shaded by what appears to be a rather unconvincing moustache. A hat is cocked on the back of his head and his legs are crossed, the trousers grubby in a suit that seems a size or two too big for him. The clean shoes of the souvenir photograph have been replaced by footwear that is dusty and unpolished.

He sits at one end of the bench, still determined not to look into the camera, and at the other end is Trifko Grabež, his old schoolmate from the High Gymnasium in Sarajevo. They had studied in the same class together, as was shown by the school report I found in Sarajevo, and had both left at the same time. In between them sits a man called Djuro Šarac, another Bosnian Serb, a few years older, who had also come to Belgrade after dropping out of the Austro-Hungarian schooling system. He is more solid, his moustache bushy. He had been accepted into the military units fighting in the First Balkan War and had proved himself in combat. The two young men on either side of him have the air of acolytes looking up to a commanding figure of authority in their midst.

When I visited the park it was laid out around a statue of Vojvoda Vuk that would not have been there when the photograph was taken. The fighter died in 1916 and the full-size statue shows him in a muscular pose, rifle in one hand, cloak across his shoulders, his left arm raised as he points purposefully onwards in battle. It is a design rich in the iconography of the Serbian epic hero, with a skull and crossbones carved prominently into the large stone pedestal on which the statue sits.

As I continued to explore Princip's trail in Belgrade, I was struck by the many streams of nationalist influence that he would have encountered during his time scrabbling to survive as a student in the city. Serbian nationalists cherish an old icon dating from Byzantium, a Serbian cross with the Cyrillic letter S arranged four times symmetrically around it, a symbol that has come to stand for '*samo sloga Srbina spasava*' or 'only unity saves the Serbs'. Yet such unity was as much a chimera in Princip's day as in more recent times. With Serbia involved in combat against the Ottomans in the brief First Balkan War of 1912 and the even shorter Second Balkan War of 1913 against Bulgaria, the most obvious stream of political opinion was the one that emphasised the interests of Serbia, and Serbia alone. This was the first south–Slav nation to have won independence and, as a Bosnian Serb, Princip would have been drawn quite naturally towards it.

But what became clear from my research was that Princip was not predominantly committed to Serb nationalism. His greater goal was freeing all south Slavs, not just ethnic Serbs like himself. Princip supported what became known as the Yugoslav ideal of driving the Austro-Hungarians back not just from Bosnia, but also from the areas to the north where other south Slavs – the Croats and the Slovenes – were under the same occupation. His goal was liberation for all south Slavs. The Serbs might have made the initial break, but out of Yugoslav solidarity they must act as the catalyst to free their south-Slav brothers and sisters – the kernel around which a wider south-Slav nation would ultimately grow, a nation that might be called Yugoslavia. 'Yug' is the anglicisation of the local word for south, *jug*.

Early indications of Princip's wider commitment beyond pure Serb nationalism can be seen in a letter he wrote in 1912, which revealed the fault lines that had already developed within political opinion. It referred to how, as a supporter of south-Slav nationalism, he had been attacked while still at school in Sarajevo by those Serb students who were only interested in their own kind. He wrote of how, for voicing his wider south-Slav commitment, he was insulted 'with the worst expressions, objecting that we were not Serbs. This caused a deep breach and hatred between us.' Princip continued to associate with Bosnian Muslims and Bosnian Croats right up to the assassination of 1914; indeed, a key introduction was made in Belgrade, when the decision was taken to procure weapons, by a man called Djulaga Bukovac, one of the many Bosnian Muslim radicals then active in the city.

At his trial and during the police investigation Princip consistently said that, even though he was an ethnic Serb, his commitment was to freeing all south Slavs. 'I am a Yugoslav nationalist, aiming for the unification of all Yugoslavs, and I do not care what form of state, but it must be free from Austria,' he told the courtroom. 'The plan was to unite all south Slavs. It was understood that Serbia as the free part of the south Slavs had the moral duty to help in the unification, to be to the south Slavs as the Piedmont was to Italy.' When later asked about how south Slavs should regard the Habsburg Empire, he replied: 'In my opinion every

Serb, Croat and Slovene should be an enemy of Austria.' Later in his prison cell he clung to the same goal, sharing his thoughts with Dr Pappenheim. 'The ideal of the young people was the unity of the south-Slav peoples, Serbs, Croats and Slovenes, but not under Austria. In a kind of state, republic or something of that sort,' the doctor recorded in his notes.

Princip can be accused of being unrealistic, of being utopian, of not thinking through how the ideal of south-Slav unity might be realised, or how the rights of the large community of fellow south Slavs who had converted to Islam could be protected. But he cannot be accused of acting out of an interest in purely Serb nationalism. In the early years of the twentieth century he was not alone, for all over the Balkans – from Slovenia in the north, through Zagreb and Sarajevo, all the way south through Belgrade – there existed a significant body of opinion that all south Slavs should live as one after ridding themselves of the foreign occupier. With a hundred years of hindsight (not least the fighting of the 1990s that destroyed Yugoslavia), it is fair to say that the south Slav or Yugoslav ideal proved to be a failure. But Princip's commitment to it should not be ignored, and the mistake should not be made of saying that he was nothing but a Serb nationalist. The difference might appear arcane, but to my eye – as someone proud to come from the United Kingdom – it feels like the difference between being willing to fight for Britain and the reductionism of being a nationalist interested solely in one of its component parts, whether England, Wales, Scotland or Northern Ireland.

As I explored Belgrade, a city that commemorates its national heroes so proudly, it was clear that Princip's Yugoslav views represented something of a conundrum. I would often see walls daubed with nationalist graffiti that referred to key dates in Serbian history, from the Middle Ages to the 1990s. There was never any mention of Princip. Hawkers in Kalemegdan Park sold self-published books that promised the 'truth about Srebrenica', denying that any war crimes were ever committed by the Serbian side; and hagiographies of Bosnian Serb leaders such as Radovan Karadžić and Ratko Mladić, rightly regarded by most objective observers as war criminals. There were no books about Princip, his commitment to the Serbian cause not being pure enough to be worthy of recognition. He was the ethnic Serb who had had greater impact on world history than any other and yet, with the exception of the signs marking Gavrilo Princip Street, I saw no statues, no plaques and very little interest when I trawled the archives. When I went to the Serb National Archive the young receptionist barely looked up from the comic he was reading, while listening to the Rolling Stones playing through some speakers on his desk. 'We have nothing on Princip,' he said before going back to his comic. 'Maybe you should try the Yugoslav Archive.'

One sunny afternoon I took tea with Ljubodrag Dimić, a professor of history from Belgrade University, and asked him why Princip is not proudly commemorated within the Serbian pantheon. 'The thing you must remember is that the Mlada Bosna movement that Princip belonged to is not typical of other nationalist movements of the Balkans,' he said. 'It was not purely a Serbian model of nationalism, more a romantic, inclusive model along the lines of Germany or France – one that sought to create something that had not been there before, one that brought together, in the case of Germany, Germans of all faiths, Catholic or Protestant. Mlada Bosna supported what you might call a south-Slav myth, one that presented a new, inclusive model for life, a style of living, of music, of poetry that was different from the individual nationalist models of the Serbs or the Croats, say. It was mythical, and although it was clear Princip was a hero who gave his life for the future of Yugoslavia, as that myth became manipulated, so his story became manipulated. When the interest died for Yugoslavia, so did the interest in Princip.'

*

On one level the plot to assassinate Archduke Franz Ferdinand, the heir to the Austro-Hungarian Empire and second only in imperial rank to his uncle, Emperor Franz Joseph, was relatively straightforward. At a time when assassination was a common driver for political change across the Balkans, Princip and his associates from Mlada Bosna had discussed for some time how they might emulate the example of their hero, Bogdan Žerajić, by killing a senior figure from within the occupying power. Princip told Dr Pappenheim that in 1913 the figure they initially planned to go after was General Oskar Potiorek, the authoritarian colonial governor of Bosnia. But in the spring of 1914 a much more tempting target presented itself, when Princip was shown at one of Belgrade's downmarket cafés a newspaper cutting that had been sent anonymously to a Bosnian friend, Nedeljko Čabrinović.

The cutting announced that in late June Archduke Franz Ferdinand would be making an official visit to Bosnia in his formal capacity as inspector general of Austria–Hungary's armed forces. Čabrinović later described how he spotted Princip dancing a traditional Serbian dance at the Acorn Wreath café, before showing him the piece of newsprint. 'I attached no importance to that communication . . . I did not think it would play such a significant role in my life,' he said.

For Princip this was the opportunity he had been waiting for. He would lead a group of assassins back across the Drina in time to launch an attack on the Archduke during his official visit to Sarajevo. It would be his grand gesture – one that would strike back against the outsider in the name of all south Slavs under occupation and prove once and for all that he was no weakling. The young idealist hoped the killing would inspire a swell of south-Slav feeling that would one day drive out the occupier, although quite how this would eventually be achieved was not of much importance to him. Striking back at the occupier was what counted most. All the evidence showed that Princip was the driving force behind the subsequent plot, persuading Čabrinović to join him, along with his old schoolmate and the young man he was photographed with in the park, Trifko Grabež. Over the next weeks the three of them met repeatedly around Green Wreath Square to plot, sworn to secrecy and constantly vigilant against spies who might betray them either to the Austro-Hungarians or to a Serbian government anxious not to provoke its imperial neighbour.

To acquire weapons the penniless group of plotters trusted a Bosnian Muslim, Djulaga Bukovac, who had trained with the Serbian guerrillas fighting in the Balkan Wars, to make a discreet approach to a man called Milan Ciganović, another veteran and one who was known to be well connected within Serbian para-military groups. After some discussions, most of which took place in and around Green Wreath Square, Ciganović said he was willing to provide some grenades, but Princip said this would not be enough. Grenades were not the most reliable tool for an assassination because of the variable time-lapse between priming the weapon and its detonation. He demanded pistols as well.

After referring back to his own contacts, Ciganović agreed to also supply pistols and ammunition, leading the would-be assassins on several occasions to an unpopulated forest called Topčider, just beyond the centre of Belgrade, which was then relatively small. There he showed the young Bosnians how to use the grenades: small metal blocks about the same size and shape as a flattened bottle, with a protective cover on the firing cap. Once the cover was unscrewed, the user would break the cap by striking it against something solid, like a rock, to start the detonation process. The user then had a few seconds to throw the grenade before it blew up. The pistols were 9mm Browning semi-automatics, originally a Belgian design and a weapon that was common among soldiers fighting for the Serbian army in the Balkan Wars. The would-be assassins took it in turns to fire at targets nailed to tree trunks in Topčider. Princip showed himself to be the best marksman.

The area where they trained has since been swallowed by the spread of Belgrade, although a small section is retained today as Topčider Park. It takes about an hour to reach the park on foot from the city centre, and as I walked there and explored its shaded footpaths, now the domain of joggers and dog-walkers, I tried to picture the scene in the early summer of 1914 when shots from the young men boomed through these same trees. As I had found out, Princip was motivated by the dream of forging Yugoslavia, a country where all south Slavs could live freely as one, and I smiled wryly at what I found in the park. Tito, the dictator who used communism to keep Yugoslavia together in the decades after the Second World War, lies buried there under a slab of white marble in a mausoleum that is open to visitors. He died in 1980 and, with him, the dream of Yugoslavia. When I joined a tour party processing past his tomb I noticed that an old map of Titoist Yugoslavia had been defaced. Sarajevo had been scratched out.

Ciganović did not just provide the three-man assassination team with weapons. He also gave them the means to smuggle themselves back across the Drina into Bosnia, handing them an envelope containing a note to be given to one of his army friends in the town of Šabac in western Serbia, close to the border with Bosnia.

The role played by Ciganović in helping Princip and his comrades complicates an otherwise straightforward plot. Ciganović was a Freemason, a discovery that led the Austro-Hungarian authorities at the trial following the assassination to suggest that the plot to kill the Archduke might have been hatched by the Freemasons, a theory that has since been discounted. But he was also an associate of the Black Hand, the secretive, ultra-nationalist Serbian group dating back to the start of the twentieth century that had been responsible for the regicide of 1903. The role of the Black Hand in the assassination of 1914 has been the subject of weighty analysis by academics and historians, although very little is undisputed. It is accepted that the weapons provided to the assassins came from the Black Hand with the blessing of its overall leader, Dragutin Dimitrijević, a powerful *éminence grise* in the Serbian security apparatus in the years running up to the First World War. Better known by his pseudonym, Apis, he was a Serb nationalist hardliner who held senior positions within Serbian military intelligence, an organisation that was used to running agents in and out of Bosnia through a network of couriers and smugglers. It was this network that was made available to Princip and his two colleagues.

It does not follow that the Serbian government knew about the assassination, still less approved of it. The hardline stance of the Black Hand group was not shared by a government that had shown from as far back as the annexation crisis of 1908 a reluctance to antagonise Austria–Hungary. Indeed, these disagreements would ultimately lead in 1917 to Apis being tried for treason by his own government, a crime that carried a death sentence. During the hearing he made extravagant and unproven claims about the central role of the Black Hand in the 1914 assassination, claiming his group had been responsible for the entire operation. While some historians have accepted Apis's claim, I accept Dedijer's analysis that it was greatly exaggerated by a man seeking to save himself from execution. It did not work. He died at the hands of a firing squad on 26 June 1917.

Decades later, further claims were made that Princip himself was a member of the Black Hand, although there is no evidence to substantiate this. The claims were recorded in the 1930s by the Italian historian Luigi Albertini, who dedicated the last years of his life to explaining the origins of the First World War, and have been used by those historians who conclude that the assassination was entirely the work of the Black Hand.

In my view, the group played a secondary, opportunist role in the assassination of 1914, after being approached through Ciganović by the three young Bosnians who had concocted the plan. Princip's commitment to freeing all south Slavs meant that he did not have the same ultimate objectives as the Black Hand, which was more exclusively committed to Serbian interests. At his trial he gave a very pragmatic answer when asked if everyone involved in the assassination shared the same aims as himself. 'Not exactly like myself,' he said. 'It was not necessary for all to be of the same opinions in the carrying out of his own ideas, nor was it necessary that every one employ the same means.'

It emerged after the First World War that word of a possible assassination attempt against the Archduke had leaked out in June and reached the Serbian government. It reacted immediately, sending orders for border guards to be on the lookout for young Bosnians trying to smuggle themselves into Bosnia. But by the time the order was given, it was too late. Princip, Grabež and Čabrinović were already on their way to Sarajevo, and with them they had all the gear they needed for their grand gesture: five Browning pistols, six grenades and a plan to take cyanide after the deed was done, so that they would not be taken alive.

They left Belgrade at the end of May 1914 on a river boat that took them all the way to Šabac, back then a busy port on the Sava River. They overnighted at one of the town's cheap hotels, paid for from a cash float of 150 crowns provided by Ciganović, stuffing their assassins' kit in a stove for safekeeping. The next day they were helped by Ciganović's contacts to take a train further west to the spa town of Koviljača, which lies on the Serbian side of the Drina River frontier. Crossing the border was the most risky part of the journey and tensions were rising among the group. While in Koviljača they made a point of sending postcards to friends and relatives as a device to conceal their true intentions, with Princip writing a message to a cousin back in Belgrade that suggested he was on the way to a monastery to study. The quiet young man who had inscribed one of his books with the quote about the importance of keeping secrets grew increasingly tetchy with Čabrinović, whom he accused of risking the mission by talking loosely and bragging about becoming a hero in the postcards he sent.

Tensions got so bad among the three young men that Princip insisted the party split up. He would continue with Grabež, but Čabrinović was told to go on alone. They did not trust him with any of the grenades, giving him just one Browning pistol and telling him to make his own way over to Tuzla on the other side of the frontier, where they agreed a rendezvous. Shortly after they split up Čabrinović got into a panic and abandoned his gun, crossing into Bosnia without incident at the main border post in Zvornik and heading to Tuzla.

Meanwhile, Princip and Grabež double backed on their trail, heading a few miles north towards a reach of the Drina River well known to smugglers. It was a stretch where the river meanders shallow and slow through a series of eyots named after the largest island, Isakovica. On one of the islands was an illegal drinking den, a shebeen where Serbian-made plum brandy was sold cheaply to Bosnian peasants, who could reach the spot across a shallow ford. At the bar they met the first in a series of couriers, who led the pair splashing across the ford into Bosnia and on foot all the way to Tuzla, with the grenades strapped to their bodies, the four remaining pistols heavy in their pockets as they struggled through muddy fields and over forested hills.

Just as for the survivors from Srebrenica who would cross this same terrain on foot eight decades later, the going was hard for Princip and Grabež. At one point they asked for their load to be carried on a peasant's cart, all the time warning their helpers that they must do everything possible to avoid the Austro-Hungarian border guards and gendarmes. The trial following the assassination heard that although Princip was the smaller of the two men, he was the most threatening, ordering all the couriers they had contact with to keep silent and warning them that they would be hunted down and killed if their mission was revealed. 'If you betray it, you and your family will be destroyed,' one of his guides remembered being told by Princip.

So filthy were they from their hike that, as they finally approached Tuzla, the pair stopped to wash the mud off their clothes in a stream, worried that it would raise suspicion once they entered the town. In 1995 I watched women driven out of Srebrenica also wash their filthy clothes in rivers near Tuzla. By the time Princip reached the city his trousers were so tatty that he bought himself a new pair, and he was soon recognised by locals who knew him from his time studying briefly in the town in 1910. They remarked that the timid, bookish boy had grown into a rather fearsome-looking young man with long hair and a very determined manner. After meeting up again with Čabrinović, the group decided it was too dangerous to carry the weapons any further, leaving them with a local man they trusted. He was told that the person who would come to collect the cache would identify himself in code by osten-tatiously showing him a packet of Stefanija cigarettes. The three then set off for Sarajevo by train, sitting in the same carriage, but apart from each other so as not to arouse suspicion. Čabrinović, whose garrulousness had so worried his co-conspirators, started a conversation with a policeman who happened to be travelling on the same train and knew his father back in Sarajevo. The subject of the imminent imperial tour of Bosnia came up, and when

Čabrinović asked when the Archduke was due to visit Sarajevo, the policeman told him the exact date: Sunday 28 June.

River boats no longer steam all the way to Šabac, so when I left Belgrade I did so on foot, taking a tram to the city's main railway station just down the slope from the old Green Wreath Square and picking my way through a hole in the fence and across the train tracks until I reached the bank of the Sava River. From there I took my leave of the city along what began as a well-marked footpath, my hazel walking stick from Obljaj at my side and my rucksack snug on my back. For company I had the thought of Princip's troika heading nervously upriver almost a hundred years before me.

The river was bridged by a number of impressive structures, and one by one I passed under them all: a box-girder railway bridge that was already in use back in 1914, followed by more modern concrete structures busy with road traffic. Down below on the river bank the scene was summery and serene, with old men shoaling in groups next to fishing rods for a long, hot, gossipy day of angling, while a bit further along a stretch of river bank had been landscaped into a lido where waiters were busy brushing the dew off tables and arranging plastic chairs. Out on the water a few energetic rowers sculled past me, while down on the beach early-bird sun worshippers doused themselves with tanning oil and took up starfish positions on towels spread out on the pale river-bank gravel. I bought an ice-cream and joked idly with a man running a rent-a-bike office about taking a bicycle all the way to Šabac.

As I walked, the loom of the city eased steadily, the buildings growing ever sparser until I found myself in open country, the noise of traffic diminishing so much that my journey's soundtrack was nothing but the tip-tap of my walking stick and the breeze through the reeds on a river bank growing ever more wild and unkempt. After five or six miles I passed a shantytown of Roma Gypsies, tucked away – as so often in eastern Europe – on land of little use to anyone else. The footpath vanished and I found myself walking along roads used by weekenders to access modest wooden houses built on floats in the river, anchored next to the river bank. Most were unoccupied, but from time to time I would see a car parked beside one, children splashing around in the shallows while the parents pootled about cleaning barbecues, fiddling with windowboxes and enjoying their riverine retreat.

After an hour or so a truck stopped and the driver offered me a lift. 'My name is Alexandre Dumas,' he said proudly after I jumped up next to him. 'My dad's family came from France and they gave me the name of the great writer. Would you like some watermelon?' It was late July and the fruit was in season, the back of the truck heavily laden with a cargo collected from a farm out on the flat plain that runs north from Belgrade. He handed me an old but very sharp knife, and would take no payment as I cut myself a generous segment from one of the fruit, the flesh perfectly firm and sweet, not yet granular from over-ripeness. He dropped me after only a few miles, but I was happy to be walking once more, biting into the fruit and leaning forward extravagantly so that the juice would not drench my clothes.

The hitch-hiking was bitty that day, with no lift longer than a few miles, but by late afternoon I made it into Šabac. My last lift came from a second-hand car dealer called Stefan Petrović, who had a very cheery attitude and drank lager from a can as he drove, singing along to the car stereo. When I mentioned Princip there was no recognition, even when I explained how his actions had led to the First World War, but he still had much to say about soldiering. 'I am only twenty-six, so I was too young for the war in the 1990s,' he said with uncamouflaged regret. 'I would have fought. There's good money in being a soldier. I only earn 180 euros a month, but in the French Foreign Legion you can earn five or six times that. I went all the way to France last year with some friends to try to join, but they failed me on the psychiatric tests.'

He dropped me in the centre of Šabac, spinning the wheels of his car as he shot off waving his beer can, and I checked into a hotel on the town's main drag. It happened to be called the Green Wreath, the same as the hotel after which the square in Belgrade where Princip plotted the assassination was named. With a wide stone staircase spiralling up three floors, it must once have been a rather smart establishment, built in the proud, early days of Serbian statehood when Šabac was a significant transport hub. In 2012 it was a dump, the receptionist sleeping on a sagging sofa behind the counter and insisting on cash up front. Outside on the pedestrian thoroughfare I found various signs commemorating the town's luminaries, such as a local nineteenth-century nobleman honoured as Lord Jevrem. The street named after him had a blue plaque recording that he was a modernist who 'brought to Šabac many things which were seen for the first time in Serbia: a piano, a bed, a window glass, a carriage, a pharmacy'. There were no plaques for Princip and his fellow conspirators.

Before sunset I walked down to the Sava River. It runs wide and deep at Šabac, but there were none of the barges and steamboats that used to carry people and cargo here at the start of the twentieth century. Roads had taken all the traffic, so where the boats used to tie up there was now a lido overlooked by a lifeguard's watchtower, the gravel rucked after a busy summer day of sun, and a boom demarcating where it was safe for swimming. A father on a mountain bike led home a daughter on a bicycle with stabilisers as I walked back in the twilight, the tops of the chimneys tufty with that most central European of sights, thatched stork nests. When I got back to my hotel room I braced a chair up against the door handle, as the lock did not work properly, and turned on the television, on which a rerun of *Mućke*, the wheeler-dealer English sitcom *Only Fools and Horses*, was being broadcast.

Rain the following morning made hitch-hiking difficult. Drivers don't like to stop for travellers with soaking-wet bags, so I had to walk about five miles before my first lift. It dropped me close to the Drina River, where I went to explore the crossing point used by Princip and Trifko Grabež. In the National Archive in Sarajevo I had come across the original map put together by Austro-Hungarian police investigators following the assassination. Dated 27 July 1914 and hand-drawn on a piece of waxed paper, it charted in royal-blue ink the meandering course of the Drina River, each branch of the stream meticulously marked where it split to create a maze of islands around Isakovica. The path of the assassins was shown by a red dotted line that led from Serbia into Bosnia, heading over the hills in the direction of Tuzla.

I found the river still runs shallow around Isakovica, although the old ford has been replaced by a ferry manned by border guards – a small and rarely used frontier crossing point between modern-day Serbia and Bosnia. The Serbian side was deserted, but over on the Bosnian side I found a bar where I bought a coffee. The only other customer, a drunk nursing a beer, sat down at my table uninvited and began to blather. 'Buy me a drink and I will tell you everything about my old friend Princip,' he said. 'I knew him really well, we were at school together.'

Storm clouds threatened but never broke as I hitch-hiked through the valleys of eastern Bosnia back towards Sarajevo, spending long hours walking, and waiting next to the road. I thought about the way anger from within this small mountainous part of Europe had impacted repeatedly on world history: the murderous fury felt by Princip towards the occupiers, and the resentment about past injustices that enabled nationalist extremism to flourish in the 1990s, along with the flowering of early jihadism.

My last lift dropped me at the edge of Sarajevo on a bypass high on a hillside. The modern road was constructed along the tunnelled route of the old mountain railway built by Hans Fronius's grandfather and gave a wonderful view of the city down below. As I walked down the slope, hungry and tired from the road, my mind was filled with the image of Princip reaching here in early June 1914 determined to commit what he regarded as a 'noble act'.

CHAPTER 11

An Assassin's Luck

König Amenhotepp XXIII
Pharao v. Aegypten

Archduke Franz Ferdinand posing as a pharaoh in 1896 while
convalescing in Egypt from tuberculosis, the same disease
that would eventually kill his killer

The last moments of Archduke Franz Ferdinand as his car
turns off the Appel Quay, his killer – not visible – waiting among
the crowd in front of the Moritz Schiller corner café

After several days of summer storms, Sunday 28 June 1914 dawned clear in Sarajevo. It was the day of Archduke Franz Ferdinand's official visit to the city. He had arrived in Bosnia by train three days earlier with his wife, Sophie, Duchess of Hohenberg, the royal party staying in the smartest accommodation then available in Austria–Hungary's newest colony, the Hotel Bosna, situated six miles west of the city in the village of Ilidža. Built as a spa resort by Austro-Hungarian colonists close by the source of the Bosna River, the hotel had been lavishly refurbished for the imperial visit, the four-storey façade bedecked with garlands and a royal suite of rooms specially constructed, complete with a private chapel where the couple could take mass.

As inspector general of imperial forces, the Archduke attended two days of military manoeuvres by soldiers from the 15th and 16th Army Corps in the plains and foothills around Mount Igman, a programme that culminated with an official dinner on the Saturday night at the hotel. The Sarajevo garrison orchestra played 'The Blue Danube' waltz by Johann Strauss while guests enjoyed a menu including *blanquettes de truites à la gelée*, *pièce de boeuf* and *crème aux ananas en surprise,* accompanied by wines shipped in from vineyards across the empire. The royal party was due to leave by train late on Sunday evening, so the ceremonial visit to the city was the only showcase opportunity that the people of Sarajevo would have to see the heir of an empire that had ruled Bosnia since 1878. As it was a weekend, crowds were expected along a ceremonial route widely advertised in advance – the streets swept, the citizenry encouraged to turn out in large numbers and to hang imperial flags prominently from windows and balconies. Local police and militia had received specific orders not to picket the route, so that the local population would have the best possible chance to see the man expected to rule as Emperor one day.

It is hard to imagine a more robust symbol of Habsburg pomp than Archduke Franz Ferdinand. Fifty years of age at the time of the tour of Bosnia, solid of build and with a bushy, upturned moustache groomed in the style of a hussar, he was known for his short temper, ardent Catholicism and hatred of Hungarians – a people he regarded as parvenu upstarts within the dual monarchy of Austria–Hungary. As a nephew of Emperor Franz Joseph, he had been brought up without any expectation of ever succeeding to the crown, launched instead on a career of military service within the imperial army, which began when he was still at school. He was only twelve when first commissioned as a lieutenant in the infantry and, as a senior member of the Habsburg dynasty, he rose quickly through the officer corps, fast-track promoted through his teens and early twenties. Photographs of him as a young man show him mostly in uniform, taking a salute on horseback, sitting in the officers' mess alongside other similarly moustachioed figures, larking about in sports kit, posing with a riding crop in his hand; and all the time his uniform was accumulating more and more insignia of rank.

When not away on army duty, he had enough inherited wealth as one of Europe's richest men to indulge his passion for hunting at the many castles and estates he owned across the empire. In one day's hunt alone he shot 2,140 game birds and animals, and he was said to be such a marksman that he could hit a coin tossed into the air. A bout of tuberculosis (the disease that would kill Gavrilo Princip) led Franz Ferdinand to travel to warmer climates to recuperate, with one of his trips taking him to Egypt. Haughty though this man undoubtedly was, he also had a sense of humour, posing for a photograph inside a stylised pharaoh's coffin, his fleshy, bewhiskered European face peeking out from an otherwise Middle Eastern framing.

His life had changed dramatically with the murky events of 1889 when the Emperor's son, Crown Prince Rudolf, died in a suicide pact with his mistress at the Mayerling hunting lodge near Vienna. Within a short time Archduke Franz Ferdinand found himself established as heir apparent, groomed to take over from the elderly uncle who had sat on the throne since 1848. Fiercely loyal to the empire, Franz Ferdinand was still enough of his own man to challenge convention on occasion, not least when he fell in love with Countess Sophie Chotek von Chotkowa und Wognin. For centuries marriage had been employed by the Habsburgs as a device to ensure the survival of the dynasty – a web of rules and traditions that demanded royalty marry royalty. As a countess, Sophie was regarded as unsuitable, not high enough in rank to marry a personage expected one day to be Emperor. Ministers met and chamberlains tutted, Franz Ferdinand all the time being put under enormous pressure to break off the relationship and make a union with a more acceptable candidate, a princess or an archduchess. Obstinately he refused and a compromise was reached in 1900 when, in front of the Emperor and an assembly of imperial archdukes and other officials, he swore a solemn oath renouncing any claim to the throne or royal privilege by Sophie and their children. The date on which he took the oath was 28 June.

At court in Vienna, the oath meant Sophie, forty-six at the time of the Sarajevo visit, could not take her place next to her husband at ceremonial events, obliged to wait in line behind archduchesses and others more favoured by protocol. The

Archduke appealed to his uncle for the rules to be eased, but his reactionary relation refused. The decision for Sophie to join Franz Ferdinand in Bosnia was made because it was a rare opportunity, so far from the imperial capital, for her to play a fuller, more prominent role in public. The photographs, taken as the couple took the short trip from the Hotel Bosna by train and limousine into Sarajevo on the anniversary of the oath, show her at her husband's side, smiling warmly under a wide-brimmed hat, wearing a flowing white dress, a parasol raised against the Balkan sun. Next to her the Archduke wears the ceremonial uniform of a three-star general in the Austrian cavalry, his corpulent frame crammed stiffly into a high-collared tunic of bright-blue cloth heavy with gold braid, buttons and medals; a sword hanging from a band straining around his waist; white gloves, spurred boots and black trousers trimmed with red. On his head he wore a cocked military hat or *stulphut* with a bushy cockade of vulture feathers, which were dyed pale green and so delicate they moved in the breeze.

At the exact moment these photographs were being taken, Princip's group of assassins was taking up position in the centre of Sarajevo, aware of another anniversary that happened to fall on that day. More than half a millennium earlier, in 1389, the medieval Serbian nation suffered a traumatic defeat at the hands of the advancing Ottoman army at the battle of Kosovo. It took place on 28 June, a day kept holy in the Serbian Orthodox Church as the feast day of St Vitus. For centuries St Vitus's Day has been enshrined in Serbian mythology as signifying the end of independence and the beginning of foreign occupation – a day of such importance that early on the morning of the Archduke's visit an annual remembrance service had been held at Sarajevo's Orthodox church for the Serbian patriots who had fallen at the battle of Kosovo.

The assassination team had grown, after Princip, Grabež and

Čabrinović arrived overland in Sarajevo in the first week of June. Although he was so careful about secrecy, Princip had written before leaving Belgrade to his old Mlada Bosna confidant and former room-mate in Sarajevo, Danilo Ilić, to inform him of his assassination plans. With more weapons at his disposal than could be used by three attackers, Princip asked for extra manpower. At the trial he said he wrote 'in a sort of allegorical form', but the meaning was clear enough to a friend with whom he had discussed many times the inspirational example of Bogdan Žerajić, the young Bosnian would-be assassin who had shot himself in Sarajevo four years earlier. Ilić recruited three more young men to take part in the assassination: Mehmed Mehmedbašić, a Bosnian Muslim carpenter in his mid-twenties; Cvetko Popović, eighteen; and Vaso Čubrilović, seventeen – the last two both Bosnian Serb students.

Some historians have dismissed Mehmedbašić's role as a deliberate ploy to camouflage what was exclusively a Serbian plot, but this ignores all the evidence from Princip and others that their plan was motivated by the Yugoslav ideal of striking back at the occupier in the name of all south Slavs, a dream shared by many Bosnian Muslim and Bosnian Croat activists. The older man had handled weapons before and knew how to use a grenade, but the two youngsters had no experience at all, so they were both given basic training once Ilić had travelled by train to Tuzla and collected the weapons cache, carefully following instructions to identify himself through the pre-arranged signal of the Stefanija cigarette packet.

Ilić stored the weapons in a bag kept under his bed at his mother's house on Oprkanj Street, taking them out surreptitiously for training purposes. On a number of days in late June the narrow Bembaša gorge of the Miljacka River, upstream from the old city centre of Sarajevo, echoed to the sound of gunfire as the new recruits were shown how to shoot. Ilić would himself be unarmed on the day of the attack, roaming among the crowds gathered for the imperial visit, but he was the one who oversaw the distribution of weapons to the six would-be attackers: Mehmedbašić and Čabrinović were each issued with a grenade, while he made sure that Princip, Grabež, Popović and Čubrilović all had a Browning pistol and a grenade. The plan to not be taken alive meant that cyanide was procured, probably from a local pharmacy, although none of the team members knew how much was needed to make up a fatal dose.

As the day for the Archduke's visit approached, Princip grew increasingly anxious. He sought the company of his books and would later tell the Austrian psychiatrist, Dr Pappenheim, how his sleep was disrupted. 'Read much in Sarajevo. In Sarajevo used to dream every night he was a political murderer, struggling with the gendarmes and the police,' the doctor recorded in his notes. Princip paid one last visit to his brother, Jovo, in Hadžići, but gave no clues about what might be about to happen, pretending that all was still on course with his academic career and lying to his brother that he had passed the Eighth Grade exams in Belgrade. Shortly before the attack Princip made a final pilgrimage to the grave of Žerajić, while various witnesses reported that on the eve of the assassination, as the Archduke's party enjoyed the grand dinner at the Hotel Bosna, the normally sober, teetotal Princip had a drink of red wine.

The Appel Quay, the wide riverside boulevard in the centre of Sarajevo constructed by the Austro-Hungarians shortly after they occupied Bosnia, had been chosen by the plotters as the site for the assassination. Josip Stadler, the Catholic Archbishop of Sarajevo, would later say that the boulevard on that fateful Sunday had become a 'regular avenue of assassins'. The crowds of onlookers were expected to be thickest here, providing good cover for the six attackers, and the Archduke's party was due to process slowly along the boulevard – which was lined by buildings on one side and open to the river on the other – pausing at various official locations, such as the main post office and a military guardhouse, before arriving for a formal reception at the large, newly built town hall at the far, eastern end of the thoroughfare. The artist Hans Fronius was a schoolboy aged eleven at the time, but as an adult he could still remember the scene as the crowd's excitement surged, imperial flags fluttered, cries of 'Long Live the Archduke' rang out and puffs of smoke emerged from cannons firing salutes in the old Ottoman fortresses overlooking Sarajevo city centre.

With military precision the convoy of cars carrying the royal party left the barracks next to Sarajevo's main railway station at 10 a.m. sharp. It drove the short distance down to the Miljacka before heading slowly along the Appel Quay, the ripple of applause and cheers through the crowd on both sides of the road warning the attackers of their target's imminent arrival. Mehmedbašić was the first of the assassination team to be passed by the Archduke's car, but he did nothing, later saying that a gendarme appeared close by him in the crowd. He said he felt he would be spotted if he tried to take out his grenade. No such restrictions hindered Čabrinović, who was next along the 'avenue of assassins', standing on the river side of the boulevard a few hundred yards further up, opposite a girls' school. As the vehicles approached he snapped the cap off his grenade and threw it at the third car in the convoy, an open-topped Gräf & Stift limousine carrying the Archduke and his wife, sitting next to each other on its bench seat upholstered with black leather. Although the grenade was well aimed, striking the folded canopy at the back of the car a few inches behind Franz Ferdinand, the timing was out. It fell harmlessly to the ground, giving the royal car enough time to drive clear, and only exploded under the next vehicle in the convoy, badly damaging its bodywork and injuring its occupants. Witnesses reported that as the grenade flew towards him, Franz Ferdinand raised his arm in reflex. More dramatic fictionalised accounts would later claim that he bravely caught the grenade and tossed it aside.

All along the route the sound of the blast was clearly audible, with many in the crowd unsure if the explosion was simply a part of the ceremonial salute, as Čabrinović jumped down the masonry wall into the Miljacka River ten feet below the level of the pavement and ran splashing through the shallows, pursued by gendarmes. Before he was grabbed he had time to gulp down his cyanide, but it failed to kill him, instead making him foam at the mouth and retch, giving his pursuers the opportunity to arrest him. Within a matter of minutes he was being bundled off to Sarajevo central police station, just as the wounded from the damaged vehicle were being tended. The scene was later captured by Fronius in a charcoal drawing that shows his father, the state doctor, standing in a landau carriage as it clatters along the Appel Quay carting some of the injured off to hospital.

The four remaining members of the assassination squad were at their pre-arranged positions among the crowd further up the route along the Appel Quay. They knew the blast had been caused by a grenade but, before they worked out that their target had been missed, the Archduke had driven safely past and had reached the steps of the town hall, where he was received by a delegation of city officials not yet fully in the picture about what had happened. The Mayor's speech of welcome was cut short by the Archduke, who interrupted him sharply. 'Mr Mayor, what is the good of your speeches?' he boomed. 'I come to Sarajevo on a friendly visit and someone throws a bomb at me. This is outrageous.' Sophie was seen to lean towards her husband and whisper a few placatory words, at which he calmed down and allowed the formal proceedings to continue. The Mayor falteringly completed his words of welcome, allowing the Archduke to give his formal reply. Franz Ferdinand spoke from notes that had to be collected from his chamberlain, who had been travelling in the car damaged by the grenade. Dedijer recorded that the Archduke frowned as he was handed the speech written on a piece of paper now marked with fresh blood. He pressed on, concluding his remarks with two lines in Serbo-Croatian that he had rehearsed specially for the visit: 'Please convey to the citizens of the beautiful capital city of Sarajevo my cordial greetings and assurances of my enduring grace and benevolence.'

The official party then disappeared up the stairs into the town hall, displaying what with hindsight appears to be remarkably careless sangfroid. In our modern age any leader whose life had just been jeopardised would be rushed away to safety, kept out of view until any remaining threat had passed. But assassination attempts were a routine enough fact of life for Europe's monarchs and leaders at the start of the twentieth century, not least in Sarajevo, where Emperor Franz Joseph's state visit of 1910 had been marked by a failed bid at assassination. 'Today we shall get a few more little bullets,' the Archduke said half-jokingly to his entourage, as various options were discussed about how to proceed, with nobody wanting to react in a way that could be perceived as panic. Sophie was led away to a formal cultural presentation by Bosnian Muslim women, and the Archduke kept to the official programme, shaking the hands of the various colonial and local delegates who had been assembled.

But as the party prepared to leave, one important change was made to the schedule. The royal couple had been due to drive a short distance back along the Appel Quay and then turn right into Franz Joseph Street to make a tour of the old city, before visiting a new museum. Among the Archduke's official party the decision was taken to skip the city tour. Instead the convoy of limousines would continue all the way back along the Appel Quay and head to the main state hospital, so that the wounded from the morning's grenade blast could be visited by the Archduke. All of those from the Archduke's inner circle were agreed, although – as would become clear at the subsequent police investigation – nobody told the drivers.

The failure of the grenade blast to kill the Archduke appears to have broken the spirit of three of the remaining four armed conspirators still milling around the crowd that stretched along the Appel Quay. Grabež, Popović and Čubrilović had all sworn they would do everything possible to kill the Archduke, but they took no further part. Princip was the only one not to be totally disheartened, instead making his way to the corner where Franz Joseph Street begins at the Appel Quay, opposite the Latin Bridge. The advertised schedule said the Archduke was due to turn from the Appel Quay onto Franz Joseph Street, so perhaps here he would still have a chance to strike.

A prominent Austro-Hungarian colonial building then stood at the corner, the ground floor occupied by the Moritz Schiller café and delicatessen, adorned with signs and window stencils advertising wine, rum, tea, cigars and local culinary specialities on sale within. The German wording of its signs had made it a regular target for student activists from Mlada Bosna, who would deface signage they regarded as a symbol of occupation. On the day of the Archduke's visit a huge cutout, twelve feet high, of a champagne-style bottle from the Hungarian winemaker Törley was attached to the façade of the café right on the corner. The shop was open for business that day, leading to fanciful accounts of Princip going inside to eat a last sandwich and take a last cup of coffee. They were a complete fiction, as the young man simply joined the crowd lining the pavement and waited.

He did not have to wait long, for at 10.45 a.m., roughly half an hour after arriving at the town hall, the official party was already making ready to leave. The Archduke took his place once more in the rear seat of the Gräf & Stift limousine on the left-hand side, his wife next to him on the right with General Oskar Potiorek, the colonial governor of Bosnia, in a jump-seat in front of him. The owner of the car, Count Franz Harrach, who had been one of the passengers sitting inside the car on the way to the town hall, gallantly took up a new position, this time standing on the running board next to the Archduke on the left-hand side – the one that would now be facing the river as they drove back along the Appel Quay. The grenade had been thrown from this side, so the count thought he might be able to use his body to shield the Archduke from any repeat attack.

Moments later the most astonishing photograph was taken of the royal party in the limousine. It captures the glare of a clear summer's day in Sarajevo, a skyline of Ottoman domes and a minaret, the sun glinting off the peak of the driver's cap, the black-eagle standard of the Archduke hanging limply next to the windscreen as the car drives slowly on its way. The crowd is thin on the riverside pavement, where a man raises his hat in salute and a child in a traditional Bosnian fez looks on in wonder. The crowd on the other side of the road is much thicker, cheering shoulder-to-shoulder, while above their heads it is possible to make out the shiny foil cap of the huge promotional bottle outside the Moritz Schiller café. Some of the onlookers are sheltering from the sun in the shade of a small tree, a woman in a white dress and summer hat standing closest to the kerb. She would have been within a few feet of Princip. The photograph was taken at the exact moment when the car began to turn right, the front wheels no longer straight, but creeping round so that the car could navigate the corner.

The driver's decision to turn into Franz Joseph Street and not continue down the Appel Quay, as had been decided back at the town hall, was a stroke of assassin's luck for Princip. When General Potiorek spotted what was happening he shouted at the driver, ordering him immediately to stop and reverse back out onto the Appel Quay. Instead of his target speeding past, Princip saw the Archduke slow right in front of him only a few feet away – the gallant count, so willing to protect the life of his liege, on the running board on the other side of the car. For the instant it took the driver to find reverse, the Archduke was a sitting duck. Princip took the Browning pistol in his hand, stepped forward from among the crowd on the pavement next to the entrance of the café and fired past Sophie, who was sitting on the side closest to him. His luck held, as the first shot he aimed at the Archduke hit home. He fired for a second time, hoping this time to hit the colonial governor, but in the melee his arm was knocked and the bullet passed through the side of the car and struck Sophie. Before he could fire for a third time, hands from the crowd knocked the weapon from his grasp and he was pushed to the ground, blows raining down on him, his hands scrabbling for the cyanide, which he stuffed into his mouth – the crowd jostling between those wanting to beat the attacker and others trying to defend him.

On board the car it was Count Harrach who first appreciated the seriousness of the situation. There were no marks immediately visible on the Archduke, as the first bullet had hit him on the high collar of his tunic where the uniform's gilt trim was thickest, leaving a barely perceptible puncture. But the bullet had then ploughed into the Archduke's neck, cutting his jugular vein. The fact that he was rapidly bleeding to death was concealed under his uniform. When blood began to trickle from the Archduke's mouth, the count took out his handkerchief to dab it away. Sophie had been hit in the abdomen, remaining conscious long enough for Count Harrach to hear her last words. 'For God's sake! What has happened to you?' she said to her husband, before slumping into the footwell, her head ending up resting on her husband's lap. The Archduke was then heard to say, 'Soferl, Soferl, don't die. Live for my children' as the count took him by the collar to keep him upright. 'It is nothing,' the Archduke assured the count before his eyes closed. He died seconds later.

Princip later spoke of the 'mystical' journey he had been on, a journey that ended in police custody around 11 a.m. on 28 June 1914. He would never again enjoy freedom, dying in an Austro-Hungarian jail emaciated by hunger, his bones eaten away by tuberculosis. Just as for Čabrinović, the cyanide had failed to make him a martyr, only scorching the lining of his mouth and making him nauseous. He was so badly beaten by gendarmes wielding sabres, and by onlookers loyal to the Habsburg Empire, that a witness reported seeing him late that evening with only his eyes and lips visible on a face otherwise swathed in bandages. The witness was Ferdinand Behr, the bystander who was photo-graphed after being arrested outside the Moritz Schiller café. This is the famous picture that so many historians, journalists and archivists (Wikipedia among them) wrongly believed to show the actual assassin being led away. Behr reported that in this early stage of the police investigation Princip defiantly refused to cooperate with the police, hoping perhaps that his fellow con-spirators might yet escape.

It was a vain hope. As an assassin Princip may have been lucky, but he was also amateur, leaving enough clues for the police to pick up all but one of his colleagues within a matter of days. When he had returned to Sarajevo from Belgrade he had registered his address on Oprkanj Street with the colonial authorities, a fact that he gave up to police under questioning less than an hour after the assassination. Officers rushed round to the house, where they arrested Ilić and found under his bed the bag used to store the weapons. With Čabrinović already in custody, the other attackers were soon all picked up, with the exception of Mehmedbašić, the only Bosnian Muslim member of the attack team. He managed to catch a train south towards Mostar before crossing the border safely into Montenegro, his role scarcely ever mentioned by Austrian police investigators. For political reasons they were anxious to emphasise the exclusively Serbian nature of the assassination plot, and it did not suit them to spend too much time chasing a non-Serbian lead. Their example would be followed by most historians analysing the assassination, with the exception of the thorough Italian author Luigi Albertini, who twenty years later tracked down Mehmedbašić shortly before he died.

After four days of solitary confinement Princip asked to see his fellow prisoners, who were being held at the military prison within the large colonial barracks built in New Sarajevo, the area developed by the Austro-Hungarians to the west of the old city. In the hours and days after the assassination the colonial authorities had deliberately stirred up a fury of anti-Serb feeling, with mobs of Austro-Hungarian loyalists being encouraged to ransack Serb businesses and property in Sarajevo and beyond. Hundreds of Bosnian Serbs who had nothing to do with the assassination plot were nevertheless arrested and maltreated. Later many of them would be summarily executed by the Austro-Hungarian authorities. Anxious to spare anyone not involved in the assassination, Princip told Grabež and Ilić, when allowed to see them briefly: 'Confess everything, how we got the bombs, how we travelled and in what society we were, so that just people do not come to harm.'

After this meeting the investigation advanced quickly, as Princip gave details of the route he had used from the Drina River frontier to Sarajevo via Tuzla, and confirmed the names of the five other armed attackers who had been deployed along the Appel Quay, as well as that of Ilić in his supervisory role. His fellow prisoners were not as steadfast in their confessions; indeed, Ilić claimed he had a change of heart and tried to stop the assassination, an account too inconsistent to convince the authorities. The one regret Princip voiced repeatedly to the Austro-Hungarian prosecutors concerned the death of Sophie. He said he had never intended to kill her, apologising on several occasions. He told the court that the bullet that hit her had been intended for the colonial governor.

Responding to this flood of information, the police were soon able to round up the various Bosnian peasants who had helped the three men smuggle themselves and their weapons from Serbia through Tuzla, along with various associates in Sarajevo, mostly fellow supporters of Mlada Bosna who had agreed to conceal the weapons. Within a few weeks, a charge sheet had been drawn up indicting Princip and twenty-four other individuals. While the group was dominated by Bosnian Serbs, four of the indictees were Bosnian Croats – including the only woman to be charged, Angela Sadilo, a Sarajevan housewife accused of helping to hide one of the pistols. Once more the Austro-Hungarian authorities sought to conceal the role played by non-Serbs, even changing the name of one of the Bosnian Croats so that in newspaper reports he appeared to be a Bosnian Serb.

The case against all twenty-five indictees – all of whom were Austro-Hungarian citizens, none from Serbia – was to be heard at a shared trial due to be held in October 1914 inside the military barracks in New Sarajevo. Although prosecutors were anxious to see those most involved in the assassination put to death, they faced a legal problem because the attackers who lined the Appel Quay were so young. The imperial criminal code allowed for a death sentence to be passed only on criminals aged at least twenty, making the five armed attackers under arrest not yet of an age to be executed. Prosecutors went to some length to convince the judges that the birth certificate of Princip in particular was wrong and he was old enough to be hanged. In the National Archive in Sarajevo I found, among the official papers connected with the investigation, a scribbled handwritten note making the twelve-day conversion for his date of birth between the old Julian calendar, which was commonly used among the Bosnian Serb Orthodox community, and the modern Gregorian calendar. It made no difference, for even after the conversion Princip's age on the day of the assassination remained nineteen.

Because of this anomaly the state prosecutors insisted on charging the indictees not just with murder, but with the more heinous crime of treason. Conspirators to treason could, under Habsburg law, face the death sentence, whereas conspirators to murder could receive nothing harsher than a life sentence. By opting for a treason charge, prosecutors ensured that those aged twenty or over, proven to have been centrally involved in the conspiracy, would hang. This way, at least someone would die to avenge the life of the Archduke.

The trial began at 8.10 a.m. on Monday 12 October 1914 and ran for eleven days. Photographs of the perpetrators being marched into court and sitting together inside the courtroom show Princip at the forefront. Although much shorter than the other prisoners, he dominates the pictures: the sharp Princip family chin prominent, his face whiskery, his eyes defiant. While the other defendants wavered during the hearing, Princip gave testimony that was steadfast and focused, explaining the rage he felt as a Bosnian peasant against the colonial occupiers who kept the rural population in dire conditions, and repeatedly stating his Yugoslav goal of liberating all south Slavs. Some of his

co-accused hinted at other motives for taking part in the assassination. One said it was because he was driven by revolutionary
socialism, another because he hoped to help Serbs alone, but
throughout the hearing Princip consistently said he had acted as
a Yugoslav nationalist, not a Serb nationalist.

While armies mobilised across Europe and the first clashes
took place on the Eastern and Western Fronts, all was calm in
the Sarajevo courtroom on Thursday 28 October 1914, when the
three judges returned their verdict after five days of deliberation.
The court found Princip guilty of murder and high treason, but
ruled that he was not of age to receive a death sentence. Instead
he was sentenced to twenty years in jail, with special orders that
he be denied food one day each month and be kept in a cell
without light on each anniversary of the assassination. The four
other armed attackers under arrest – including Čabrinović, who
had thrown the bomb at the Archduke – were also too young to
be executed, receiving instead stiff jail terms. However, five of
the older prisoners, including Ilić, were convicted of treason and
sentenced to be hanged – although two of them would have their
death sentences later commuted to life. Nine of the co-accused,
including Mrs Sadilo, were acquitted of all charges.

The three men on death-row were hanged on 3 February 1915,
using nooses strung over coarse wooden columns driven into the
ground within the military barracks in New Sarajevo. Witnesses
described how drums rolled as the executions were carried out
one after the other on a clear winter's day, the peaks of the mountains surrounding Sarajevo white with snow. Ilić was the last to
be executed, the hangman later saying: 'The third, who had the
greatest guilt on his soul, was serene.'

By this time Princip had already been moved from Sarajevo,
taken by train in December 1914 to serve out his sentence in a
military prison within an old Habsburg fortress at Theresienstadt,

in the far north of the Austro-Hungarian Empire. Shackled night and day with leg irons weighing 22 lbs, his condition worsened steadily, tormented all the time by cold, malnutrition, loneliness and the refusal of his jailers to give him anything to read. The occasional snippet of news reached him about the war that his actions had precipitated, about the invasion of Serbia by Austro-Hungarian troops, about the death and suffering endured among the south-Slav people he had hoped to liberate. The last known photograph of Princip was taken around this time. He stands shirtless in a jacket next to a studded prison-cell door and what looks like a privy. It was while at Theresienstadt that he was interviewed by Dr Pappenheim, and the clinical notes record how the prisoner ached for something to read, his spirits declining to the point of attempting suicide: 'It is very hard in solitary confinement, without books, with absolutely nothing to read, suffering most from not having anything to read. Sleeps only four hours in the night. Dreams a great deal. Beautiful dreams. About life, about love, not uneasy.' When the doctor handed over a pen so that Princip could jot down some thoughts about social revolution, the prisoner said it was the first time in two years that he had handled one.

Following Princip's journey had shown me how it touched repeatedly on events from the later twentieth century, and so it was in Theresienstadt. While there as a prisoner he was treated for tuberculosis by a local doctor called Jan Levit, then a loyal medical practitioner of the Austro-Hungarian Empire. Two and a half decades later the same doctor would return to the same fortress, but in very altered circumstances, born from the fallout of the events sparked by his patient. In 1942 Theresienstadt, now called Terezin, had been turned into a Nazi concentration camp, and Dr Levit, a Jew, passed through this time as a prisoner, locked up and eventually transported to Auschwitz where he was murdered.

Dr Pappenheim recorded the spread of tuberculosis through the prisoner's body. On 18 May 1916 he noted 'wound worse, discharging very freely, looking miserable, suicide by any sure means impossible, "wait to the end", resigned but not really very sad'. The notes for his fourth and final visit a month later ran to only one line: 'When permission has come, arm to be amputated, his usual resigned disposition.' Princip's right arm was removed for medical reasons some time later, although he lingered on through 1917, the disease spreading all the time. When death came at 6.30 p.m. on 28 April 1918 the death-certificate recorded tuberculosis as the cause. On the wall of his cell two lines of verse were later found:

> Our ghosts will walk through Vienna
> And roam through the Palace, frightening the lords.

Under cover of darkness, his corpse was handed over that night to a burial party of five Austro-Hungarian imperial troops. They were under orders to place the body in an unmarked grave already dug in the local graveyard, and not leave any traces when they filled it back in. The Austro-Hungarian authorities hoped it would never be found.

CHAPTER 12

More Than One Shadow

After the 1941 Nazi occupation of Bosnia, the plaque in
Sarajevo commemorating Princip as a 'herald of freedom'
is ripped down and presented to Adolf Hitler

The last known photograph of Princip, circa 1915,
before dying in prison from tuberculosis

The assassination on the morning of 28 June 1914 might have been the end of Gavrilo Princip's 'mystical' journey, but for the rest of the world it was just the beginning. Look carefully at the photograph of the Gräf & Stift limousine as its wheels turn to make the corner outside the Moritz Schiller café and it is possible to make out that by some strange synchronicity the car's number plate can be read A111118. It was a sequence with no great resonance before the First World War, but when the four bloody years of fighting eventually ended, it did so on Armistice Day, the eleventh day of the eleventh month in 1918: A 11-11-18.

The checks and balances of the grand strategic alliances between Great Power rivals had for decades prevented continental war from erupting in Europe, not least during the 1908 crisis when Austria–Hungary annexed Bosnia. So when news broke of the Archduke's death there was no immediate sense of any impending crisis that might destroy the old order. At first, the death of Franz Ferdinand prompted nothing but sympathy from the established European powers – a mood perfectly reflected by an editorial in *The Times* newspaper published in London the day after the assassination:

With the deepest and most profound regret we record today the tragic news of the assassination of the Archduke Franz Ferdinand and his wife, the Duchess Hohenberg . . . The sympathy of the whole world will go forth to the bereaved emperor and all Englishmen will pray that he may be able to bear this final affliction with the fortitude he has never failed to show his deepest trials.

Within weeks, those same Englishmen were being urged not to pray for the Emperor Franz Joseph, but to take up arms against him and his allies. The sense of security guaranteed by the grand alliances proved to be an illusion, a collapsing house of cards, unable to contain any longer the rivalries of the Great Powers, especially that between the era's global superpower, Britain, and the relatively new but ambitious German empire. No matter how many times the treaty matrix had worked, it took only one failure for the whole edifice to come crashing down.

So it was that in July 1914 a series of strategic manoeuvres, under the cover of agreements intended to protect peace, acted like tumblers falling into place, one after the other, locking Europe onto a war trajectory. A shooting on a street corner in Sarajevo was leveraged into a *casus belli* for continental conflict through a staggered sequence of falling diplomatic dominoes, one well visited by historians. Austria–Hungary used the assassination as grounds to declare war on Serbia, provoking tsarist Russia to mobilise forces in defence of Belgrade, a move that led the Kaiser's Germany to attack France pre-emptively through Belgium, leading Britain to declare war on Germany at midnight on 4 August 1914.

The trigger for it all had been the shooting in Sarajevo, an event that on a simplistic level could be plotted through artefacts I explored through my journey. Before travelling to Bosnia, my research had taken me to Austria's military museum at the Arsenal in Vienna, where items connected with the assassination remain on public display, including the original Gräf & Stift limousine. With the passing of the years the dark paint of its bodywork was not quite as polished as it was on the day of the assassination, but it was still possible to see the bullet-hole on the right-hand side made by the shot that killed Sophie, and the portentous number plate. The Archduke's uniform was laid out in a display cabinet, the feathers on his *stulphut* a little limper than they had been on the day of his grand visit to Sarajevo, the breast of his blue tunic still torn where doctors hacked desperately through the material in the mistaken belief that he had been shot in the heart. The shirt he wore, black with his dried blood, is kept in a special presenta-tion case elsewhere within the collection, too delicate for daily display.

I rode a train west along the Danube River valley to Artstetten castle, favourite among the Archduke's many properties. Sophie's lowly status in the eyes of Habsburg traditionalists meant she could not be buried alongside the imperial forebears in Vienna, but love meant that the Archduke did not want to be separated in death. So, today, they lie side-by-side in a modest crypt beneath the castle, fresh flowers being laid each year on the anniversary of the assassination. Just as in my village of Hellidon and countless others all across Europe, the small Austrian town nearby has a memorial listing the names of locals who fell in the world wars. But the grey slate plaque in Artstetten can claim something unique. It bears the names of the first two fatalities, Archduke Franz Ferdinand and Sophie. Touring the museum with its array of family photo-graphs and memorabilia, I was moved to read that the couple's two sons both paid a high price when Austria was caught up in events rooted in the war that began with the murder of their parents. For opposing the Nazi occupation of their homeland in the late 1930s they were both sent to Dachau, although both survived.

Nearing the end of my own journey, I was able to follow the exact route taken into Sarajevo by the Archduke on the day of his death. The Hotel Bosna had been through turbulent times, occupied by Bosnian Serb forces during the war of the 1990s when, in its grounds, they dug in the guns that used to fire upon the mountain road I had driven so perilously across Mount Igman. After the war ended, the hotel building was one of many taken over as the headquarters of the NATO force sent to enforce the terms of the Dayton peace treaty, but when I arrived in the summer of 2012 it was in the late stages of refurbishment, the receptionist totally unaware of the royal party that once stayed there. The spring of the Bosna River still lies close by, reached by a long, straight gravel avenue lined by plane trees, another instance of Austro-Hungarian outsiders seeking to order Bosnia's wild landscape. Today the avenue is plied by horse-drawn carriages, dating from the Habsburg colonial era, that carry tourists and visitors.

The Archduke's party took a train into Sarajevo on 28 June 1914 and I followed by tram, stopping outside the old military barracks in New Sarajevo, where he had formally inspected troops before boarding the car convoy into the city centre. I had known it as the Marshal Tito barracks during the war of the 1990s, a briefly fought-over piece of military real estate that would be occupied by Ukrainian UN peacekeepers who flogged black-market diesel by the jerrycan through holes blasted in the perimeter wall. Only a small section remained when I visited in 2012, its plaster blackened in places from flames that went out twenty years earlier, its masonry still marked with what we called 'Sarajevo sunflowers' – the scar left by a shell-strike that would create a deep central crater surrounded by radiating petals of smaller holes gouged by shrapnel.

I walked the route of the limousine convoy from 1914, one that passes close by the National Archive of Bosnia, where relics from the assassination are still to be found: police paperwork filled in by the authorities over in Obljaj when Princip's parents were hurriedly taken in for questioning; references to the long-gone

Vlajnić pastry shop in central Sarajevo, where some of the weapons were distributed by Danilo Ilić on the morning of the attack; a piece of stationery from the coffee-grinding business in Sarajevo owned by Nedeljko Čabrinović's Habsburg-supporting father; a postcard written in pencil by Princip to a relative, with an Austro-Hungarian postage stamp bearing the bewhiskered likeness of Emperor Franz Joseph.

I walked the length of the old Appel Quay alongside the Miljacka. The river ran calmly by at its low summer level, the even flow broken only by an occasional weir where the water bubbled and churned, plastic bottles bobbing frantically where they were trapped in back eddies. A woman fished for her dinner right there in the centre of this small city, casting her line from close by the spot where Čabrinović launched himself down the stone-lined river bank after throwing his grenade. No plaque marks the spot of his attack, but photographs taken from 1914 show a building that is still there today, the façade unchanged after a hundred years.

At the end of the boulevard I came to the remains of the old town hall, where the royal party was photographed arriving that sunny Sunday morning, its steps then lined by serious-faced dignitaries, some wearing fezzes, others with top hats doffed – yet to receive the imperial dressing-down from the royal visitor so enraged by the grenade attack. A photographer was on hand to capture the departure from the same steps half an hour later, the limousine pointing this time back down the Appel Quay, the gallant count taking up his position on the running board facing the river, the plumes on the Archduke's *stulphut* momentarily flattened by a gust of wind.

By the time the Bosnian War broke out in 1992 this monumental building was no longer the town hall, converted instead into the National Library, a building of such prominence it drew fire from Bosnian Serb gunners. In the summer of 1994 I had walked up its steps and taken photographs of what remained, a roofless hulk, the stone columns lining the atrium blistered by the blaze ignited in the bombardment. The striped pink, pseudo-Moorish façade that Rebecca West had derided prompted a more sympathetic response from me, its stonework smudged with soot where the fire had vented through the windows. Almost two decades on, when I visited in 2012, the building was yet to be put right, muffled by scaffolding as it underwent slow reconstruction.

It took me just minutes to walk back down the river past the same domes and minaret captured in the remarkable photograph of the Archduke's car approaching the turn where Princip was waiting. I passed the spot where the man raised his hat at the royal party and the little boy looked on in wonder, the masonry walls lining the river bank unchanged. The sky above me was as cloudless as on the day of the assassination and, when I arrived at the turning, I rested just opposite on an old stone seat prominent at the end of the Latin Bridge. It was built by the Austro-Hungarians as part of an elaborate memorial to the Archduke, one that was pulled down shortly after the end of the First World War when the occupier was finally driven out of Bosnia. The seat had somehow been spared from destruction, its stencilled Latin legend – 'siste viator' or 'stop traveller' – allowed to fade with the years.

The riverside road was busy with trams, cars and other city traffic, but from the seat I had a clear view of the spot, just thirty feet away, where the assassination took place. Sarajevans bustled past what was, for them, just another busy street corner; a traffic warden ticketed an illegally parked car, and an elderly woman, doubled over with age, sat crumpled on the old flagstones of the bridge begging for money, quietly yet insistently.

There was little to tell passers-by of the significance of the street corner opposite me, just a modest plaque set in the wall at ground level with a message that read: 'From this place on 28 June 1914

Gavrilo Princip assassinated the heir to the Austro-Hungarian throne Franz Ferdinand and his wife Sofia.' The neutrality of the wording jarred as I set off on the last leg of my trip.

I knew exactly where I was going. I started along what used to be Franz Joseph Street, the road that begins at the corner where the Moritz Schiller café once stood and is today called Green Berets Street, in honour of fighters who protected Sarajevo during the war of the 1990s. My route then took me across Ferhadija, the pedestrian avenue linking old Ottoman Sarajevo to the new city shaped by Austria–Hungary. It was a street Princip used as a schoolboy on his daily walk to the Merchants' School. Today it bears scars still livid from the siege, memorial stones to Sarajevans killed by Bosnian Serb shells.

On I walked, nearing the end of a journey that had rumbled over the frets of history. It had taken me from Obljaj through parts so wild they are still roamed by wolves; into archives in Sarajevo missed by observers for whom Princip remained only a half-formed, incidental figure; through a land where the twentieth century's most influential political force – nationalism – had shown its power both to unite and to divide. Through the course of the journey, and with the help of Arnie, Mile, Džile and many others, I had been able to strip away the filters of history that can obscure the outsider's view of the Balkans, bringing into focus my mental picture of the young man whose actions led to the First World War. And the journey had gone far beyond the story of an individual, touching a region that cast more than one shadow over world history. I had passed through the same mountains where Tito wooed the West, trapping the south Slavs for decades on the communist side of the Iron Curtain, and had trudged through the killing fields of Srebrenica that brought about NATO's coming of age and drove others to jihad.

As I walked purposefully through the back streets of Sarajevo for one last time, the dominant impression I was left with was one of distortion. Ever since those Edwardian statesmen and diplomats in the summer of 1914 accepted the misrepresentation that Princip was acting solely for Serbia when he fired the pistol, his story has been twisted. From the moment Austria–Hungary, in the face of clear evidence to the contrary, wilfully misconstrued Princip's motives in order to justify its attack on Serbia, distortion was inserted into the founding narrative of the First World War. For their own reasons of strategic ambition and hubristic self-confidence, the other Great Powers acted without challenging the misrepresentation, too focused on finger-pointing, mobilisation and retaliation to properly explore what lay at the very beginning.

Princip's real story – his dream of all south Slavs living together – was left behind, overwhelmed by the scale of the events he had brought about. I felt that therein lay the cause of the unsettling feeling that still dogs the First World War, the unease over the senselessness of the sacrifice. My great-uncle, Captain Alyn Reginald James, had died along with millions of others in a war started after the motives of a young Balkan assassin were distorted. From this instance of original sin ran all the attendant feelings of futility that still weigh down the calamities of the Great War.

The twisting meant that the story of Princip was no longer tethered in reality, but was free-floating and bendable to the vision of any beholder. The plaque that today marks so blandly the site of the assassination replaced earlier versions, each worded according to the political authority of the day. When Austria–Hungary was still in control of Sarajevo, a plaque was installed at the site of the shooting that denounced Princip as a 'murderer'. The next plaque went up in the 1930s when Bosnia was part of royalist Yugoslavia, a country founded for all south Slavs. This time the plaque referred to Princip as a 'herald of freedom', pointedly dating the shooting as having taken place on St Vitus's Day, the day kept sacred for the Serbian heroes of the battle of Kosovo. When Nazi troops swept into Sarajevo in 1941 one of the first things they did was to tear down the plaque and present it as a birthday gift to Adolf Hitler in Berlin. A powerful photograph exists of the moment it was handed to the Führer, a man who – like Princip – was born a subject of the Austro-Hungarian Empire and who was also driven by notions of nationalism.

After the Second World War a third plaque was erected at the street corner in Sarajevo, this time by the Titoist communist authorities. The wording on this occasion was more heroic, describing Princip's actions as expressing 'the people's protest against tyranny and the age-old longing of our peoples for freedom'. So by the time the war of the 1990s broke out, Princip himself cast more than one shadow: a scapegoat for all seasons, who could be described in turn as a murderer, a liberator, a socialist hero of the people.

After twenty minutes of walking I approached the spot I was looking for, recognising the red-roofed building I had first seen that summer's day during the siege in 1994. The chapel in the Archangels George and Gabriel cemetery had been restored in the years since the war ended, the damaged door repaired, the broken roof tiles replaced and the filth cleaned up. But the same black plaque I remembered being so unnerved by all those years ago was still there, Princip's name etched prominently in Cyrillic: ГАВРИЛО ПРИНЦИП.

A member of the burial party that dumped Princip's body in an unmarked grave at Theresienstadt came forward after the First World War. With his help the remains were exhumed, on the orders of the authorities in nascent Yugoslavia, and the identity of the skeleton confirmed because, following the amputation, the remains had no right arm. The bones were brought back to Sarajevo in 1920 for a ceremonial funeral in this graveyard. In 1939 Princip made the very last stage of his journey, dug up one final time and moved to this chapel, where he was interred alongside the remains of his friend from school, Trifko Grabež, his room-mate, Danilo Ilić, and other conspirators involved in the assassination of 28 June 1914. The bones of their role model, Bogdan Žerajić, the would-be assassin from 1910 whose example they sought to follow, were also brought here to lie among those he had inspired.

Inside the small chapel the air was still, the sound of the city outside muffled by thick, bare walls lined with fragments of old gravestones. Once again the chapel was a sombre, dusty site of quiet remembrance.

Through my journey I had heard Princip referred to by some as a hero, by others as a terrorist, yet I had come to see him as an everyman for the anger felt by millions who were downtrodden far beyond the Balkans. He was a dreamer whose short life had exposed him to the same political streams that inspired so many others fighting for freedom from unelected, reactionary structures. Empire had had its day and, like so many others at the start of the twentieth century, Princip was struggling to shape a new reality to take its place. The essential idea he stood for, the dream of liberation, was shared not just across the Balkans but across the wider world, whether by Irish nationalists struggling for Home Rule or Russian revolutionaries plotting against the Tsar, and it reached far beyond Europe through India, Africa, the Middle East and elsewhere. The violence to which he resorted was no different from that employed by freedom fighters the world over.

But as the events of the twentieth century showed, through the rise of extremism and fascism, the nationalism he espoused had the potential to be toxic. His goal of all south Slavs living together was ultimately not strong enough to defeat chauvinism from within his own community. The concept of nationalism carries with it a reductionist edge – the sense that in seeking to define those who belong to a nation, others who do not belong can become a threat, an enemy to be confronted. This dangerous potential was what those I had met on the trip had helped me better understand, a corruption so strong it was able to distort the utopian dream of Princip, a young Bosnian Serb who had come to trust those Bosnian Croats and Bosnian Muslims who shared his vision of south Slavs in union.

I felt the Princip I had got to know would have been appalled by the war that first drew me to Bosnia. He was a Bosnian Serb who was brave enough to stand up to those from his own community who accused him of betrayal by aligning himself with Bosnian Muslims and Bosnian Croats. And yet I could now see why some in Sarajevo during the worst days of the siege might regard him with so much contempt that they could desecrate his grave. By that time the south-Slav nationalism he championed had failed and his message had been so distorted that he could be vilified, not just because he was a Bosnian Serb like the gunners firing their shells into the city, but because the Yugoslavia he had worked for had failed so completely to protect one of its component parts, Bosnia.

As my time in the chapel came to an end, I watched the caretaker as he carefully locked the door to Gavrilo Princip's tomb. For me, the time had come to let him rest in peace.

LIST OF ILLUSTRATIONS

Maps by Paul Simmons
All photographs are the author's own, unless stated

For more photographs, video and historical material go to: www.tim-butcher.com

NOTES AND BIBLIOGRAPHY

Over the past hundred years much has been written about Gavrilo Princip and the Sarajevo assassination, often in dramatic detail. We have been told that: Princip jumped on the running board of the Archduke's limousine to take his shot, the Archduke's wife was pregnant when she died, the shooting happened on the anniversary of their marriage, the car did not have a reverse gear so was incapable of correcting the driver's error, the Archduke caught the grenade thrown earlier at the couple and tossed it away safely, and Princip stopped to eat a last sandwich at the corner café before emerging to take his shot.

The problem is that these details, and many more besides, are not true. Some might appear unimportant, ignorable perhaps as fanciful trivialities. The 'sandwich' was concocted for television, entering historical orthodoxy to such an extent that the ingredients used for its filling became a subject discussed by schoolchildren studying the origins of the First World War.

But other errors are much more important. The extent to which Princip was, or was not, under the influence of the Serbian authorities when preparing the assassination speaks directly to any meaningful assessment of who was to blame for starting the First World War, a question that today remains far from settled. Austria-Hungary had a clear political motive in representing Princip as an agent of Serbia, so historians must tread carefully when assessing claims about Princip that could have been made for political reasons.

Panning away a century of muddle and misinformation was the challenge I faced when researching *The Trigger*. My strategy was to go back, as much as possible, to primary sources, not least because familiarity with them would allow me to assess the reliability of works of history that have been published subsequently.

The discovery of Princip's school reports at the archives in Sarajevo, Tuzla and Belgrade provided, for me at least, a series of goose-bump moments, bringing alive the young boy sent to study in the big city. They allowed me to prove what other historians had only been able to infer: it was during Princip's schooling that he lost his way. This was charted clearly in the worsening grades logged by teachers, blissfully unaware of the bloody impact their failing student would have one day.

Documents from the initial police investigation into the assassination were enormously useful, kept at the National Archive of Bosnia and Herzegovina in Sarajevo. No police work can provide the whole picture but it can give important and reliable information. Similarly, the transcript of the court hearing, put together from the stenographers' notes held at the same archive, allowed Princip's voice to be heard clearer than anywhere else with the exception, perhaps, of the clinical notes of the psychiatrist who visited him in prison.

Some of the books I used for research are given below but special mention must be made of Vladimir Dedijer's great work, *The Road to Sarajevo*. In its wide scope, grasp of detail and historical rigour, I found it without equal.

There was one final aspect that needed to be considered when researching Princip, the very powerful and occasionally toxic nature of Balkan nationalism. The war of the 1990s in Bosnia taught me how dangerous ethnic loyalties can be, a lesson that had to be borne in mind when dealing with any local assessment of Princip, whether by his ethnic kin from within the Bosnian Serb community, or from the rival groups of Bosnian Croats and Bosnian Muslims. Objectivity is difficult to maintain if you have lived through the siege of Sarajevo, say, or the fall of Srebrenica.

This was brought home all too clearly in February 2014, the centenary year of the assassination, when mobs took to the streets of Sarajevo angry at the ongoing failure of government structures created in Bosnia at the end of the war in the 1990s. Fires lit by the protestors damaged badly the National Archive of Bosnia and Herzegovina, the place where I had carried out some of my research.

After surviving two world wars and a civil war, original documents concerning Princip were destroyed. History does not rest easily in Bosnia.

SOURCES ON GAVRILO PRINCIP

The school reports – original records from Princip's secondary education in Bosnia are held at the Sarajevo Historical Archives www.arhivsa.ba and at the Tuzla Cantonal Archive www.arhivtk.com.ba

From Princip's schooling in Serbia some reports are held at the Belgrade Historical Archives www.arhiv-beograda.org

The police investigation – original paperwork from the Austro-Hungarian investigation in 1914 was lost, last seen in a chest with serial number IS 206-15 around June 1915 in the custody of the Habsburg imperial commandant in Vienna

Copies of some documents are held today at National Archive of Bosnia and Herzegovina in Sarajevo. A more complete collection of copies is held at the Austrian State Archive in Vienna www.oesta.gv.at

The trial – original stenographic notes from the 1914 trial of
Gavrilo Princip et al. are today held at the National Archive of
Bosnia and Herzegovina in Sarajevo

In 1930 they were abridged and published by Albert Mousset as
Un Drame Historique – L'Attentat de Sarajevo, Payot

In 1954 a more complete version was published by Professor
Vojislav Bogićević as *Sarajevski Atentat,* Izdanje Drž. Arhiva
Nr BiH

In 1984, an English translation was published in two volumes by
W. A. Dolph Owings, Elizabeth Pribić and Nikola Pribić as *The
Sarajevo Trial,* Documentary Publications

The clinical notes of Princip's psychiatrist – originally published
in German as *Gavrilo Princips Bekenntnisse,* 1926, Lechner &
Son

Translated into English and published as *Confessions of the Assassin
Whose Deed Led the World War,* in periodical *Current History,*
August 1927, Vol. XXVI, Number 5, pp. 699–707

OTHER READING

Luigi Albertini: *The Origins of the War of 1914,* 1953, Oxford
University Press

José Almira and Giv Stoyan: *Le Déclic de Sarajevo,* 1927, Éditions
Radot

Ivo Andrić: *The Bridge over the Drina,* 1994, Harvill Press

– *Bosnian Chronicle* or *The Days of the Consuls,* 1996, Harvill
Press

Karl Baedeker: *Austria–Hungary including Dalmatia and Bosnia
– Handbook for Travellers,* 1905, Baedeker

Gordon Brook-Shepherd: *Victims at Sarajevo – The Romance and
Tragedy of Franz Ferdinand and Sophie,* 1984, Harvill Press

Rupert Brooke: *The Collected Poems With a Memoir*, 1931, Sidgwick & Jackson

Lavender Cassels: *The Archduke and the Assassin – Sarajevo, June 28th 1914*, 1984, Dorset Press

Christopher Clark: *The Sleepwalkers – How Europe Went to War in 1914*, 2012, Allen Lane

Roger Cohen: *Hearts Grown Brutal – Sagas of Sarajevo*, 1998, Random House US

Nada Ćurčija-Prodanović: *Yugoslav Folk-Tales*, 1957, Oxford University Press

Muriel Currey: *Dalmatia*, 1930, Philip Allan

Wade Davis: *Into the Silence – The Great War, Mallory and the Conquest of Everest*, 2011, The Bodley Head

F. W. D. Deakin: *The Embattled Mountain*, 1971, Oxford University Press

Vladimir Dedijer: *Diary*, 1946, Državni Izdavački Zavod Jugoslavije Belgrade

– *Tito Speaks – His Self-Portrait and Struggle with Stalin*, 1953, Weidenfeld & Nicolson

– *The Road to Sarajevo*, 1966, MacGibbon & Kee

Robin S. Doak: *Assassination at Sarajevo – The Spark that Started World War I*, 2009, Compass Point

Robert J. Donia: *Sarajevo – A Biography*, 2006, University of Michigan Press

Lawrence Durrell: *White Eagles Over Serbia*, 1957, Faber and Faber

Charlotte Eagar: *The Girl in the Film*, 2008, Reportage

Modris Eksteins: *Rites of Spring – The Great War and the Birth of the Modern Age*, 2012, Vintage Canada

Ralph Erskine and Michael Smith, editors: *The Bletchley Park Codebreakers*, 2010, Dialogue

Arthur John Evans: *Through Bosnia and the Herzegovina On Foot*, 1876, Longmans, Green and Co.

– *Illyrian Letters*, 1878, Longmans, Green and Co.

Tony Fabijančić: *Bosnia – In the Footsteps of Gavrilo Princip*, 2010, University of Alberta Press

Hans Fronius: *Das Attentat von Sarajevo*, 1988, Styria

Misha Glenny: *The Fall of Yugoslavia – The Third Balkan War*, 1992, Penguin

– *The Balkans 1804–1909: Nationalism, War & the Great Powers*, 1999, Granta Books

Richard Greene: *Edith Sitwell – Avant Garde Poet, English Genius*, 2011, Virago

John Gunther: *Inside Europe*, 1938, Harper

Max Hastings: *Catastrophe – Europe Goes to War in 1914*, 2013, William Collins

Richard Holmes: *Soldiers – Army Lives and Loyalties*, 2011, HarperPress

Rezak Hukanović: *The Tenth Circle of Hell*, 1997, Little, Brown

Dobroslav Jevdjević: *Sarajevski Atentatori*, 1934, Binoza

Vladimir Jokanović: *Made in Yugoslavia*, 2000, Picador

Robert D. Kaplan: *Balkan Ghosts – A Journey Through History*, 1993, Picador

John Keegan: *The First World War*, 1998, Hutchinson

Greg King and Sue Woolmans: *The Assassination of the Archduke: Sarajevo 1914 and the Murder that changed the World*, 2013, Macmillan

Clea Koff: *The Bone Woman – Among the Dead in Rwanda, Bosnia, Croatia and Kosovo*, 2004, Atlantic Books

Hans Konig: *Death of a Schoolboy*, 1989, W. H. Allen & Co

Michael Lees: *The Rape of Serbia*, 1990, Harcourt Brace Jovanovich

Franklin Lindsay: *Beacons in the Night*, 1993, Stanford University Press

Alistair MacLean: *Force 10 from Navarone*, 1968, Collins

Fitzroy Maclean: *Eastern Approaches*, 1949, Jonathan Cape

– *Private Papers*, Special Collections Library, University of Virginia, Charlottesville, Va.

Rory MacLean and Nick Danziger: *Missing Lives*, 2010, Dewi Lewis

Margaret MacMillan: *The War that Ended Peace – How Europe abandoned peace for the First World War*, 2013, Profile Books

– *Paris 1919 – Six Months that Changed the World*, 2003, Random House

Geert Mak: *In Europe – Travels Through the Twentieth Century*, 2008, Vintage

Noel Malcolm: *Bosnia – A Short History*, 1994, Macmillan

Mark Mazower: *The Balkans*, 2000, Weidenfeld & Nicolson

Christopher Merrill: *Only the Nails Remain*, 1999, Rowman & Littlefield

Frederic Morton: *Thunder at Twilight – Vienna 1913/1914*, 2001, Da Capo Press

Robin Okey: *Taming Balkan Nationalism*, 2007, Oxford University Press

Ratko Parežanin: *Mlada Bosna and the First World War*, 1974, Munich Iskra

Said Halim Paša: *L'Empire Ottoman et La Guerre Mondiale*, 2000, Isis

Roland Penrose: *The Road is Wider than Long*, 1939, London Gallery Editions

Kemal Pervanić: *The Killing Days – My Journey Through the Bosnian War*, 1999, Blake

John Reed: *War in Eastern Europe – Travels Through the Balkans in 1915*, 1916, Scribners

Joachim Remak: *Sarajevo – The Story of a Political Murder*, 1959, Criterion Books

David Rohde: *A Safe Area – Srebrenica*, 1997, Farrar Straus and Giroux

Jasper Rootham: *Miss Fire – The Chronicle of a British Mission to Mihailovich*, 1946, Chatto & Windus

Joseph Roth: *The Radetzky March*, 2000, Penguin Classics

P. J. O'Rourke: *All the Trouble in the World*, 1994, Atlantic Monthly Press

Susan Schwartz Senstad: *Music for the Third Ear*, 2001, Black Swan

Bonnie Kime Scott: *Selected Letters of Rebecca West*, 2000, Yale University Press

Laura Silber and Allan Little: *The Death of Yugoslavia*, 1995, Penguin

David James Smith: *One Morning in Sarajevo – 28 June 1914*, 2008, Weidenfeld & Nicolson

A. J. P. Taylor: *War by Time-Table – How the First World War Began*, 1969, Macdonald & Co.

Jassy Torrund: *Wenn Landsleute Sich Begegnen*, 1913, Phillip Reclam

Nikola Trišić: *Sarajevski Atentat u Svjetlu Bibliografskih Podataka*, 1960, Izdavačko preduzeće Veselin Masleša

Peter Villiers: *Gavrilo Princip – The Assassin who Started the First World War*, 2010, Fawler Press

Ed Vulliamy: *Seasons in Hell – Understanding Bosnia's War*, 1994, St Martin's Press

Evelyn Waugh: *Brideshead Revisited*, 1951, Penguin

Nigel West: *Secret War – The Story of SOE, Britain's Wartime Sabotage Organisation*, 1992, Hodder & Stoughton

Rebecca West: *Black Lamb and Grey Falcon*, 1942, Macmillan

– *Selected Letters*, edited by Bonnie Kime Scott, 2000, Yale University Press

Richard West: *Tito and the Rise and Fall of Yugoslavia*, 1994, Sinclair-Stevenson

Friedrich Würthle: *On the Trial of the Sarajevo Assassins – Is there an Authentic Text of the Trial Records?* 1966, Austrian History Yearbook, Vol. II, Rice University

– *Die Spur führt nach Belgrad: Die Hintergründe des Dramas von Sarajevo 1914*, 1978, Fritz Molden

Rudolf Zistler: *How I Came To Defend Princip and the Others*, 1937, Ljubljana

ACKNOWLEDGEMENTS

The journey at the spine of *The Trigger* was made in the high Balkan summer of 2012 yet important steps began long before and continued long after. For the help I received from many people over many years, I will remain eternally grateful.

No traveller in Bosnia could ask for a better companion than Arnie Hećimović. And old friends who helped me in the 1990s as an ingénu foreign correspondent again gave generous support: Amela Filipović, Tamara Levak Potrebica and Aleksandra Nikšić.

My journey through the place and history of Bosnia and Serbia was added to by many including: Mile Princip and his family, Zdravko Lučić, Josip Tomas, Avdo, Adis and Tess Hećimović, Eloise Grout, Nick Penny, Božo Čičak, Ljupko Kuna, Kemal and Elma Tokmić, Muzafer Latić, Ahmed 'Sini' Begičević, Nadja Ridžić, Drago and Marija Taraba, Damir Osmanović, Father Branko, Paul Lowe, Elma Kafedžić Haverić, Ed Serotta, Jakob Finci, Jan Munk, Ivar Petterson, Mirsad Kurgaš, Džile Omerović, Sefer Zahid, Martin Böhnlein, Paul Leslie, Svjetlana Trifković and her colleagues at the Bosnia and Herzegovina Mine Action Centre, Nigel and Clare Casey, Rob Tomlinson, Fikret Kahrović, the band Franz Ferdinand, Mirza Ibrahimović, Graham Binns, Dan Bradbury, David Harland, Shahid Butt, Darius Guppy, Jo and Carolina Menell, Jamie Maclean, Richard Greene, Celia Hawkesworth, Peter Villiers, David Mantero, David McNeill and colleagues at the Royal Geographical Society, Amber Paranick, Margaret Hrabe, Marian Eksteen, Josh Irby, David DeVoss, Ian

Mathie, Sylvie Nickels, Cherie Collins, Michael Smith, Mike Smith, Nick Alexander and Maggie Matheson.

And archival research was made easier by many. In Austria – Klaus Honisch, Helga Fichtner, Brigitte E. Leidwein, Gerhard Floszmann, Georg Rütgen, Christoph Hatschek and Sue Wodmans. In Turkey – Murat Siviloglu, Ayten Ardel and Sinan Kuneralp. In Germany – Angelika Betz and her colleagues from the Bavarian State Library and Count Rupert Strachwitz. For RAF/RFC history – Gareth Morgan, Oliver Woodroffe, Andy Kemp and his colleagues from The First World War Aviation Historical Society, Andrew Renwick and colleagues at the Royal Air Force Museum and Thomas Allen and his colleagues at the Special Collections department of the University of Texas.

In Sarajevo, I was helped immensely by Haris Zaimović, Saša Beltram, Jasmin Halilagić and their colleagues at the Sarajevo Historical Archives. Further assistance came from others including Sandra Biletić, Mihret Alibasić, Alma Leka, Adnan Busuladžić, Andrea Dautović, Hrvoje Potrebica, Salmedin Mesihović, Amir Duranović, Edin Radušić, Goran Milkulvić, Bruno Peskovan, Amra Madžarević, Mirsad Avdić, Guido van Hengel and Paul Miller.

In Belgrade, Miloš Paunović and Gavrilo Petrović assisted tire-lessly and skilfully. Others included Slobodan Mandić, Vladimir Tomić, Danica Jovović Prodanović, Miladin Milošević, Ljubodrag Dimić, Andzelija Radović, Sladjana Bojković, Mirjana Slaković, Ivan Obradović and Biljana Grujović.

Special thanks to Poppy Hampson, my editor at Chatto & Windus, and Rebecca Carter, my agent from Janklow & Nesbit. Only we know how much they have added to *The Trigger*. It has been long in gestation so thanks to Elizabeth Sheinkman and former colleagues at Curtis Brown who helped at its conception.

No author could ask for finer pastoral care than that given by

Stanley and Lisette Butcher, Patrick and Marilyn Flanagan and Susanne Bittorf, who provided the perfect writing space. And, as ever, my greatest debt is for the love of Jane, Kit and Tess.

INDEX